JMK

THE
MEDLEY
OF
MAST AND SAIL
II

The French schooner BRETONNE and ketch VIGILANT ready to sail.

THE MEDLEY OF MAST AND SAIL II

A CAMERA RECORD

525 photographic illustrations of many of the world's vanished sailing craft, both great and small, accompanied by comment and description by experienced ship-masters and other experts.

WITH AN INTRODUCTION BY ALEX. A. HURST

NAVAL INSTITUTE PRESS

Copyright Notice
© 1981

Published and distributed in the United States of America by the Naval Institute Press, Annapolis, Maryland 21402

Library of Congress Catalog Card No. 80−85162
ISBN 0−87021−940−5

All rights reserved. No part of this publication may be reproduced, stored in a retrieval system, or transmitted in any form or by any means, electronic, mechanical or photo-copying, recording or otherwise, without permission of the publishers.

Printed in the United States of America

CONTENTS

	Publishers' Note	VII
	List of Illustrations	VIII
	Acknowledgements	XV
	Introduction	1
1	Sailing with the Finland Line, *by the late Captain Sten Lille*	20
2	Too Close Encounter near the Line, *by Åke Rosenius* ..	44
3	French Schooners in the Bristol Channel, *by Jack Neale* ..	45
4	The L'AVENIR, *by Captain R. H. Turner*	69
5	The Buginese and Makassarese Tradition, *by Adrian Horridge*	80
6	Working Ship, *by Alex. Hurst*	94
7	Some Junks and	115
8	. . . Some Indian and Country Craft, *by Captain R. H. Turner*	121
9	The Deutscher Schulschiff Verein, *by Captain Gerhard Eckardt*	138
10	The Farmers' Boats of Torreira – (1) The Xavega, *by Major David Goddard*	152
11	The LADYE DORIS *(Photographs by Captain John Hay)*	163
12	Some Ships which made News, *by the late Captain Severin Waage et aliis*	196
13	Some Ships of Statistical Interest, *by sundry contributors*	211

14	Pataholm, and the Matter of Snows and Brigs, *by Torsten Cervin, Martin Ohlsson et aliis*	219
15	Ironwork Aloft, *by Richard M. Cookson*	234
16	Giant Schooners and Others, *by the late Captain Archie Horka*	248
17	Sink Me the Ship, Master Gunner, *by Alex. Hurst*	283
18	Disorder and Desinence, *by Alex. Hurst, Åke Rosenius et aliis*	292
19	Spars by the Shore-Line, *by sundry contributors*	325
20	The Farmers' Boats of Torreira – (2) The Moliciero, *by Major David Goddard*	341
21	Winter Weather, *by Alex. Hurst, Anders Westermark et aliis*	349
22	The Firewood Fleet, *by Captain R. H. Turner, Anders Westermark et aliis*	355
23	The Photographic Portrayal of Merchant Sail, *by sundry contributors*	370
24	The Tasman Sea and South Australia, *by the late Captain Jim Gaby and Captain Frank Walker*	403
25	A Mix of the Medley, *by sundry contributors*	433
	Index	461

PUBLISHER'S NOTE

When the first volume of *The Medley of Mast and Sail* was published, it was made clear that, because the intention was to present all manner of merchant sailing craft within the age of the camera without favour or distinction between the humblest and the proudest, the book would not be set out in sections or chapters.

In the event, that volume proved to be so popular and we were so inundated with contributions that it was considered that there was a case for presenting this second volume in loose chapters, in order to differentiate the work of one contributor from another. In some instances this has proved to be possible but, Alas! some of those who associated themselves with the project have not lived to see its fulfilment. Since some of their contributions were incomplete and others short, which were best incorporated into other sections which they enhanced, textually or pictorially, a measure of editing was required and, in consequence, the names of the *major* contributors to each section appear in the Table of Contents.

In a book devoted to Mast and Sail we make no apology for the inclusion of the Xavega, which has neither, since we believe her to be of sufficient interest to take her place with those vessels so equipped, nor is apology needed for the vessels of the Deutscher Schulschiff Verein which, if they carried no cargo, were producing crews for others which did so. Some pictures are of very high quality: others are of exceptional interest. For the rest, we trust we have produced a satisfactory mix of the Medley which will give much pleasure.

LIST OF ILLUSTRATIONS

	Plate
Abner Coburn . .	492
Abraham Rydberg	100–261/3–267–312
Actie . .	316
Ada	312
Adelaide, Port . .	350
Adolf Vinnen, see *Somali*	
af Chapman . .	1
Ahti . .	407
Alaska Packers ships	490
Alastor . .	393–397–408
Albatross	176
Albert Rickmers (bq), see *Penang*	
Albert Rickmers (4-m. bq) see *Herzogin Sophie Charlotte*	
Albyn . .	365
Alcaeus Hooper	273
Alexa . .	453
Alexander	246
Alexandra	251
Alma Doepel . .	465
Almee . .	71
Alpha . .	437
Amasis, see *Schulschiffe Pommern*	
Amelia . .	250
Amicizia, s.s., see *Carmen*	
Amor . .	513

	Plate
Ancyra, see *Wandsbek*	
Anemone, see *MacCullum More*	
Anirac . .	315
Annie M. Reid . .	444
Antofagasta . .	206–358
Antuco, see *Søm*	
Arcadia, tug . .	98
Archibald Russell	411/20
Ardencraig	318
Ardente	72
Arethusa, see *Hippalos* (sh)	
Argus	495/6
Asgerd. see *Kilmory*	
Asia Island	35
Astur, see *Anirac*	
Athena	443
Atlas, see *Bertha L. Downes*	
Austrasia, see *Gustav*	
Baghla	117
Bago, see *Pajala*	
Bandi, see *Elizabeth Bandi*	
Barcore, see *Songvaar*	
Barque with damaged bows . .	311
Barque off Sandy Hook . .	522
Barque with spencers in R. Nene	515
Bellhouse, see *Regina Elena/Ponape*	

	Plate
Bérengère	505
Bertha L. Downes	298
Besian	83
Bessfield	36/7
Bhyalkshmy	137
Bianca	286
Bolt, Daniel R...	2
Bosphorus craft	509
Bowen, Frank C.	3
Boy Clifford	107
Bradford C. Jones	293
Bretonne	Frontis-59
Bridgetammal	126/7–129–131/2
Brigs, Collier	240–246/58
Brigs, HM training	508
Brig, Indian	126/134
Brigantine entering Colombo	134
Brigantine leaving Littlehampton	442
Buenos Aires Maru, s.s.	118
Calcutta	365/6
Caledonia, see *Olivebank*	
Camilla	359
Cape Town	362–364
Carey of Blyth	246
Carmen	429
Carolina	246–51
Carpenter caulking	173
Carrier, see *Ungdoms Venner*	
Cassius, see *Kilmory*	
Castleton, see *Skaregrom*	
C. B. Pedersen	Front endpaper & 458
Champigny, see *Fennia*	
Charles Racine	220/2
Charlotte, see *Diego*	
Chinchas, anchorage off	32
Christiania	381
Christian Radich	62
Cidad de Porto, see *Hans &*	302
Circular Quay, Sydney	355/6
City of Orange	284

	Plate
Cleomene	367
Cleta, see *Frideborg*	
Colbert, see *Prinzess Eitel Friedrich*	
Colombo	128/30
Colonel de Villebois Mareuil	504
Commerce	247
Commonwealth, see *Sofia*	
Concorde	52
Conqueror, tug	308
Cora F. Cressey	278
Coringle	461
County of Anglesey, see *Gladbrook*	
County of Inverness, see *Carmen*	
County of Peebles	426/7
Craggs	250
Craigisla	362
Crane	253–263–266
Cromdale	336
Crown Zellerbach No 1, see *Somali*	
Cumberland Queen	288
Dar Pomorza, see *Prinzess Eitel Friedrich*	
Desdemona	497
Dharma, see *Ladye Doris*	
Dhows	117/25–128–130
Diego	231
Dione	391
Dora, see *Carmen*	
Dog Watch	172–213
Domino	46–60/1–63–65
Dorothy M. Palmer	279
Dreadnought, see *Moshulu*	
Drogden, see *Nina Podesta*	
Duen	317
Duke of Sutherland	356
Dunboyne, see *at Chapman*	
Duncan Dunbar	355
East African, see *Ada*	
E. A. Whitmore	283

IX

	Plate
Ebba	402
Edna Hoyt	289
Eglantine	58–65
Elfrieda, see *Schulschiffe Pommern* &	
	145
Elizabeth Bandi	217
Ellen	519–521
Elsa Olander, see *C. B. Pedersen*	
Emile	60/1–71
Emmanuele Accame, see *C. B. Pedersen*	
Endurance	382
Esmeralda	320
Esquimaux (aux)	385
Esthonia	392
Ethel	331/4
Eufrozine	275
Evaleeta	458
Fair Wind	448
Favell 18–27/30–33/4–37/9–394	
Fennia (2)	24/5
Ferm, see *C. B. Pedersen*	
Fitzjames, see *Pinnas*	
Flats, Mersey	175
Fleet	463
Flora, see *Potosi*	
Foam	462
Forest Dream	285
Förlig Vind	235
Fort Laramie	287
Fortuna	338/9
France (2)	10
Frazer, Captain	164
Fredique	246
Frexas, see *Anirac*	
Frideborg	403
Fritz, see *Ellen*	
Garthneill, see *Inverneill* &	518
Garthsnaid	321/2
G. D. Kennedy, see *af Chapman*	

	Plate
Genoese wine trader	491
George W. Wells	277
Gerda	236/9
Gill-netters in Alaska	493/4
Gladbrook	454/5
Glenard	19/23
Glycine	44–56
Goeland	64–66
Grossherzog Friedrich August, see	
Statsraad Lemkuhl & ..	144
Grossherzogin Elizabeth	
139–141–143–148	
Gustav	436/8
Gustave	41
Half-deck	166
Hamburg	360/1–363
Hamilton, Mr	164
Hampshire, Charles	2
Hannah and Eleanor	246
Hans, see *Cidad de Porto* & ..	301
Hawaiian Isles, see *Abraham Rydberg*	
Hawkesbury	356
Hay, Captain J. .. 164–166–172	
Helen Denny	449/50
Henriette, see *Anirac*	
Hereford	365
Hermann	49/50–55
Hero, see *MacCullum More*	
Herzogin Cecilie .. 1–325/7–423	
Herzogin Sophie Charlotte	368/71
Hibernia, tug	417
Highland Chieftain	247
Hilda	398
Hippalos (sh)	101
Hippalos (4-m. bq)	432
Holkar, see *Hippalos* (4-m. bq)	
Hoppet, see *Novo*	
Hougomont	323/5–327
Howard D. Troop, see *Annie M. Reid*	

	Plate
Hunier à rouleau (diagram) ..	43
Hylton	253
Ideal	69
Imacos, see *Ahti*	
Indian Country craft	117/38
Indian Empire	365
Ingrid, see *Rigdin*	
Inverneill, see *Garthneill* & ..	517
Inversnaid, see *Garthsnaid*	
Iquique 195–197–199–204–208/10	
Irene	501
Iris	51–71
Isabel Llusa	335
Isis, see *Narcissus*	
Isobel Browne	193
Jacob M. Haskell	272
Jane Palmer	276
Janes, see *Diego*	
Jasper	445
Java	337
Johanna, tug	78
John and Helena	248
Junks, Chinese	110/15
Junks, Japanese	108/9
Kagosima	244
Karima	125
Katherine Mackall	291
Kerroch	54
Ketch, South Australian ..	457/8
Ketches, British and French 40–68–71	
Ketches, Tasmanian jackyard ..	462/4
Killoran	97/8
Kilmory	367
Knight Errant, tug	518
Knight of the Thistle, see *Novo*	
København	15
Kommodore Johnsen ..	11/2
Kotia 118–120–122/5	

	Plate
Kurt, see *Moshulu* & ..	303–307
La Belle Poule	62
Ladye Doris 163/6–168/75–177/92–	
193/6–198–200/1–203–205–	
208–210/13–215/6–523	
La Hogue	356
Lambo, see *Pajala*	
L'Avenir	73/82–404
Lawhill 104–253/7–265/6–351–	
406–433/4	
Leicester Castle, see *Vik*	
Leon	67
L'Etoile	62
Lille, Captain Sten	26
Lilly G	506
Lingard	408
Lisbeth	352–354
Loch Carron	313
Loch Linnhe	396
Lorcha, nitrate	202–207
Lord Ripon	430
Louisa Craig, see *Raupo*	
Lyra	249
MacCullum More	93
Maco, see *Søm*	
Macquarrie, see *Fortuna*	
Madby Ann	314
Mae Dollar, see *Somali*	
Magdalene Vinnen, see *Kommodore Johnsen*	
Mahamedeli, Captain	129
Maid of Judah	356
Maine	400
Manurewa	451
Mariendorff	248
Marjorie Brown	274
M. C. Weatherall	271
Medical inspection	174
Medusa	395

	Plate
Melbourne (sh), see *Fortuna*	
Melbourne (4-m. bq.) see *Gustav*	
Mermaid	241
Mertie M. Crowley	280
Middleton	240
Mincio, see *Cleomene*	
Minnie A. Caine	340
Miro	485
Mneme, see *Pommern*	
Moliciero	372/80
Montgomery, A.	164
Morten Jensen, see *Niobe*	
Moshulu, see *Kurt* &	4–6–304/6–back endpaper
Mount Hamilton	294
Mount Stewart	226/30
Mozart	234
Nal, see *Lord Ripon*	
Nancy	292
Narcissus	224
Nautilus, see *Christiania*	
Neale & West trawler	68
Nelly and Mathilde, see *Frideborg*	
Nemrac, see *Carmen*	
Newcastle, NSW, loading coal	188–190/1
Nimrod	389
Nina Podesta	299
Niobe	218
Nithyakalyani	135
Nora	246
Norden	264
Norman, tug	61–67
Novo	99
Ocean	248
Oceanide	45–48–53–70
Odessa, see *Hippalos* (4-m. bq.)	
Oliva, see *Ladye Doris*	

	Plate
Olivebank	39–106–348/9
Oriente, see *Isabel Llusa*	
Ostend	359
Ottone, see *Christiania*	
Outrigger canoes in Ceylon	116
Pajala	92
Pamir	16/17–95–258/60
Parvatharthaniamma	136
Passat	309/10
Patorani	85
Patrie	317
Payne, Arthur	2
Pehr Ugland	233
Penang	341–343/7
Pendragon Castle, see *Lisbeth*	
Peru, see *Raupo*	
Peter Rickmers	428
Pinisi	86–88/91
Pinnas	214
Pintado	186
Piri	468/84–486
Pisagua	308
Plus	386/8–390
Pola, see *Richelieu*	
Polaris, see *Endurance*	
Pommern	5–96–102/3–349
Ponape	421/2
Port Blakely	352
Port Lincoln	369
Port Victor	517
Port Victoria	357
Potosi	9
Poyser, Captain Fred. C.	2
Prahus	83/92
Preussen	7/8
Prinsessan	383
Prinzess Eitel Friedrich	140–142
Prompt	394
Protector	251

	Plate
Quathlamba, see *White Pine*	
Queen	251
Queen Margaret	176–498/500–502/3
Raupo	452
Regina Elena, see *Ponape* &	424
Revel	94
Richelieu	447
Rigdin	441
Risør, see *Ada*	
River Indus	167
R. J. Hayes	251
Rochambeau	13
Roller topsail (hunier à rouleau) diagram	43
Rooganah	459/60
Rose Mahoney	290
Rosenius, Åke	1
Rousseau	497
Runnelstones, the, map	31
Sailmaker	170
St. Elvies, s.s.	230
Samuel Plimsoll	342
Sanita, see *Anirac*	
Saxon, see *Schulschiffe Pommern*	
Schliebracht	520
Schooners, unnamed:	
Off Asia island	35–37
Baltic	397–399–405
Banks	270
British, Breton and Irish	40–42–68
Wrecked off Deal	330
Leaving Falmouth	353
Beating out of New York	268
In the Nene	245
New York pilot	269
Scottish Isles	207
Scottish Lochs	435
Schulschiff Deutschland	143–146–149/52

	Plate
Schulschiffe Pommern, see *Elfrieda* &	147
Sedov, see *Kommodore Johnsen*	
Seth Jr	384
Seeute Deern, see *Elizabeth Bandi*	
Shakespeare	401
Shippen, Mr	164–172
Shoe, upper topsail	255
Sivasuramaniapuravny	138
Skaregom	514
Skomedal, see *Ada*	
Smack, coasting	507
Smart	516
Snows/Snow-brigs	236/52
Sobraon	356
Søfararen, see *Scottish Lochs*	
Sofia	37
Solblomsten	446
Søm	425
Somali	512
Songvaar	328/9
Sound of Jura	510/11
Southern Cross, see *Ysabel*	
Souverain, see *Hippalos* (4-m. bq.)	
Speedwell	464
Star of Greenland, see *Abraham Rydberg*	
Star of Peace	355
Star of Ocean	330
Statsraad Lemkuhl, see *Grossherzog Eitel Friedrich* &	153
Suecia, see *C. B. Pedersen*	
Sunlight	232
Sunshine	47
Susanna	307
Svalen, see *Skaregrom*	
Sylvabelle	41–57–60–67
Tangaroa, see *Piri*	
Tarapaca	319
Terrier	242/3

                        Plate

Thomasina, see *Thomasina McClellan*	
Thomasina McClellan	223
Thomas W. Lawson ..	295/7–300
Thorsten	316
Tomaso Drago, see *Diego*	
Torrens	225
Truss	253–255–262
Two Sisters	41
Tyholm, see *Niobe*	
Ungdoms Venner	316
Urania	62
Vale Royal, see *Manurewa*	
Varuna	507
Vellore	365
Vema, yacht	404

Vesores	439
Vigilant (ketch)	Frontispiece–59
Vigilant (bg)	250
Vik	219
Viking	14–105–367–440
Vimiera	409/10
Vittoria, see *Anirac*	
Voorburg, see *Alexa*	
Waimana	466
Wandsbek	431
Wathara, see *Lingard*	
Wells, Mr.	164
Xavega	154/62
Zealandie, s.s.	321

ACKNOWLEDGEMENTS

The Publishers have so many people to thank for their co-operation in making this book possible. It is not merely a matter of those who have contributed text, anecdote or pictures, but of the many who have not, in fact, produced any of these things yet who have pointed the way to others who could, or have in some cases acted as voluntary translators or agents for us in different parts of the world. People who said to us: *'Why don't you contact so-and-so?,* even if they contributed nothing directly to the book themselves, are no less deserving of our gratitude.

As explained in the Publishers' Note, it was intended that this second volume should be divided into sections, each of which would have its own author. In some cases, notably where Richard Cookson, Major David Goddard and Professor Adrian Horridge are concerned, this aim has been more than fulfilled. In others, the material arrived in somewhat different form. Captains Lille and the late Archie Horka, amongst others, wrote long and fascinating letters, touching on the subjects in question, saying: *'Use any of this you wish'.* Thus, since it is their material, they are accredited as authors and, in such instances, drafts or proofs were sent to them for their approval. In one case, a great deal of material had to be reduced in length and, in others, matters of language were involved while, in the course of a world-wide and massive correspondence, other people added facts or confirmed details, or provided additional pictures which were used to swell the original 'pieces' in some instances, and in others they were included in Sections 13, 23 and 25.

Regrettably there have been delays in the production of this volume, mainly because the publishers* have been in litigation (as plaintiffs!) with the Provincial Insurance Co, and British readers will be aware of the implications when a mere mollusc† finds itself pitted against a firm of such monolithic structure – quite apart from the inordinate delays in bringing actions to the British courts. Thus time passed and, as a result and with infinite sadness, we have to report that some of those who had associated themselves with this enterprise have passed on to Fiddler's Green – that Valhalla of deep-water sailors – during the interval, while others of the older ones have become stricken with illness. We mourn those who have died and who were our very good friends – Captain Jim Gaby of Balgowlah near Sydney: Tomaso Gropallo of Genoa, Carl-Gustav Holm of Varburg; Captain Archie Horka of New York, Captain Severin Waage of Flekkefjord, and others whose names were probably household ones to many readers‡. We much regret, too, that they are no longer with us to enjoy the fruits of the finished book on which they had set so much store. Since some of the contributions were incomplete, and others short, which were best incorporated with other sections which they enhanced, whether in the form of text or pictures, there has been a measure of editing required to balance the book and, in consequence, only the names of major contributors appear in the Contents, where several people are involved in a section.

Captain Severin Waage provided information in Flekkefjord and on the nearby island of Hidra about the *Charles Racine,* in which he had been mate while his father was master. He died very shortly afterwards and his dog, which was his constant companion, followed him within days – a testimonial to the man if ever there was one. Åke Rosenius I met over lunch one day quite by chance when the book was already well advanced, and I

---

*   i.e. The British Publishers
†   Teredo Books Ltd. (Weak joke!)
‡   To this unhappy obituary list must now be added our good friend Captain Sten Lille of Espoo, Finland.

1. One of the contributors to this book, Åke Rosenius, in the days of his youth at the double wheel of the HERZOGIN CECILLE as she passes the Swedish training ship Af CHAPMAN, which started life as the Whitehaven DUNBOYNE: was later the Swedish G. D. KENNEDY and is now at Stockholm as some sort of hostel, and by no means properly 'preserved'.

believe that others will find his anecdotes about his time in the *Olivebank* and *Herzogin Cecilie* as interesting as I do myself.

Jack Neale must be acknowledged as the expert on the Breton schooners which used to visit South Wales, and it is hoped to expand this subject in much greater depth. Captain Turner, a ship-master of great experience, has not only contributed, but helped in many matters concerning this work. Space has precluded a further section by him on the *St. George,* which we hope will appear in a further volume. Captain Gerhard Eckardt of Bremen provided the information for the text on the Deutscher Schulschiff Verein and most of the photographs, while Major David Goddard, whose Maritime museum at Exeter is an object lesson in all that ship preservation should achieve, provided the text and pictures for the two sections on the Farmers' Boats of

Torreira. When he went back the next year (1980) to take yet more pictures, he found that the xavega had become extinct in the intervening twelve months. Thus do the sands of time run out . . .

Captain and Mrs John Hay, who both appear in Pl. 172, are relatively near neighbours, and I do not think I let any cat out of the bag when I state that he is ninety-four, since a quick calculation must make this obvious, but he is none the worse for that, and both he and Mrs Hay (who has far more experience in square-rig than most men alive today) have been veritable mines of information. Herr Thorsten Cervin is another to whom our grateful thanks are due, not only for his own contribution, but for his contacts with Martin Ohlsson, who must be the last European to have sailed as mate in a trading brig. The whole matter of the so-called 'snow' has been the subject of infinite discussion with a large number of people, who have all been so generous in giving their time and expertise to this rather academic point. If the names of some of those who have contributed to the text are missing, it is because it is difficult to identify their contribution to the reader, where the text has become an accumulation of various statements and records.

Equally, we extend our thanks to all those who contributed photographs, including – and the numbers refer to the Plates:– The American Museum of Natural History in New York, 242/3-268/70-497-513-520-522: the late Dewar Brown, 151: Frank G. G. Carr, 240: Mrs Ruth Carr, 411: Thorsten Cervin, 235/9: Captain G. V. Clark, 135/8: The Columbia River Maritime Museum, 354: R. M. Cookson, 139-146-330-253/7-261/7-443: the late C. E. Davies, 233-391-407-417-419: Captain Gerhard Eckardt, 140/1-144-148/50: the late A. D. Edwardes, 327/9-331/4: the late Basil Fielden (many of which were taken by the late H. N. Cooper), 15-24-74-217-219-258/60-275/6-288-294-401-403-433-435-447/8-510/11-516-519-521: C. H. Friberg, 297-363: the late Captain J. Gaby, 453/5-461-487-489: Messrs Gieves, 105: Major David Goddard, 154/62-372/80: the late Dr Tomaso Gropallo, 424-491: Captain J. Hay, 163/74-177/98-200/205-207/13-215/6-523: the late H. O. Hill, 30-145-401-408-439: the late Carl-Gustav Holm, 402: John F. Holm, 449/50: the late Captain Archie Horka, 37-176-228/9-271-283/5-289-291/3-298-300/1-409/10-425-430-436/8-495/6-507-514: Professor Adrian Horridge, 83/92: the late Major Jones, 362-364-501: Captain Sten Lille, 20/23-26/8-30-33-35/7-95-396-400-414/5: Captain J. E. F. Lionnet, 231: Captain P. A. MacDonald, 304-306: the late Captain F. Maltby, 18-82-102/4-106-234-392-406-416-421: the late Captain J. M. Mattson, 326: Dr Jurgen Meyer of the Altonaer Museum, 361: J. K. Neale, 40/61-63/71: the late Edgar Newgass, 394: A. R. C. Osmond. 14-16/17-323/4-340-357-368/71-440-457/8-517: Paull Bros, 336: the late A. H. Payne, 393-407: the late Captain Hermann Piening, 12-346/7: Å. Rosenius, 1-38/9-325: San Francisco Maritime Museum, 176-352-452: (Swanley Coll.) 490-492/3 (Larsen Coll.) 494-498/500-502/4: the late Captain Schutze, 467: Captain R. H. Turner, 73-75/81-108/132-134-226-230-299-309/10-335-337-342-387-389/90-397/9-404-434-459/60-509: the late Captain S. Waage, 221: Dr P. Ransome Wallis, 152: Captain Frank Walker, 469/86-518: Captain T. Walker, 343: Anders Westermark, 383-386/7: Wisbech & Fenland Museum, 245/52-515: State Library of South Australia, 331/4. Others came from the late Captain F. C. Poyser (*infra*), some from the Northern Publishing Co. and some I took myself. No. 508 supplied by Tracy, of Dartmouth.

Captain Frank Walker, now in Mississippi, has contributed a lot, and his name was omitted from the list of authors since he first contacted me when he read a previous book and realized that he and I had trodden the same paths in and around Gravesend at much the same time, and that we must have many friends in common. Thus, in a book devoted to the Medley of Mast and Sail, I have little compunction about including the men in Pls. 2 and 3, since they recorded so much of its history as to become a part of it. Frank Bowen's name as an author is a by-word. He was not 'a' marine journalist, but *the* marine journalist, writing in innumerable periodicals and producing a multiplicity of books for all tastes on *all* aspects of the sea. His knowledge was encyclopaedic, and he possessed by far the largest private nautical library in the world in his offices in the Custom House Building, which looked up and down the length of Gravesend Reach. Almost deserted now, in an age when sea transport is transformed and when the upper docks have virtually died as a result of restrictive practices by their stevedores and by failure to modernise them, it is now difficult to believe that that bustling tideway was then so busy as to represent a veritable microcosm of the world's trade in its everlasting movement of every sort of vessel, from passenger liners to coasting schooners and sailing barges in profusion; tramps from the ends of the earth and square-riggers towing past after Cape Horn passages, or barques and lesser craft from the Baltic. There were deck cargoes of esparto grass and timber; the 'butter' boats from Denmark, banana

*   i.e. Near to the publishers of the British edition.

2. *Left to right: Fred. C. Poyser, A. H. Payne, Charles Hampshire and Daniel R. Bolt.*

3. *Frank C. Bowen in his office in the Custom House Building at Gravesend.*

ships from Jamaica, Dutch schuyts, vessels and companies of all sorts and of nations without number, besides the mass of tugs and various local craft – even the bawleys (shrimpers): all these were there, and so much more.

Bowen broke with his family auctioneering business to make his life one of sheer vocation, not only pursuing his own interest in ships, but helping and encouraging others with the same bent. It was he who founded the original 'Shiplovers Association' (What a terrible name that was – to 'love' ships!) and branches still survive, but his original society was composed almost entirely of men who were expert within their own fields and whose names have, in many cases, become enshrined on the spines of classic books in the maritime libraries of the world. They were no mere 'arm-chair escapists'. Some were old clipper ship men and others were of the same ilk, with such accumulated experience that they knew the sea and ships through and through. As a boy and young man, I learnt much forgotten lore in the swirling pipe-smoke of their meetings!

As a man, Bowen was over-weight and over-worked. He lived in the old Three Daws Tavern adjacent to Gravesend's Town Pier and Crooked Lane. He had once visited the tavern for twenty four hours, and stayed the night there, but he never left again until, after the 1939–45 war, his life fell apart. Each night he took back from his office a bag full of wax cylinders (seen in the picture) and was even dictating into them in bed far into the night. Next day his secretary, Aileen Bolt, daughter of Daniel Bolt (*infra*) transcribed them. Generally, his suits were stained and spotty: the whites of his eyes were yellow, and his colour was bad. Latterly, he suffered from diabetes and, unfortunately, could not take insulin. Finally, and sadly, he was knocked down and killed by a motor-bicycle.

He was a most hospitable man, but seldom accepted hospitality himself. He took me under his wing when I was still about ten years old, and I can state without equivocation, both from my own experience and from that of others, that he was the kindest man I have ever encountered, whilst I believe that he was also the most knowledgeable on maritime affairs at large. He inspired trust, and my own parents, acting against all the precepts and instincts of their generation, gave me almost unlimited freedom to spend days and nights away from home in tugs towing sailing ships in and out from sea, or going over to the Continent, when I was still at preparatory school, which was a measure of their confidence in anything on which he set his seal. (This was long before people were going abroad *en masse,* even as adults.). He knew everyone in nautical circles and amongst his achievements was the founding of the Nautical Photo Agency which was run by his friend, Fred Poyser, and his sister-in-law, Mildred Vincent.

Poyser was a charming fellow, equally abounding in kindness and knowledge, who built up the greatest collection of marine photographs then extant – (many being used in these books). Here, again, was a man whose life was sheer vocation. The enterprise made him no money, but he loved it. Fortunately, due to family connections with Madame Tussauds, profit was not of paramount importance. When he died, it was a problem to know what to do with his vast collection of negatives – many of them old plates – which were liable to deteriorate alongside the River Waveney in Suffolk. Miss Vincent, by then, had damaged an eye and then had a succession of strokes: Mrs Poyser was chair-bound with acute arthritis. Some people started to gather as vultures hover over a dying beast. Mrs Poyser was not impressed. She asked me to take over the main collection, but this was impossible. Finally, after various schemes had been discarded, I suggested that they should be offered to the National Maritime Museum at Greenwich, of which the then director was an old and trusted friend of all parties. This was done, in essence, but shortly afterwards, to the accompaniment of furious controversy, the repercussions of which still reverberate down the corridors of time, change was made at the head of that institution, for better or for worse. As time went by, Grace Poyser, Fred's widow, came to feel that the terms of the transaction had been abused* and lived to regret her decision as, indeed, I have lived to regret my advice to her. Later, those remaining portions of the collection were diverted elsewhere, as were Poyser's splendid collection of models and other ephemera.

En passant, many of the negatives were returned to the original photographers: but many did not go to the Museum – at first by accident, but later by design – and many are now held in the original by this publishing house. It was thus astonishing to discover many of these, including some reproduced in the first volume of this work, published in another book to which reference is made in a footnote elsewhere, stating that the copyright belonged to a certain Photograph Agency†. Some are in the public domain: others not, and we therefore draw particular attention to the fact that the copyright notice in this book means precisely what it says. Nor have the

---

* Though she was gratified to learn of the excellent manner in which the collection was filed and dealt with physically.

† Oddly, the Agency claims to have bought them at an 'executors sale'. Odd, because I was sole and specific legatee of all the Poyser material relating to the sea and ships! There were, by then, no negatives in the estate, of which I possess the inventory.

National Maritime Museum the power to farm out the copyright, (which they have not, in any case, done). Pirates used to be hanged on Execution Dock!

Certainly, if posthumously, Frank Bowen and Fred Poyser must take much credit for the very possibility of this book and its predecessor, not only for the legacy they left but, although I must admit that the conception of the volumes – again for better or worse – was mine alone, had it not been for the good offices of these two men, it is doubtful if my own interest in these matters would have blossomed at all – let alone that I should have gone to sea in sail myself.

Charles Hampshire was, perhaps, the inspiration of modern miniature model-makers. Even now I have before me, amongst others, his model of the barque *Inverness* together with the salvage tug *Crocodile*, in the first of which Fred Poyser served his time, and the second he commanded at Gibraltar in the first world war, and used, incidentally, as a platform for photographing square-rigged ships at sea! (Even some of these are now 'claimed' as copyright by the Agency mentioned, together with a variety of photographs, whose sources, in this country and the USA we know very well!). Hampshire's work can still be seen in a number of museums.

Payne was an indefatigable photographer of ships and craft, and many of his pictures have appeared in our pages. He, too, was a walking mine of information, and anything which floated was grist to his camera. On the right of Pl. 2 is another man whose name – or initials – are known to anyone who has researched sailing ships. Daniel Bolt's father was master of Black Ball; Anderson, Anderson and Devitt & Moore clippers, and he made a couple of voyages as a youth with his father in the lofty *Harbinger*. He became the deputy Borough Surveyor of Poplar, and his great collection of records, notes and ephemera is housed in the library there today*. Oddly, perhaps, he did not write books, by which the world must be accounted the poorer, but, like those kindred spirits, his friends Captain Daniels of Montevideo, who served in such ships as the *Wanderer*, and 'Bull-dog' Woods on the Mersey, he garnered infinite information about sailing ships while the going was still good. The rich harvest of their sowing is still being reaped.

Have these men really a place in these Acknowledgements? And, if not, why are they here? I think they *do* belong for, if they were all dead long before this book was conceived, and long before they could make any positive contributions (as they surely would have done), their influence lives on and has affected others besides myself, whether longshoremen or sailors, and led them into fields of both research and experience. There was no National Maritime Museum in those days: no Maritime Museum in San Francisco (for which the world must thank Karl Kortum), and much else did not exist. Many an author of that time owes his means of research to Frank Bowen and his library, which was virtually an 'Open House'. Were I to catalogue the men I had met there, it would embrace almost every classic maritime author of a generation. Perhaps, taking a break, we would ascend to the roof, to look down on a newly-arrived full-rigger drying her canvas in the sun. As Swinburne wrote: *These things are over, and no more mine.*

Acknowledgements are usually terribly boring (which is why they tend to be in smaller print!), but although these are longer than most, I hope that, because the names of these men are still so well-known, if they themselves have become shadows to a new generation, the foregoing notes and pictures will raise them above the normal level of a soporific!

Alex A. Hurst

---

* Though, in local government re-organisation, it is no longer called Poplar.

4. *'The Trade wind in our hair'* – the MOSHULU.

'Weary am I of the tumult, sick of the staring crowd,
  Pining for wild sea places where the soul may think aloud,
Fled is the glamour of cities, dead as the ghost of a dream,
  While I pine anew for the tint of blue on the breast of the old Gulf Stream.

I have had my dance with folly, nor do I shirk the blame;
  I have sipped the so-called Wine of Life and paid the price of shame;
But I know that I shall find surcease, the rest of my spirit craves
  Where the rainbows play in the flying spray, 'mid the keen salt kiss of the waves.

Then it's Ho! for the plunging deck of a barque, the hoarse song of the crew,
  With never a thought for those we left or what we are going to do;
Nor heed the old ship's burning, but break the shackles of care,
  And at last be free, in the open sea, with the Trade wind in our hair.'

From 'Free', by Eugene O'Neill (see page 205)

5. *Swaying through the Trades in the moonlight — the POMMERN.*

INTRODUCTION

Pictures of sailing ships engender different emotions in different people but, in almost every case, they do summon up a feeling of nostalgia for times now past. Those vessels designed with beautiful lines, together with almost all those shown under sail, undoubtedly hold an aesthetic appeal and, for some, they embody all that is understood by the expression 'The Romance of Sail'.

Past time is like remembered pain, for its rough edges are smoothed and all its poignancy is dulled. 'Romance' is a strange word to use of the sailing ship era because, although there is more than one meaning to the word, it is one which generally implies a fiction or exaggeration and, if some of us were fortunate enough to strike up with the craft in which we sailed some sort of *rapport,* or harmony, that remained with us throughout our lives, it was based on the hard reality of experience rather than on a nostalgic romance.

The sheer splendour of a lofty square-rigger swaying through the Trades in the moonlight under a star-studded sky, with the curves of her canvas caught in ghostly light and strange shadows as the ship swayed almost imperceptibly through the night in a silence broken only by the lap of the water about her bow: when even the warm wind seemed to be gently caressing men and ship alike: when the stars and moonlight faded in all the glory of a tropic dawn to tinge, at first, the upper sails with ethereal pink until the warmth of the rising sun embraced the steady, sail-crowded masts with the gleaming white of virginal chastity as she sped effortlessly over the blue sea flecked with foam, with only the flying fish and the odd whale to sense her passage: − all this, and so much more besides, could lead a man to fancy that he was flirting with that fiction which some liken to 'Romance'.

No picture, particularly in black-and-white, can capture all that magic, for this is the weakness of pictorial representation, save only, perhaps, in exceptional paintings by a few great artists. In this book we shall see pictures of ships and, sometimes, of their men, and all are accurate enough. Inevitably, two things are lacking – the appreciation of sensations and of skills. A sailing vessel in high gale could, sometimes only for the merest instant, pluck even more strongly at a man's soul, almost as though she was making manifest the whole purpose of the pagan gods of old as he struggled aloft, fisting frozen canvas in a night as black as pitch, punctuated with blinding snow squalls. Perhaps that moment of inspiration, amidst all the waste of the winter wildness of the Southern Westerlies, might come in a mere flash of moonlight, momentarily breaking through the storm-wrack to illumine half a mile of white water racing to leeward: to catch the crests of the long Cape Horn greybeards relentlessly pursuing the driven ship, to spill hundreds of tons of ice-cold water over her decks and race on . . . and on . . . to the uttermost horizons far beyond the compass of human vision. That same gleam would glint, perhaps, on the thin, straining arches of canvas on another mast and, above all, he would be left with an appreciation of his part, and the part of his ship, in all that elemental wilderness of wind and water.

Some men never discovered these things and, of those few who did and whose misery was temporarily lifted to a sense of exultation in the very power of their vessel and in the sense of their own place in the whole order of creation, all appreciated that the sailing ship had many deficiencies. There was no Romance about being wet and cold for weeks on end; about suppurating salt-water boils or fighting for hours aloft with recalcitrant sails, nor even about a constant diet of unpalatable food which, sometimes, resulted in beri-beri. Indeed, there was no Romance to be found in so many of the jobs in sail – the chipping rust in the holds: the use of caustic soda in appallingly cold weather, let alone when washing unbelievably greasy dishes with cold sea water in a rolling ship after working on deck and aloft, soaked and chilled to the marrow, any more than there was in trying to free a blocked latrine of primitive design or to clear a wash-port as icy seas crashed over the bulwarks.

6. *The glint of light on a straining sail in high gale – the MOSHULU.*

7. *The PREUSSEN, of some 8,000 tons d.w. was the only five-masted full-rigger ever built and undoubtedly contained a measure of German jingoism in her conception. In certain conditions she was barely manageable. There was insufficient cargo from . . .*

The sailing ship — and the bigger she was, the greater the truth of this statement — either wove a spell on a man and blinded him to all her defects, or she repelled him. There was no middle way. All those dreadful days of desolation, of discomfort and despair, are lost in retrospect, and it is amusing to listen to many of those who attend the Congresses of the *Amicale Internationale des Cap Horniers* — the men who have rounded the Horn under sail. Memory, fortified by books they have read in the intervening years, leads them to aver that it was a hard and tough life, but they have forgotten the *real* sensations as they forget the intensity of toothache directly the offending molar is extracted. *'Yet'*, one asks oneself, *'if they say it was so bad, why are they here to commemorate such misery? Were they, in fact, so attached to "sail"? Did, then, an apprentice, on completing his time, go back as second or third mate?'* Not very often, one discovers. *'Did the younger generation of them'* (now mainly in their fifties and sixties), *'who made but a single passage to or*

8. *. . . Hamburg to Chile to load her sufficiently and, although Laeisz built more splendid sailing ships, they never repeated this experiment, from which conclusions may be drawn. After being in collision with a cross-Channel steamer, she went ashore near the South Foreland and disintegrated through weather and the hand of man.*

from Australia, go back for a second voyage?' Only seldom does one find such a one and he, had he had the opportunity, would probably have been wedded to the sailing ship for all his life. Indeed, some were so wedded simply because, in their eyes, the advantages outweighed the disadvantages, but they constituted a small minority. Others, it is true, might have stayed, but saw greater opportunities to further their careers in steam. So it is that many of the Cape Horners are looking back with longing to the youth which they lost so long ago, rather than to the ships in which they spent it. Yet, it is a good enough club and, when all is said and done, why should they not do so? They are but human.

All, I submit, were the better for their time in sail, since it is undeniable that the character-training it provided was a marvellous by-product of the vessels, but the sailing of those merchant ships has become so remote that those who sailed only for a few months (during which their tasks were generally pretty menial) now speak loudly with an authority to which they

9. *Laeisz's POTOSI preceded the PREUSSEN. Both, in virtue of their length, were fast and magnificent vessels, but the company found four-masted barques slightly in excess of 3,000 tons to be the best proposition. As the Chilean FLORA, she was lost by fire and shipwreck in 1925.*

are not entitled, for many of them never went to sea again in *any* ship. Indeed, some could not leave that one vessel, of which they now speak so proudly, fast enough when she reached port!

The tradition is more thinly spread than is commonly believed. The British section of the Cape Horners recently had at the head of its hierarchy two men, the one of whom, by his own account, had made only one Cape Horn passage during which he was virtually a passenger with his arm in a sling after an accident ashore, whilst the other had made an unexceptional passage of a mere three months in the course of which the captain reported to the owners that *'he is not cut out for the life.'* Other members are now yachtsmen who have rounded the Horn in purpose-built craft, worked mainly from their cockpits and with little going aloft. Excellent fellows all, but with totally different experience. The few old sailing ship masters and others with great experience who are left merely

10. *Prentout-Leblond's FRANCE — the second five-master of the name — was the largest square-rigger ever built, of 5,633 GRT. Originally with two 295 n.h.p. auxiliaries and twin screws when launched in 1911, these were removed about 1920, after which her general performance improved. She went ashore on New Caledonia in 1922. The auxiliaries might have saved her. There was a world slump and she was left to lie there, with no attempt made to salve the big ship.*

raise their eyebrows in silent disapproval for . . . they are old and, if they can take nothing with them to their own Valhalla, equally they cannot leave their accumulated lore and learning behind them.

When the first volume of this work was published, it was in no spirit of nostalgia, looking backwards through rose-coloured spectacles, but in an endeavour to set some records straight and to provide a sense of perspective to the age of sail, which did not comprise merely those famous vessels which fill the history books and which were, in fact, very much the minority. This second volume seeks not only to perpetuate this theme, but also to serve as some sort of springboard from which to view the future dispassionately, since much oil has flowed out of the wells since the first was published.

That man must look to the wind for motive power once again in the foreseeable future is now beyond question, and it is therefore the more

11. Superficially like the Laeisz four-masters, the N.D.L. sail-training ship seen here arriving in the Thames in January 1938, had a longer midship section, steel well-decks and a 128 hp auxiliary which was used little. Built in 1921 as the MAG-DALENE VINNEN, she was a happy ship: as the KOMMODORE JOHNSEN she was over-manned and over-disciplined and, ceded to the Russians after the 1939–45 War, she became the SEDOV. Judging by her odd appearance since, it was some time before her new owners came to understand the sailing of her.

important that a proper understanding and perspective of the ships of the past be maintained, since the wish is often father to the thought in the minds of many of those who are making proposals for the wind-driven ships of the next century, and who are, often enough, aero-dynamicists rather than sailors. (I use the word 'sailors', as distinct from 'seamen' advisedly, since there is a great difference between the two terms.)

In the age of sail, it is probably true to say that some of the small, local types and rigs were the most efficient for their purposes and could scarcely be bettered. The bigger ships grew, the more improvements

12. *The KOMMODORE JOHNSEN with a shifted cargo of bulk grain when bound from Buenos Aires towards Hamburg in March 1937. In very strong winds and with so heavy a list – here at some 55° – it was not possible to make a good job of stowing her courses even with her large crew of some 72, all told.*

might have been made. (e.g. Perforated sails and the abolition of staysails and of square sails on the after masts of square-rigged ships, as instanced in Volume 1.) That they were not generally adopted was due either to some innate conservatism, which is almost beyond comprehension, or because no-one had applied their minds to better methods which were acceptable. When improvements were made, they were often for the wrong reasons. Thus the French built vessels with long shelter decks to increase their gross tonnage and thereby qualify for a higher government bounty, but *all* square-riggers trading through the Southern Ocean should have been so built as a contribution to both safety and comfort.

Much can be gleaned from pictures, but some aspects of the sailing ship can only be spelled out in words of warning which, often enough, nobody wants to hear. Whether or not wind-driven vessels of the future will be of conventional types is still uncertain. All we can say is that we know that those rigs proved to be practicable, within the limitations of their size and despite all their defects. Thus it is fortunate that, approached with the necessary caution, all the past experience of the development of the sailing ship in its multifarious forms is there to be drawn upon, as though from a bottomless pit, although the practical experience of sailing them is all but dead.

Theorists can be very dangerous, especially when they say that sailing ships of the past could have been improved (which is true) but infer, in the same breath, that ship-designers, owners and masters of that era knew less than they do. This is far from the truth. Moreover, there is a growing propensity nowadays to sweep unpalatable facts under the table where they may not be seen. When the four-masted barque *Pamir* foundered in 1957, the Court of Enquiry convened at Lübeck glossed over the essential factor – that she was loaded with a cargo known to be unsafe in a sailing ship. After I went to print on the subject*, I was called to account by the foremost living authority – a German – for 'stirring up dirty water'. When I pointed out to him the implications of the erroneous beliefs which had been propagated, and that schemes which had no relation to the *Pamir* disaster were being cancelled, he wrote back that I was perfectly right†, and that he had not appreciated these things. He had said that *'It could never happen again, anyway,'* which seemed to be true enough at the time but . . . in the light of the fossil-fuel supply situation, it *could*

*The Call of High Canvas, Cassell & Co, 1958.
†Square-Riggers – The Final Epoch, 1921–1958, Teredo Books, 1972.

13. The French barque ROCHAMBEAU, of 2,725 GRT, was the last big square-rigger built at Nantes (in 1902). She had a continuous shelter deck to increase her gross tonnage and thus her government subsidy. It kept her decks much dryer. She was wrecked 25 miles from Tchio in August 1911, and eventually broke up.

happen again, as I am sure he would agree were he alive today and, even now, official bodies are considering the future of merchant sail.

This book is not about yachts but, some years ago, I was asked to review an excellent work* by the eminent yachtsman, Adlard Coles, which, although it did not spell out the situation in words of one syllable, led me to write:

'. . . (the book) . . . should be compulsory reading for the ocean-racing fraternity and must be absorbing reading for all with an interest in seamanship, even if the latter may ponder on questions outside the scope of the text . . . designed with an element of cunning to incorporate strength and speed, one suspects that that other element of prudence may have been lacking in these yachts when catering for what the author terms 'survival gales'. . . . When Mr Coles writes: 'It looks uncommonly as though there is a minimum speed necessary to provide steering control

*Heavy Weather Sailing, Adland Coles Ltd, 1975.

when running before gales', he may be guilty of gross understatement but, in any case, one can run too long, particularly when single-handed. Thus it is odd that we find no mention of streaming an oil-bag to a sea-anchor. If these craft have insufficient grip on the water forward to lie to it properly, we must ponder again. . . .'

The fact is that these craft are so cut away forward that they cannot heave to conventionally and are therefore unseaworthy in the true sense. Certainly they sail faster thus in normal circumstances, and they may never encounter a 'survival gale'. This implies luck, but all will know of the tragedy and fiasco of the 1979 Fastnet Race which involved much loss of life and yachts, besides such a vast rescue operation*. Whether the results of the subsequent enquiry are considered to be any more useful than those pertaining to the *Pamir* may be open to question. One survivor stated that his yacht was hove to when knocked down by a big sea on her beam. How could that be, if she was hove to properly?

The sea is an element which does not suffer fools, gladly or otherwise, and she is not to be flouted. Some safety precautions in modern ships have, perhaps, been taken to absurd extremes, but the dictates of common prudence can only be neglected at the peril of those who sail on her waters. It is all the more important in vessels whose crews are amateur and who cannot, in the nature of things, have much experience of gales. That of the Fastnet Race could well have been of even greater intensity. If the unhappy events which followed had not taken place then, they must inevitably have occurred somewhere, at some time.

Today we see a craze for sailing deep-water single-handed, and races are sponsored by yacht clubs and commercial enterprises who are deemed to be responsible. Let us suppose that we all forsook our motor-cars and decided to go sailing single-handed about the world. Is not the prerequisite of seagoing prudence to keep a proper lookout at all times? How can a single-hander do this? Were we all to behave in such an irresponsible manner, chaos would quickly ensue on the sea-lanes. Surely no-one would suggest driving along a motor-way, freeway or autobahn with his eyes shut, or asleep? Yet . . . there is no difference.

Some good did emerge from the enquiry into the 1979 Fastnet Race debâcle. Comments on stability were valid, together with those on rudder failure and other matters. It was clear that many of the men involved had

*Costing the British taxpayer alone £350,000.

14. Fresh water was always a problem on long sailing ship voyages and even drinking water in the ship's tanks could become short — let alone that for washing. This latter was collected from scuppers from the poop or midship section or, as in this case aboard the shelter-decked VIKING, by means of a rain-sail.

no proper understanding of their life-saving equipment, and pertinent conclusions were drawn from the flooding which arose when washboards were lost as the yachts capsized. When the term 'capsizing' is used, it does not merely mean going over onto their beam ends, but going through 180° and, in some instances, 360°!

I found nothing in the report to suggest that such behaviour was utterly unacceptable, nor that a craft which was incapable of being hove to properly was not really seaworthy, however well she may have been handled.

If yachtsmen choose to put their lives at risk by going to sea in unseaworthy craft, that is a matter of supreme indifference to everyone else, always providing that they do not expect other people to imperil their own lives in rescuing them – as was, in fact, the case. The main blame was laid at the door of 'the deadly enemy, the sea'. If this finding were to become established as some sort of precedent – blaming weather for disasters in merchant sailing ships of the future – it would be an ominous and dangerous one. Competently handled, any vessel should be able to weather any conditions which she might encounter, and she must be sufficiently seaworthy and capable of being handled efficiently to this end. If she is not seaworthy in the true sense, she should not venture into waters where she may encounter conditions beyond her capacity. Adlard Coles' book, and my review of it, were written long before that fatal race. For differing reasons, many people do not always want to face the consequences of reality.

Of course, there have always been disasters at sea, and so there will always be. It can be said that most – if not all – of them are caused by error of human judgement at some point, if only with the benefit of hindsight. The various forms of craft generically termed 'dhows' were excellent for their purposes within the seas through which they traded, but it would have been the height of folly to have attempted to beat such a vessel to the westward around Cape Horn. Their rig was not suited for such a passage. Similar examples could be quoted, and will be quoted in this book, but this does not infer that the craft concerned were not ideal for the purposes for which they were built.

It is easy to say that merchant sailing ships of the past were often too conservative in form and rig; that owners, designers and masters tended to cling too hard to old and tried ideas and generally eschewed experiment. Such criticism is basically fair but, having made it, it should be qualified by saying that changes should have been made gradually and by stages. In the years following on the 1939–45 war, apart from phenomenal advances in navigational equipment and the like, many merchant ships have advanced in size to hundreds of thousands of tons, and yachts have altered radically in form, being lighter with quite different stability curves and with less grip on the water. Since statistics are dangerous and can always be slanted, let me merely cite the case of two sister ships of some quarter of million tons apiece which both went missing in a relatively short space of time*. No-one knows for certain what happened to them, though most competent naval architects have a pretty shrewd idea.

*The *Berg Vanga* and *Berg Istra*.

15. *The last five-master was the Danish sail-training ship KØBENHAVN. She had an auxiliary, but went missing after a few years of life. It is widely believed that she hit ice near Tristan da Cunha.*

The vessels seemed to be excellent enough on their drawing boards, which did not take account of the fallible human element, for their size was such that their tanks could not be – or were not – cleaned out properly after discharging volatile cargoes, with the probable result that they exploded and sank. So, in the loss of these two vast vessels*, disappeared the equivalent of fifty or sixty pre-war ships in terms of tonnage!

In much the same way, designers of off-shore racing yachts, untested by extreme weather for some years, made change after basic change in their quest for lightness and speed. The ultimate proof of any pudding always lies in the eating – or, in these cases, the sailing – *in all conditions*. The yachts were tested in that fatal Fastnet Race and were found wanting. Whether in a yacht, in a vast bulk carrier or in a more conventional sailing ship, change in design and size must be gradual and, when the sailing ships of the future come to be built, theorists must only be given a limited amount of head at any one time, in order that their beliefs may be tested fully, step by step. If innovation in ships of the past was too slow, that was

*Lineal descendants, by house flag, of the *Charles Racine* (page 203).

surely a lesser fault than making extreme changes too quickly! It is useless to say that a huge vessel is more economic if she cannot be relied upon to stay afloat.

Seamen today lead a far more sybaritic existence than in the past. A superficially pleasanter and more profitable one, no doubt, if more soulless and with apparently unlimited leave, but their ships are often so large that they are far more divorced from the sea itself and from the weather and, in truth, they do not have the same immediate and personal control over their vessels. The old skills have vanished and pride in ship has diminished in almost inverse ratio to the increase in what materialists term 'better conditions'. If these words seem harsh or extreme, let the reader refer to the records. The facts speak for themselves. Moreover, in how many modern vessels can one sense the 'pride in ship' which used to exist? Not very many, yet it is a quality essential to a successful sailing ship. Perhaps its absence today is as much the fault of the designers as of the men since, for all their modern innovations and gadgets (which do not always seem to achieve the expected benefits), the modern functional ship lacks personality and does not engender pride. I doubt if many VLCC* masters could even sail a Thames barge today. How, then, shall we man the sailing ships of the future, even if they approximate to their predecessors, let alone the monsters dreamed up on the drawing boards?

Man may have landed on the moon and performed similar exploits of greater or lesser worth, but he has not yet learned to conquer the elements, and the old, fundamental principles are no less binding than they were a century – or five centuries – ago. Today we hear of proposals for a five-masted barque half as big again as the almost unmanageable giants of the past, and more than twice the size of any sailing ship in which anyone alive has sailed. One such craft is no good: there must be whole fleets to maintain trade when oil becomes intolerably expensive or unobtainable. No-one, *alive or dead,* has experience of such vast sailing ships and, although it is true that square-riggers (and others) were sometimes sailed across the world by shanghai-ed, hobo crews in the past, there was always a *cadre* of trained men aboard, while the master and mates had years of experience behind them. This state of affairs does not exist today and all the old skills need to be re-learned. Moreover, really successful ships were under masters who had not only developed a *rapport* with them, but who

*Very Large Cargo Carrier.

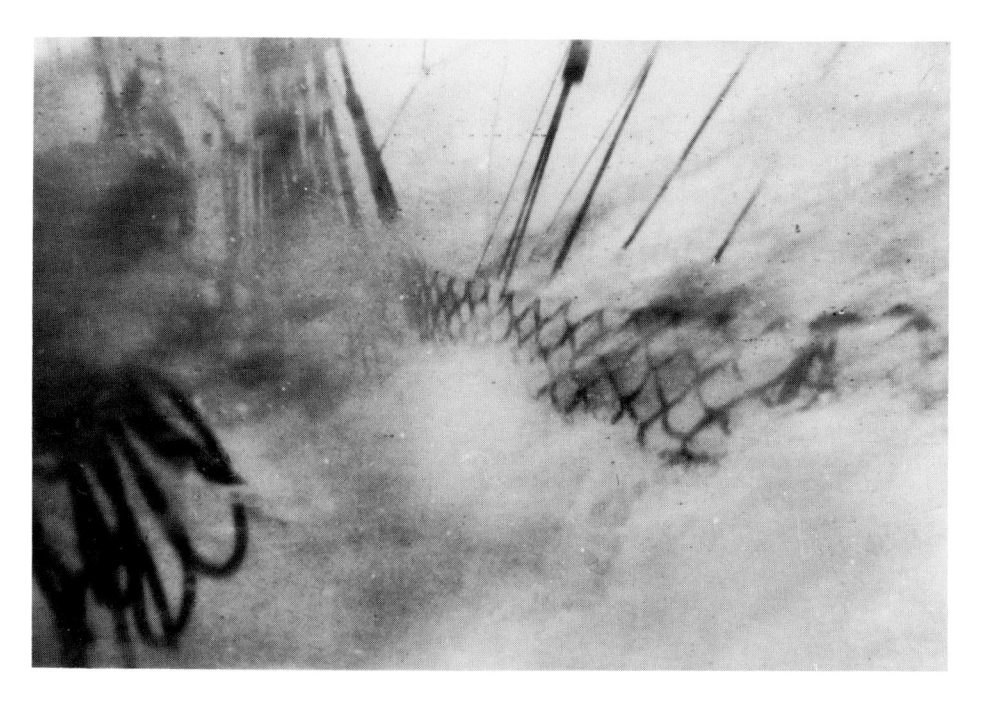

16. As the PAMIR makes a deep-loaded passage round the Horn, the air is almost solid spray as seas sweep over the decks and the braces rise out of the Southern Ocean itself. The need for the life-nets is obvious. Even without bringing home the intense cold of the scene or the relentless roar of the wind, the picture bears ample testimony to the incompatibility of square-rigged ships and modern seamen's union practices, for their material expectations have risen enormously since the sailing ships became defunct. Where shall the sailors of a new era of sail come from? And where shall officers, with experience in high latitudes, be found today?

possessed some sixth sense involving the very elements themselves. Whether this was inherent or acquired is open to opinion, but it is as indisputable as it is unquantifiable, and it is the reason that some ships shone only under certain individual masters, but not under others. If anyone thinks that radar and other modern navigational aids supplant this sixth sense, which seemed to be some sort of mystique to those who did not possess it, he has only to scan the current Lloyds casualty reports to perceive the fallacy of his belief.

To send a large sailing ship to sea with insufficient trained and qualified men at all levels would be to put her at risk — a risk which would extend far beyond her crew and her cargo to the future of any such enterprise. This would be illogical, since it is almost always men, and not ships, which are the cause of maritime disasters, but logic does not always attend enquiries. To start any such operation with an outsize vessel, by sailing ship standards, before skills had been re-acquired, would be the height of lunacy yet . . . it could . . . and may . . . happen. Conrad wrote that any ship would sail without ballast . . . until she turned over. The *Pamir* and her consort made several voyages with grain in bulk before Nemesis struck. It was only a matter of time. Lessons there are in plenty, writ clearly on the tablets of the past.

Nevertheless, we hear proposals for schooner-rigged vessels of tens of thousands of tons . . . and so on. This book will explain the troubles of giant schooners of the past on ocean voyages and, if the proposed schooners have lighter gear, they must have considerably more sail area if they are to overcome the very wind-surfaces of their vast hulls. I believe that the aero-dynamicist can contribute much that is new and useful to the sailing ship of the future and, for all my personal regrets for the ships in which I served myself, I should be sorry to think that an improved form of vessel could not be produced. Even if it be a negative argument, the past holds such a wealth of experience that it should be possible to avoid many of the pitfalls inherent in the future, provided that some of the sacred cows can be kept at bay. Two of these are the insensate and twin desires for speed, and for size.

Obviously, the larger a ship and the more cargoes she can carry in a given time, the more economically viable she will prove to be, always providing that she can be kept fully employed, sailed safely and that she can be loaded and discharged with expedition. To say that these latter qualifications do not always hold good in practice would be to understate the case in this age when dockside labour calls the tune to which governments and managements dance, and when economists (who have appalling track records) are treated as though they were major prophets. Nevertheless, in the new era of the silicon chip which is already beginning, it is

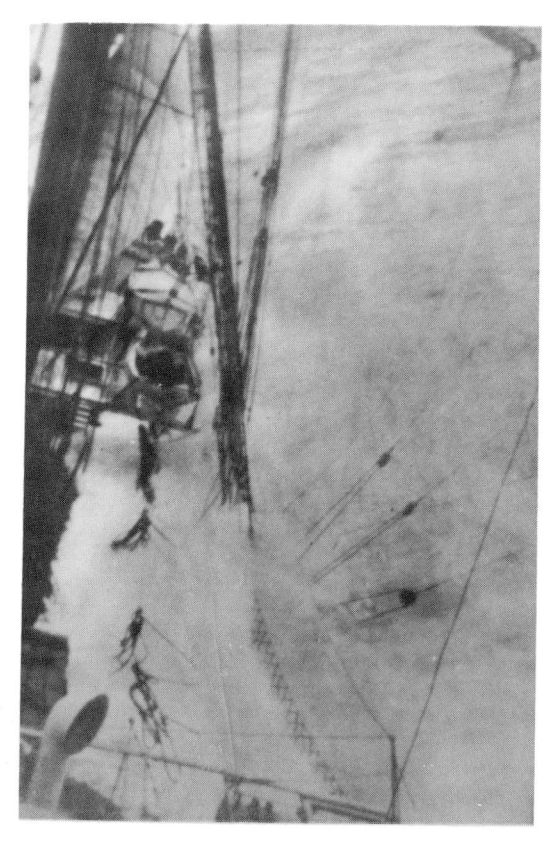

17. With running gear made up on the lifelines, the PAMIR battles with the Horn.

predicted that whole employment patterns will be changing radically with, perforce, entirely new philosophies for living. I wonder how large these factors of speed and size will loom in such changed conditions?

Unashamedly, this book is once again looking back into a past which, whether or not people choose to call it 'Romantic', was at least fascinating. It does not look into the future, since the authors have not the ability to do so with any conviction but, if it serves to persuade those who are engaged in this activity to walk before they can run – or whatever the nautical equivalent of this metaphor may be – it will have served a dual purpose.

Alex A. Hurst

18. *Pilot aboard, the FAVELL ghosts past Dover. Unusually, she was built under the cover of a shed before launching at Bristol by Charles Hill on their own account. She was named after Miss Favell Hill, of their family.*

This is an age when terminology and, indeed, language generally is being abused with joyous abandon and when it is common enough for some vessel, often peculiarly converted to indulge in what is euphemistically described as 'sail-training' frequently to be described as a 'Tall Ship' and sometimes, for good measure, as a 'Clipper'. So an American yacht club recently issued a handbook which, it claimed, was *'all you want to know about sailing in a nutshell'*. No-one connected with the writing of this book accepts that anyone can sail in a nutshell!

Certainly it is an age when the school-ships, possibly because they are, to all intents and purposes, the only true square-rigged ships left in commission, receive publicity and attention far in excess of their deserts, thereby acquiring adulation and photographic coverage to a degree formerly accorded only to Hollywood film stars, so that it is sometimes easy to suppose that they are themselves turning into some sort of nautical sex-symbols. It is always dangerous to generalize, but most of the purpose-built school-ships, which do not, of course, carry cargo, are of necessity over-manned, usually providing relatively short sea-going courses which operate within tight schedules. They seldom encounter hard weather or high latitudes and have never termed themselves (however other people may describe them) as 'sail-training' ships, since it is manifestly impossible for them to produce sailors in the real sense of the word. As 'drill' ships, instilling a sense of discipline, they often do an excellent job.

Sail-training ships were a different matter altogether. Their total crew, including cadets, was generally larger than that of a conventional merchant sailing ship, and they did carry cargo which, of itself, precluded running to pre-determined schedules dovetailed with courses in shore-based establishments. They traded wherever their freights took them, and thus their boys had a longer and more concentrated experience in sail, usually in all latitudes. Any man who served in square-rig became 'sail-trained', but the sail-training ships, fitted expressly for the purpose, usually provided more for their cadets than the run-of-the-mill merchantmen provided for their apprentices, both in theoretical instruction and, often enough, in conditions of accommodation and the like. The line of demarcation between sail-training ships, built or converted for the purpose, and some merchant ships which carried a number of apprentices who were not treated merely as 'cheap labour', was not always clear, and the most famous of the former were probably those of the Nord Deutscher Lloyd (which never owned many vessels) and Devitt & Moore, whose first cadet ships were clippers on the Australian run.

However, there were many more sail-training schemes than is popularly supposed but, as the ships tended to go about their business without the flourishes and fanfares which seem to attend the school-ships today, they did not always receive the meed of attention which they merited. One of the most successful and long-lived schemes was that of the Finska Skolskepparederiet – The Finnish School-ship Association – which was, I believe, the only such company to utilize the words 'school-ship' for cargo-carrying vessels. In fact, and mainly for accounting purposes, this was a subsidiary of the well-known Finska Ångfartygs AB (The Finland Line), which was building up a large fleet of steamers, and the *emminence grise* behind the sail-training enterprise was Mr Lars Krogius of this company, who backed it until the last sailing ship was broken up in 1934. Of course, until Finland achieved independence after the 1914–18 war, the ships were wearing the Russian ensign. Initially the company was called the Finska Rederi Aktiebolaget, and the manager was Captain Gunnar Rydman until 1921, when he was dismissed by Mr Krogius after misuse of the company's funds had been called into question.

The first three ships were purchased almost simultaneously from the same owner, J. W. Söderlund of Raumo, and comprised the bald-headed full-rigger *Glenard* of 1,937 tons, built on the Clyde in 1903 for the Glasgow 'Glen' Line: the four-masted barque *Fennia,* of 2,262 tons, and built in Belfast as the *Goodrich* for the local firm of Boyd Brothers, and the Bristol-built and, originally-owned, three-masted barque *Favell,* of only 1,309 tons. They had passed to Raumo ownership in 1900, 1895 and 1897 respectively and had been well maintained. In fact, the *Goodrich* had been only three years old when sold to Söderlund, doubtless having been considered by her previous owners to be rather small for her rig in the light of the economic situation then prevailing. After ten years of general trading, this vessel was requisitioned by the British Shipping Controller in 1917 and converted to a full-powered tanker – the *Fiona Shell* – though this unhappy transformation was not completed until after hostilities had ceased.

19. The GLENARD after being re-rigged as a barque. She was bald-headed as a full-rigged ship previously.

In 1919 the *Glenard* was almost totally dismasted in the Bay of Biscay and was towed by the French steamer *St Patrice* into Brest, where she was re-rigged as a barque. It is generally believed that this mishap occurred in the Bristol Channel and was only a partial dismasting, but this was not the case*. The facts of the case were that, after discharging a cargo of linseed from the River Plate in the Thames, she was loaded with a part-cargo of cement. The chief mate was new to the ship, and this cargo was loaded too low in the hold, with the result that she was terribly stiff and, when she struck a heavy gale in the Bay, her masts were literally rolled out of her*. However, after being re-rigged, she was kept in trade, despite the slump that was setting in and, with the consequent fall in values, the Finland Line purchased the fine four-masted barque *Champigny* which was then laid up with so many other French square-riggers in The Cemetery – the Canal de la Martinière.

*An error perpetuated in Square-Riggers – The Final Epoch, 1921–58.
†Predictably, perhaps, this matter was hardly raised at the enquiry! See page 10.

20. After dismasting, the wreck of the GLENARD's mainmast . . . .

21. . . . and the mizzen. Note the damaged catwalk, rails, etc.

22. The GLENARD dismasted. Note damaged lifeboat.

23. A weather side view, looking aft.

24. The second FENNIA, ex-CHAMPIGNY, dropping the Mersey pilot when outward bound on her last voyage . . .

Built in 1902 under the French bounty scheme, which put a premium on gross tonnage, this vessel had a long shelter deck and was thus ideal for conversion to a cadet ship while, with a net tonnage of 3,112, she was a good deal bigger than her predecessor for, on purchase, she was also named *Fennia*. When she was converted and ready for sea, it was decided to sell the old *Glenard* for scrap, and she was duly towed to Sunderland breakers after discharging a cargo of saltpetre at Hull. Although conversion from full-rig to barque rig was often beneficial (since the after yards on a full-rigger often do more harm than good), this had not proved to be altogether the case where the *Glenard* was concerned, and the re-rigging had not only detracted from her appearance, but also from her performance.

The second *Fennia* was a fine vessel and excited admiration wherever she appeared – in the Mersey; at Gulfport, in Australia and on the West Coast of South America but, on passage from Cardiff with a cargo of patent fuel towards Valparaiso, she encountered appalling weather off

25.   ... and making sail, showing her elongated poop and foc's'le head, increasing her gross tonnage like so many French-built vessels of her period, which thereby increased their 'prime', or bounty, enabling them to undercut ships of other nations.

the Horn early in February 1927, and was almost totally dismasted, apart from her fore lower-mast and a portion of her jigger, which was just enough for her to limp back to Port Stanley under jury rig. She was the last square-rigger to be dismasted off the Horn but, by that time, a dismasting of that order was a virtual death sentence, freights and profits being much depressed, and she was condemned in the Falklands.

So the *Favell* was left. One might say 'the little *Favell*', since she was small by the standards of the square-riggers left afloat and trading deep-water although, of course, she was a great deal larger than many of the famous clippers and other vessels of previous decades. 'Big' and 'Little' are two other adjectives which mean different things to different people! She was an attractive vessel to the eye and, like her Finland Line consorts, it was not immediately apparent that she was any different to a normal trading square-rigger, although an extra deck-house had been fitted aft when she was converted for sail-training. With a crew of between 30 and 35 all told, against 18 when under British ownership (and perhaps 26 in

26. Captain Sten Lille as an apprentice aboard the GLENARD.

the biggest of the undermanned Erikson four-masters, more than twice her size), she still had the original galley, store-rooms and water tanks. There was only the master's lavatory aft, and the mates had to go forward under the foc's'le head (which one would suppose to be most irritating for them) and thus it is apparent that she had not been altered to any great extent. Certainly she was always a very happy ship, and no-one ever deserted from her, as was so common in the Erikson ships with which she was so often running.

Like the *Glenard,* she was mainly painted with a white hull although, in her last years, she was black. In these plates she may be seen in both states, and readers may form their own opinions about which was the more pleasing.

The painting of a ship's hull is surely as much a matter of personal taste as a painted picture. White always enhances size and is thus, perhaps, unsuited to a large vessel with a shelter deck (vide Pls. 82 and 423) because it gives the impression of increasing the bulk of the hull in comparison with the masts and spars, but it is excellent for smaller craft with cleaner sheers. It may well be thought that the green hull with a gold stripe of the Aberdeen White Star clippers and the great fleet of Rickmers of Bremen was amongst the most inspired conceptions, although the Bordes' nitrate vessels, with their painted ports below a black stripe of only bulwark depth, and light grey between the white stripe of the ports and the boot-topping, invariably looked not only distinctive but exceptionally smart. A line of painted ports on a white stripe on an otherwise black hull tended to make a ship look heavy and, the bigger she was, the greater was that effect (Pl. 307).

Consciously, no photograph of the Russian school-ship *Krusenstern* is included in this book, but her picture is to be seen almost everywhere today, perhaps because she is the largest square-rigger still to be commonly seen. It is true that the Russians, carrying so large a crew, have had no option but to spoil her appearance with the many deck erections and so forth which were not necessary when she was in trade as Laeisz's *Padua* and painted black with, as usual, her midship section picked out in white. Grey and, particularly, red hulls tended to have a utilitarian look, while the colour blue can hardly have been seen by anyone alive today, as it was practically confined to Hine's Sunderland 'Holme' barques running to New Zealand. They were small, and could doubtless get away with it!

As to the *Favell,* she was undoubtedly lucky in her last master, Captain Sten Lille, who has supplied most of this material and who had been in the *Glenard* (taking the photographs reproduced of her dismasting) and also in the *Favell* as both third and first mate before being appointed to command, for he was devoted to the ship although, unlike Captain Waage*, he regarded her rather as a stepping stone to promotion than because he was wedded to the ideal of sail *per se*. The responsibility for painting her black was his and, as he points out with justice, he had restored her to her original state when running for Charles Hill, of Bristol, who had built and owned her†.

Captain Lille is one of the last surviving masters in sail, and his appointment to the *Favell* throws an interesting sidelight on the opinions

---

*Page 203.

† I have joined issue with Captain Lille on this matter. Many ships have had their painting altered over the years, sometimes for better, sometimes for worse. My old ship, the *Moshulu,* started life as Siemers' *Kurt* with painted ports on a black hull (Pl. 303) which made her look very heavy indeed. Later, for a short time, she was white, which did not suit a three-island vessel, and she was probably at her best when black latterly. No doubt, were they alive to read this, Siemers would disagree! (Ed.)

27. *The FAVELL painted white and . . .*

of his peers at the time, since all had been in sail. In his own words:

> *'Promotion in those days was slow and there were many Chief Mates in the fifties* (in the Finland Line) *and I was only thirty-three. I was promoted master of the FAVELL in 1929 only because none of those older mates wanted to leave their families and good table on the passenger ships for 'salt horse' and months at sea in a sailing ship. I was serving as second mate in a small two-watch, coal-burning steamer running between Finland and the UK at the time, when I was called to the office to see Mr Krogius, Chairman of the Board. . . . He told me bluntly:*
>
> *'We need a new master for the FAVELL. You, Mr Lille, have all the qualifications for the job except your age. You are altogether too young.'*
>
> *'Excuse me, Sir', I ventured, 'but being too young is a defect that will disappear over the years.'*
>
> *The old man laughed. 'In God's name then, go to Liverpool and take command'. I left the room walking on air.*

Latterly, the ship was employed in the so called Australian 'Grain

28.   . . . 'as idle as a painted ship upon a painted ocean'.

29. The FAVELL anchored off Falmouth awaiting orders for discharging port.

Race' — a strange sort of race when the last ship could sail long after the first had arrived! — but her relatively small size and build militated against her ever being in the first flight. It is doubtful whether she made much profit in Captain Lille's first year, as freight rates had slumped and she only got 20/− per ton, which was below the generally accepted break-even point, but thereafter the market improved and there was also the odd timber cargo to South Africa on the way out. She lost the best part of a suit of sails in a cyclone off the Azores outward bound in 1929, on his first voyage as master, and subsequently suffered a minor collision in Durban and, when making about nine knots down Channel in 1933, a small coasting steamer, the *Asteria,* tried to cross her bows and caused a collision for which her owners admitted full liability. The *Favell* could not heave to quickly, since her headgear was gone and she was thus in the same sort of position as the *Preussen* after her famous collision, since precipitate action could have lost the masts and, in any case, as pointed

30. *The FAVELL becalmed again – now painted black.*

out on page 108, a sailing ship does not have hydraulic brakes and cannot 'stop' quickly at the best of times. However, she put into Falmouth for repairs which were, fortunately, all above the waterline, and it was not a matter of great consequence in the event.

On her return from Australia, she had been sold to shipbreakers near Wiborg and the return passage after discharging was, as Captain Lille put it, 'a melancholy one'. To deliver a ship like that, of which one has almost become a part, must be a thankless task, and to that must be added, again in his own words:

> '... My own future also looked bleak. After five years in command, I did not know if I would have to start again as an officer in one of the Finska Ångfartyg's steamers, now that the company had done away with its training ship organisation.... None of my older colleagues had envied me my promotion to the FAVELL, but now it was a different matter. Could Mr Krogius give me command of even one of the Company's tugs without evoking the wrath of all senior officers? Most of those who had refused the FAVELL away back in 1929 were still waiting for commands....'

33

In the event, Mr Krogius *did* give him command of one of the Company's vessels running to South America, to the ill-concealed annoyance of many older chief officers who held to the doctrine that one should have one's cake and eat it! However, bringing the *Favell* home for the last time, under sentence of death, with 1,000 tons of bunkering coal for the FÅA steamers in lieu of ballast, she sailed down the Bristol Channel easily enough, after leaving on 5 October, 1934:

> 'The second night out found us tacking between the Scilly Isles and the Cornish coast without making much southing. The FAVELL was a nice easy barque to manoeuvre in narrow waters and always came about well with an experienced crew and smooth sea, but this time the wind seemed to work against us, so that we were always on the 'wrong tack'. I was also somewhat short-handed, as many of the senior apprentices and the third mate had left the ship in England to enter navigation schools in Finland which start their academic year on 1 September. By daybreak we were over on the Scilly Island side and, when I went about, I thought that we should clear Land's End on the starboard tack.
>
> But again the wind seemed to draw more to the south and freshened at the same time. I stood on, hoping for the best. Visibility was good and the high headlands of Land's End stood out clearly. . . . There is, of course, a group of rocks called the Runnelstone less than a mile from the shore and marked by a buoy. I sent the mate for'ard to look for the buoy and he called out that it was straight ahead and that we should never clear it. I gave the order 'Ready to go about!' but then hesitated. In an astonishingly short time a choppy sea had got up and I was not sure if the FAVELL would stay with her light draft . . . and, looking to leeward, it did not seem that we had room to wear. I had stood on too long! In desperation, I took a glance at our old 'blue-back' chart and **thought** I could see a clear channel between the Runnelstone and the shore, so I gave the helmsman the order to pay off a point and keep the ship 'full and by'.
>
> The next twenty minutes were a nightmare that I can never forget. With her big topgallants full, the FAVELL increased her speed and did not make so much leeway. The breakers over the rocks could be seen plainly, but inside them the passage seemed clear. Not much room to be sure. The headland seemed to hang over us and, for a few seconds, it seemed as if the lee yard-arms would scrape against it. To this day, I believe that the backwash of the seas striking the land saved us. With immense relief I saw Mount's Bay opening on our lee, and soon we had room to wear ship – but it was not necessary. In fact, the wind veered a few points to the Sou'west and we cleared the Lizard with ease and were then able to square up and set the royals for a fine run up Channel.
>
> Owing to the early hour, I did not think we had been observed from the shore, but some 'early bird' of a Cornishman had been about and later

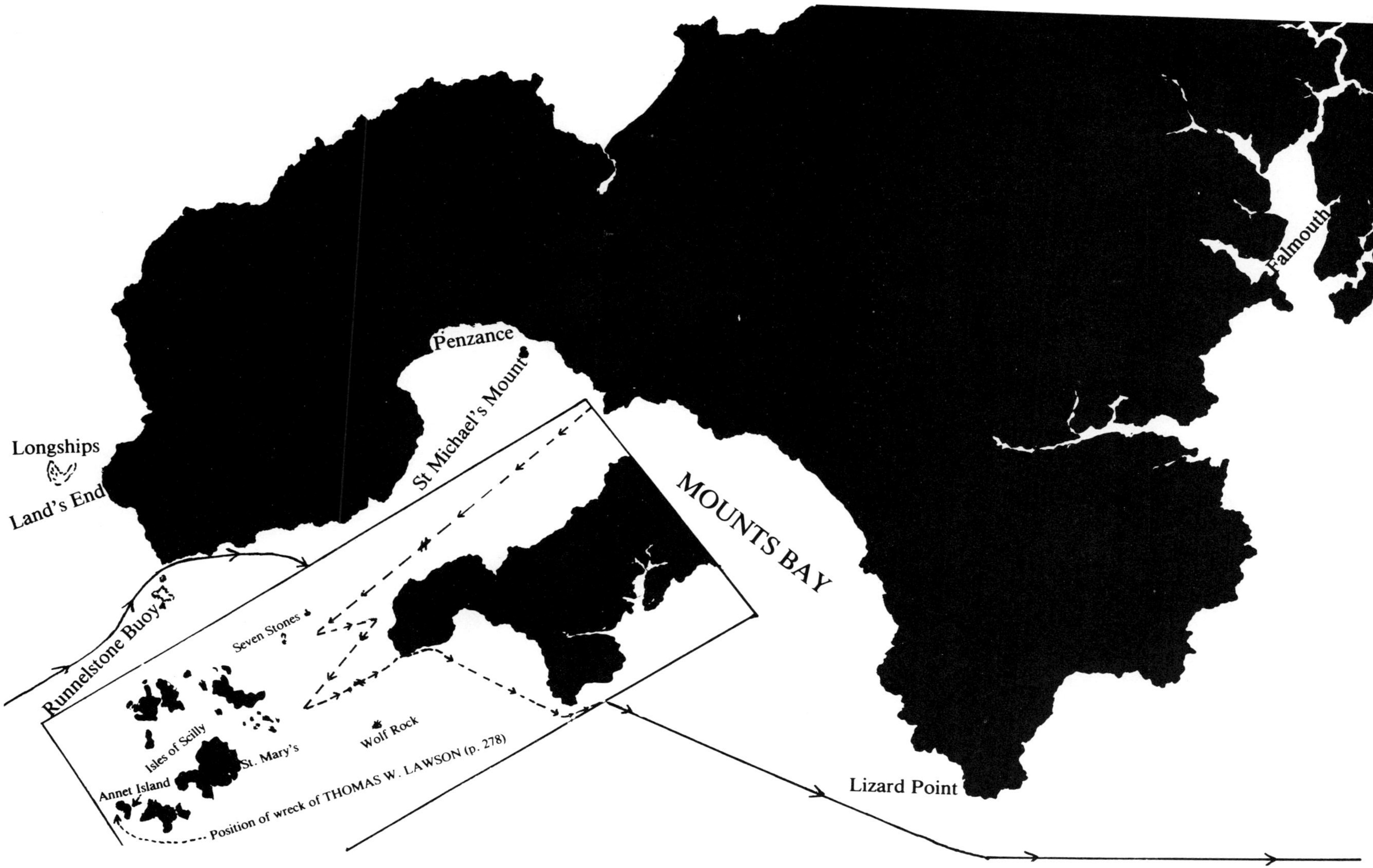

31. The FAVELL's dramatic passage inside the Runnelstone.

32. *The Chinchas – circa 1871.*

mentioned it in some Falmouth newspaper. Months afterwards, I received some clippings in which I was given credit for 'a splendid act of seamanship'. Never was praise less deserved! It was a desperate act which, combined with a measure of good luck, had saved me from a situation into which I had got myself by crass stupidity. . . . Every time I passed the Runnelstone in the ensuing thirty years in command of steamers and motor ships, the sight of that buoy gave me the shudders and, looking at an up-to-date Admiralty chart, it seems impossible to take a ship through inside the rocks. There is even a wreck marked today which blocks the passage completely, except for small boats.'

Reference to the sketch map may indicate the critical situation of the *Favell* that dawn but, to anyone who knows the coast there, the incident will savour of the miraculous, since it is no passage for a deep-water square-rigger. The story is related here, not only as an example of one of the many unsung sagas of sail, but also, perhaps, as a source of inspiration to some marine artist who may be running short of ideas (which seems to be a common condition amongst some of them!). Previously, Captain Lille had been third mate of the barque when, like so many vessels, she had loaded guano at Asia Island, off the coast of Peru.

This was one of the most unpleasant of all sailing ship cargoes, both on

33. The *FAVELL*, with black hull and light ship.

34. The FAVELL getting along nicely in the Nor'East Trade, full and by.

account of its very nature and of its location. The guano islands first became known in 1843, and brought a great fillip to a most depressed shipping economy at the time, when many ships were promptly commissioned and sent out to load – initially to the island of Icheboe off the west coast of South Africa and to the three Chincha Islands (though others, in the Seychelles and elsewhere, were opened up subsequently). None had the resources of the Chinchas, which lie in the Humboldt Current. This is a basically cold-water flow of water which is bent northwards when the westerly drift of the 'Roaring Forties' strikes the southern end of South America and, marvellously rich in anchovy and other fish, it sweeps up the arid Chilean and Peruvian coasts to become a breeding ground for myriad upon myriad cormorants and sea birds which prey on the fish and had roosted and left their droppings on the islands for centuries beyond calculation.

There was some half a ton per cubic yard deposited – and in places the deposits were 200 feet thick. Initially, the ships' crews had to dig it out and take it down to the landing stages by wheel-barrow. It was a dreadful job, since the smell was indescribable, while the fumes of ammonia were intense and irritated the nostrils, often causing nose-bleeding. It was soft and powdery, much of the consistency of pepper, and was mixed with old, rotting feathers and skeletons of dead birds. Being so light, those working in it were usually sinking up to their knees, as it was often loaded in bulk. (If and when it was loaded in bags, these had usually rotted by the end of a voyage and, as a rule, it was deemed provident to send down the sails while loading, as the fumes tended to rot them, too.) Men buried by falls of the walls of the guano pits were usually dead before they could be dug out.

Later, Chinese coolies were shipped out to the workings and, in 1862, roughly at the time of Pl. 32, the second mate of a Boston ship – the *Astrea* – wrote that the guano was 175 feet deep, and that the Chinese coolies, obliged to work naked in the hot sun, were in such condition that he believed that they would rather die than live, but that their guards watched them too closely for them to make away with themselves. *'When one dies, they throw a little guano over him, which the dogs and vultures tear up and then pull him to pieces. All over the graveyard may be seen heads and legs of the poor wretches.'* Little could the cormorants and booby-birds of previous generations have foreseen man's inhumanity to man to be occasioned by their droppings. There were about 100 ships at the anchorage when the letter was written, off the North Island.

Later still, the Peruvian government, which earned a considerable revenue from the export of the material due to its excellence as a fertilizer, supplied convicts to work the deposits both in the Chinchas and on Asia Island, and these transported the dug guano in handcarts to a point above the landing stage in the former, where it was shot down in chutes to waiting lighters which each held about ten tons and were then taken out to the anchored ships, when the cargo was loaded by the crew. On Asia Island, there was no proper jetty, so two bags at a time were sent down on an endless lift.

The islands are simply covered by the guano, for no trees or plants can grow: there is no water; no animals and, apart from some lizards, nothing

35. *Asia Island, with two local schooners in the foregound. The dark patches show where the guano has already been dug out.*

except thousands upon thousands of wheeling seabirds and the odd sea-lions basking on the rocks on the tide-line. At one point, towards the end of the last century, all loading was stopped in order to allow the stocks to build up again – a somewhat optimistic expectation in view of the fact that the accumulation of whole millennia had been almost dissipated in the space of a mere half century!

The *Favell* had discharged a cargo of coal from Newcastle, N.S.W., at Callao in the autumn of 1923 when she was ordered to Asia Island, and was towed the odd sixty miles along the coast while, at the same time, the *Glenard* and the German ship *Bertha,* which had recently been H. H. Schmidt's *Mimi,* and was previously the British *Port Logan,* belonging to Crawford & Rowat, went to the Chinchas. The *Bertha* loaded for Jacksonville, via Panama, and then loaded phosphates for Hamburg, but went missing *en voyage.* It was the time of soaring inflation in Germany, and there had been a good deal of trouble with her crew.

The only other square-rigger loading at Asia Island was the Norwegian barque *Bessfield,* which had been strike-bound in Newcastle with the *Favell,* but these two were later joined by the Peruvian barque *Tellus,*

36. *The Norwegian barque BESSFIELD leaving Asia Island in 1923. The FAVELL is visible at anchor under her stern.*

originally the Dutch *Evertsen,* built at Rotterdam in 1891, which had also been briefly Hamburg-owned and which was finally broken up as late as 1956 when, still on the Peruvian coast as the *Malaboo,* no bidders came forward when she was put up for auction, and also by the *Sofia,* which had been one of the London fleet of John Stewart's and was built as the *Commonwealth* away back in 1873. Subsequently she was sold, in 1907, to D. Loero & Buccelli of Genoa and became the *Cavour,* but was sold to Peru in 1916 and became the *Cuatro Hermanos* before being named *Sofia*. These two ships were also towed up to Asia Island, but were also towed away again, not even having sails bent, and at that time were not classed. Indeed, four years later, after lying idle for six months off Antofagasta at anchor, the *Sofia,* which had presumably accumulated loose water in her holds, started to heel over and then, rather spectacularly and with cameras focussed on her, simply sank! There were also some schooners, coasters and ketches loading for local ports with the *Favell* (Pl. 37).

The guano on the island was then about two feet thick, and the lee side of it was being harvested: the labourers, presumably convicts, doing the digging and bagging and being supervised by armed guards. The ships'

37. Off Asia Island. Left to right: the SOFIA, BESSFIELD and FAVELL with her upper yards sent down since she had towed up to Callao with standing ballast only. Two Peruvian schooners are closer inshore.

crews were free to go ashore after working hours to collect shell fish or to hunt sea lions, so long as they did not approach the convict camps. The guano birds were nesting on the other (weather) side of the island, where they covered almost every inch of ground until the dawn came, when they rose in dense clouds which actually darkened the rising sun until, when they located a shoal of fish, they dived down and the water seemed to boil as each bird emerged with a fish in its beak. The crews of the ships also obtained plenty of fish (though not by the same means!), the most common being a variety of mackerel, and delicious oysters could be trawled up from the motor boat. Normal sailing ship menus of salt pork and beef, stock-fish, weevily pea soup and so forth were, of course, a by-word, but in the Peruvian guano islands the crew began to complain of so much fresh fish and to demand the usual fare!

The anchorage was completely unprotected, and the ships rode with springs on their cables in the open Pacific but, being on the edge of the Trade Wind belt, the weather was mainly fair, though there were 'surf days' when no lighters could come out. These were towed by a motor boat manned by a single negro. The ship had to send men down to the barge to send the bags aboard in a sling, hoisted by the ship's winch, and these, landed adjacent to the hatch, were then cut open and the contents

38.   The FAVELL coming up on the OLIVEBANK (see page 44).

dumped down into the hold – the bags being made up in piles and returned ashore. The smell was not so bad away from the workings, but the ammonia fumes were so strong that it was found to be impossible to trim the cargo, even when men had wet towels round their faces, and finally the carpenter cut holes in the decks through which guano was bled to this end. A midship shifting board had been erected, but this was really academic, as the cargo set so hard that it would not have shifted had the ship gone over onto her beam ends.

   On good days, some 50 or 60 tons could be loaded, so it was all a very slow business, especially taking account of the time taken to discharge the ballast and the odd surf days. The *Bessfield* was ready first and received the customary 'West Coast' help with her anchor and halliards when she sailed, going home south-about via Cape Horn, but the *Favell* was lucky and received permission to come home via Panama, finally discharging in London.

39.

In 1932, when both ships were homeward bound from Australia with grain, the *Favell* and *Olivebank* fell into company near the Line and visits were exchanged, the *Olivebank,* which had hove to, presenting the *Favell* with half a pig which had just been slaughtered. Passing under the four-master's stern, the *Favell* ranged close alongside the *Olivebank's* port (lee) side but, as she slowly came up, she lost the wind in her headsails and, trying to tack, would not answer her helm at the low speed and, in fact, boarded the bigger ship, the rather remarkable Pl. 39 being taken as her bowsprit swept across the *Olivebank's* deck. (There is little time to set camera speeds in such moments when an easy afternoon turns into crisis within seconds and the sails – but only the sails – have been touched up.) Fortunately, neither vessel suffered damage which could not be repaired at sea, and it would be interesting to know whether it was recorded in either log-book!

40. English, Irish and Breton schooners waiting to dock on Cardiff West Mud in 1933.

After some schooners had ceased to cross square topsails on their mains early in the nineteenth century, a topsail schooner was, by definition, one which set one or two square topsails on her fore. There were a variety of types, for some set a single sail: some double topsails, and some set a topgallant or even a royal as well. A square foresail was sometimes set flying when running and there were a few vessels – mainly larger ones – which sometimes begged the question whether they were really brigantines or barquentines. The latter types of vessel do not carry a lower abaft the foremast, but staysails between main and fore, and are thus dependant upon the use of some square sail for their sail balance* at all times when sailing. A schooner, on the other hand, can work under fore-and-aft canvas alone on all points of sailing at all times, without necessary recourse to her square sails.

Most topsail schooners were relatively small and, due to their profusion on the British coasts, it was easy to believe that they were peculiar to the Red Ensign, but this was by no means the case. As the medium clippers in the 1850s started to divide their huge single topsails into upper and lower sails, so the same principle was adopted in the more humble topsail schooners, both in Great Britain and elsewhere, but it was the Bretons who, towards the end of the nineteenth century, introduced what they termed the *hunier à rouleau* or, as it is more generally known in

*See page 94 (Ed.)

45

41. *Lying off Penarth on Cardiff West Mud. Left to right: English ketch TWO SISTERS, two-master GUSTAVE and the Breton schooners SYLVABELLE and YVONNE in 1930.*

English, the 'roller topsail'. More pedantically, it is sometimes called a 'self-reefing topsail' and, indeed, the German name for it is *Selbsttätiger reffender Marssegel,* though there seems to be no evidence that the Germans ever adopted the idea while, in fact, only about three of the myriad British coastal schooners are known to have followed the French example, which must be a measure of the innate conservatism which characterized British shipowners and masters in the days of sail.

The idea was an excellent one and it worked splendidly. Taking in the square topsails of a small schooner did not entail anything like the effort of a big square-rigger but, in a so-called age of enlightenment, there was nothing to be said in favour of going aloft to furl sails on the yards. Some square-riggers had been fitted with patent reefing gear on their topsail yards in the mid-1850s – mainly Cunninghams (which presumed a single topsail)* and Colling and Pinkney's patent gear which assumed that sails could be both reefed and furled, in each case by yards rotating and rolling the sails up like blinds. These systems did give some satisfactory results, but they came at a time when the size of ships was generally increasing and this militated against their efficacy. Of course, this is not to suggest that *all* vessels were becoming bigger, but the fact is that, whether partly due to the conservatism already mentioned or for other reasons, these two

*See plates 242 and 243.

42.   Two Breton schooners making up to Penarth Docks in 1930.

methods did not survive very long, although Howe's patent system, on the other hand, evolved as the double topsails which became commonplace.

The *hunier à rouleau* was essentially Breton and became a hallmark of their schooners which became instantly recognizable by this feature alone. In fact, the sail reverted to a single topsail and was worked in the manner detailed in Pl. 43. With no need to go aloft, since the work was all done on deck, and with a single sail which is always more efficient than two smaller ones, it was a great advance. At sea, the rig was pretty and eye-catching, whilst in port the clews, or 'pigs' ears', did not look so neat as a conventionally furled sail but, since the majority of double topsail schooners on the British coasts, with no topgallantsail, had a bald-headed look when the sails were not set, the Bretons looked none the worse on that account.

So far as I am aware, the principle has never been incorporated into larger craft and the inference is that, as with previous patent reefing gears, there are limits to the size of yard and sail on which it would operate successfully. Some three-masters of around 350 tons used it, but this was probably the top limit.

Although the roller topsail was not introduced until the end of the last

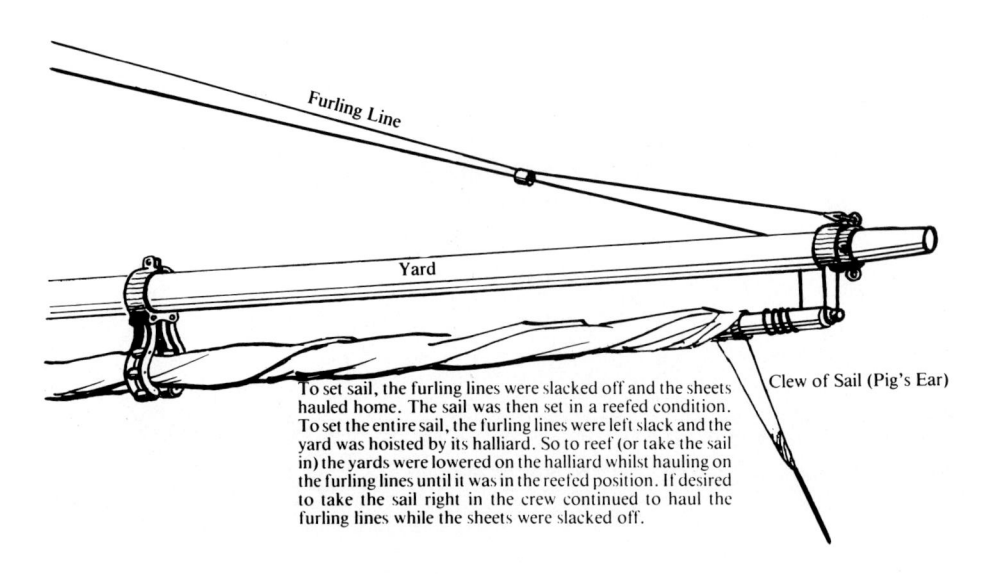

To set sail, the furling lines were slacked off and the sheets hauled home. The sail was then set in a reefed condition. To set the entire sail, the furling lines were left slack and the yard was hoisted by its halliard. So to reef (or take the sail in) the yards were lowered on the halliard whilst hauling on the furling lines until it was in the reefed position. If desired to take the sail right in the crew continued to haul the furling lines while the sheets were slacked off.

43.   Diagram, looking from abaft yard, showing working of a 'hunier à rouleau'.

century, Breton schooners were still being built in large numbers and almost all carried this rig once it had been proved. Perhaps the most famous were the schooners which went over to the Iceland Banks, mainly for cod, which were termed the *Morutiers d'Islande* – or *Islandais* – and were amongst the largest, whilst rather lighter and faster ones were the *Chasseurs*, which sailed out to Portugal with potatoes about a week after the *Pardon* – or blessing – which preceded the mass departure of the *Islandais*, and then loaded salt which they took over to a specific *Morutier* and then, in Reykjavik or some other Icelandic fjord, transferred their salt aboard, whilst at the same time loading the first of her cod which was then sailed home: the little schooner being driven like a racing clipper to make the best of the new market. Then they would go into general trade until the next season, joining a whole host of schooners with basically the same rig, if sometimes with variations in size, which traded round the European coasts – mainly to the British Isles – with a variety of cargoes, not least of which were the onions which Brittany used to grow in such

44. The GLYCINE making sail and sweating up the fore peak halliards.

profusion. These were termed the *Caboteurs*. On arrival, the supernumeries would go ashore with bicycles festooned with strings of these vegetables and sell them from house to house – and very good value they used to be! Then they would pick up such cargo as they could – scrap iron, cement, china clay, or anything else which offered – for the homeward trip. The supernumeries might or might not sail with her, as they would sometimes return in some other schooner.

I have confined my pictures to one trade: that from the Breton ports to South Wales, often bringing over pit-props from the softwood forests of Brittany and taking coal back. Thus, as these illustrations are concerned rather with the trade than with the specific rig, I have included some of the French ketches (or *dundees*) which were runing in parallel with the schooners*.

The square topsail was almost always set in the schooners. From force 6 to 8 it was reefed until the yard was lowered to the cap, but in stronger winds it was usually taken right in. The square foresail, which they called

---

*The origin of the French word *dundee* is not clear. It may be a corruption of 'Dandy', though this rig was properly yawl rigged with a jib-headed mizzen.

49

45. *A pretty little Breton schooner caught against the sun as she runs up the Bristol Channel past Flat Holm and Steep Holm (on the horizon) with a fair wind and her flying foresail (fortune) set. She is probably the OCEANIDE and her crew are on deck to watch the passing of the four-masted barque VIKING, from which this picture was taken.*

the *fortune,* was set flying in fair winds up to about force 6, the fore staysail being run down, since it would have been fouled by the *fortune* and would fulfil no function anyway, whilst the fore lower sheets were checked in, so that the sail would not blanket the square foresail. (The main sheets, of course, were slacked well off, for the *fortune* was a 'running' sail.) These schooners had a smart rake to their masts which enhanced their appearance and, although they could sail without ballast in light weather, they would never have thought of making a passage without it, although they sometimes discharged it at sea before arrival in good conditions.

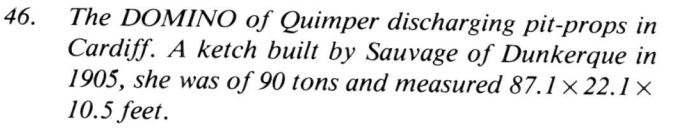

46. The DOMINO of Quimper discharging pit-props in Cardiff. A ketch built by Sauvage of Dunkerque in 1905, she was of 90 tons and measured 87.1 × 22.1 × 10.5 feet.

47. The roller topsails were so peculiar to Britanny that these four sails drying in Cardiff West Deck were almost symbols of a national flag. In the foreground is the YVONNE, alongside the ketch SUNSHINE, both coal-laden and ready to sail home.

48. Dwarfed by the factory chimneys and the Welsh hills beyond, the OCEANIDE sails up to Cardiff West Dock.

Loaded, the ships had a freeboard of only about 15 inches, and many were driven very hard: a fact which has been the basis of many an epic tale. Some of them crossed the Atlantic, perhaps to or from St Pierre or Miquelon, in wild conditions. Hove to, with a trysail set in place of the normal mainsail, and with the inner jib sheeted to windward to slow her down, the square yards were then braced aback to the same end, since the windage of the roller topsail and its gear could present enough surface to give her additional way and make her unduly wet forward. Latterly, all these Breton schooners had roller reefing on their boomed lowers.

They often attained speeds of 10-11 knots, and sometimes slightly more, while a round voyage could often average 8 knots. These schooners were marvellously handy in all weathers, and frequently used to enter and leave docks under sail until most of them had had auxiliaries installed. When there were tug strikes in Cardiff (and there is nothing new about the British workman's propensity to strike) they exhibited their skill by sailing up to the Cardiff West Bute Dock with its seaward dock gates. Sailing a 100-foot vessel in this narrow basin might appear to be daunting, whilst the narrow approach, known as 'The Drain', with its large adjacent buildings, caused fickleness and fluctuations in the wind. The craft needed good steerage way to get through the dock gates, yet not so much that they could not be stopped in time, and it would have been easy to

49.
The HERMANN of Treguier drying her sails in Cardiff West Dock in 1938. One of the smartest and hardest-worked schooners, loading 180 tons, her hull was painted black.

50.

51. *The Treguier dundee (ketch)* IRIS *in the sunshine off Lundy Island. Built at Paimpol by Binne, she was of 86 tons nett and 85.1 ' long.*

have buckled a bowsprit, at best. Moreover, there were mud dredgers and hoppers; steam trawlers, coasters and a multiplicity of other craft on the move, yet these French schooners sailed in and out, time and again, in the manner born, without the slightest trouble or damage. Sometimes, shifting in dock, just the square topsail was used, much as Thames barges shifted in London docks under their topsails.

A schooner was once making the narrow entrance to Quiberon Bay off Port Navale, and making some 9-10 knots through the water, but the tide was coming out like a mill-race and, for half an hour, she was stationary over the ground! Sometimes these craft would leave the estuary stern first when there was a headwind but a strong outgoing tide, not only demonstrating consummate seamanship but watermanship of the highest order.

Everyone knows that the French for 'schooner' is *goelette* but, in fact,

52. A fine view of the CONCORDE of L'Orient, of 95 tons nett, which was built at St Malo in 1908. Painted black with bright green bulwarks, she is seen in tow. In 1922 she crossed the Atlantic eastwards in 20 days.

53. *The clutter of the OCEANIDE's deck in port as she discharges sand ballast, of which she carried some 60 tons in winter and 40 tons in summer when no cargo offered to South Wales.*

the most famous of these craft were always built in Paimpol, and the word derived from the district of Goelo, in which the port lies. Thus, although the French word came to have a general application to any schooner, it was properly applied to that *élite* from Paimpol. A large book could be written about the *goelettes* built there, although there were also *dundees* and other types, including some of the larger *Terre Neuvas* and, if I be accused of giving undue emphasis to the *Oceanide* and *Hermann* in my pictures, it is because these two schooners were both built there and were great rivals in the South Wales trade, apart from the fact that I knew them both very well and had tremendous admiration for their two masters, who invariably made more round trips each year than their consorts on the same run.

The *Islandais* and some of the *chasseurs* had jibbooms and martingales

54. *The three-master KERROCH of Paimpol was one of the bigger schooners to carry the Breton roller topsails.*

which were, naturally, run in when in dock, but most of the *caboteurs* had spike bowsprits, since they were always in and out of dock and the constant running of them in and out would have been a needless chore. All the Breton schooners were delightfully colourful and their hulls were never tarred all over like their British counterparts. In truth, some were painted black, with red below the waterline, but the majority of the fishermen had white or grey topsides. Some of the *caboteurs* and *chasseurs* were black, with white bulwark rails, trailboards and deckhouses, but some had topsides of light or dark green, light or cobalt blue, or of pale grey, while some had black topsides with dark green bulwarks. Almost all had fancy scroll-work on their transoms. It was all rather imaginative.

The *morutiers* were seldom sailed hard, except when acting as

55. *Working aloft in the HERMANN.*

chasseurs, which occasionally happened and when, at all events with a fair wind, they did well on account of their larger size. The *chasseur* was probably the most efficient, economic, handy and seaworthy schooner of her size ever built and, although not a noticeably better performer than a *caboteur* off the wind, would lose her going to windward because, although their outward appearance was similar, the latter had a shallower draft, and the deeper keel and the rise of floor of the *chasseur* reduced her leeway whilst, with her better grip on the water, she was handier in stays. On the other hand, in general trade, she needed more water to float and sometimes needed to await a spring tide when a *caboteur* would already be on her way. The *morutiers,* which fished with hand-lines from on board (unlike the dory fishing of the *Terre Neuvas)* carried about 23 men – the large number being in order to man the fishing lines – but the complement of the *chasseurs* and *caboteurs* was normally about six – a

56. *The GLYCINE, from her lee bow, when homeward bound.*

57. The bows of the SYLVABELLE of Bayonne as she lies on the Cardiff grid-iron.

captain; mate; a couple of ABs, a novice in his 'teens and a *mousse* (or cabin boy) who was latterly about fifteen, but formerly much younger than that.

Handling their own cargo in port, using the fore gaff as a derrick, with the master often ashore and the two younger members unable to do the work of a grown man, there was little rest in a Breton schooner, whilst anyone with a knowledge of the Bristol Channel will know that it is no picnic ground for any sailing ship in winter time with its iron-bound coasts, bad weather and few points of refuge.

The sea-going traditions of Brittany can vie with those of any European community, and its individualistic people are splendid seamen. The exploits of their corsairs in the pre- and post-revolutionary period have become legendary, and it was a rare Breton who was not an asset to any ship's company. It was fitting that their long and glorious tradition in sail

58. *Off Penarth, the EGLANTINE dries her fortune, as the Bretons term the flying foresail.*

59. *The BRETONNE and the ketch VIGILANT coal-laden, waiting to sail in the West basin of the Bute dock. The VIGILANT was built by Deryksen in Dunkerque in 1903, of 79 tons. Dunkerquois ketches usually had straight stems, unlike the Bretons.*

60.

61. With the DOMINO, once in the cod fishery trade, leading, the 80-ton EMILE and schooner SYVABELLE tow in line astern of the tug NORMAN, which always handled these craft in the inter-war years. French square-rigger men always joked that they took so much coal from South Wales that it would one day fall into the sea. The schooners and ketches made their contribution and . . . who knows? – they may prove to be right!

should close on the chapter of these Breton schooners – perhaps in the form of the *Glycine* which made the last Iceland voyage under sail in 1935 and was the last of the *caboteurs* in 1951. It was a further tribute to these craft that, when the French Navy decided to built two small training ships, they modelled them on the Paimpol *goelettes,* since they were convinced that no other type of vessel could fulfil the training programmes so satisfactorily without being interrupted by weather. In the event, they were built with more yacht-like, finer sterns, but in essence the principles were maintained in *L'Etoile* and *La Belle Poule.*

62. The French naval training schooners LA BELLE POULE and L'ETOILE lying ahead of the Dutch naval ketch URANIA from Den Helder and the Oslo school-ship CHRISTIAN RADICH in the Dart in 1962. Their appearance compared unfavourably with the merchant schooners due to the inevitable fore deck-house. The large pig's ears in port were aesthetically a disadvantage to the appearance of roller topsails.

63. The DOMINO, reflected in the receding water on Cardiff's West Mud, but . . .

64. The Bristol Channel offered little enough of shelter. The ketch GOELAND . . .

65.   . . . here, off Penarth Dock, sails up past the anchored EGLANTINE in 1938

66.   . . . with her sails blown out was driven ashore on Friar's Point, Barry, in September 1935.

67. The NORMAN was not a tug to catch the eye, but she did a fine job for these small sailers. Here she tows the SYLVABELLE and the 72-ton ketch LEON, built at Dunkerque in 1906. Such a sight was common enough at the time – October 1937.

68. The industrial chimneys to the left: the steamer being manoeuvred into the Queen's Dock entrance on the right, and all the steamers within it, with the (then) modern Neale and West trawler astern of them, the British and French ketches in the foreground, with the Breton schooner beyond them, seem to belong to the wrong age. The picture was taken about 1930.

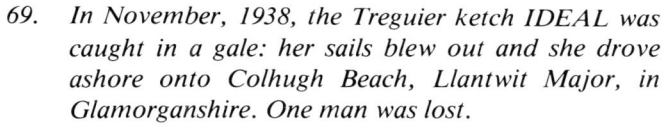

69. In November, 1938, the Treguier ketch IDEAL was caught in a gale: her sails blew out and she drove ashore onto Colhugh Beach, Llantwit Major, in Glamorganshire. One man was lost.

70. The 100-ton OCEANIDE, the HERMANN's great rival, making a good departure off Penarth Head.

71. Perhaps the foreground of foliage is more in keeping with small sailing ships – the IRIS with blue-green hull; the white EMILIE and the black ALMEE. The Drain is in the left distance; the West dock entrance on the far left and the Queen's dock entrance on the extreme right, with Cardiff on the skyline.

72. Light ship, the ARDENTE, built in 1903, passes down by Dover cliffs.

The *L'Avenir* was built in 1908 to be a Belgian sail-training ship by Rickmers of Bremerhavn for the Association Maritime Belge SA which had started its operation with the full-rigger *Comte de Smet de Naeyer*. This ship was ordered from the Grangemouth & Greenock Dockyard company and launched in 1904. Her poop extended forward to the mainmast, to accommodate her large complement including 80 cadets, and her deadweight was slightly in excess of 3,000 tons. In the event, when she sailed on her maiden voyage the next year, from Antwerp towards Valparaiso, she had only 28 cadets aboard, and she arrived back in Antwerp early the following year with a cargo of nitrate. She left again on 11 April that year and proceeded down Channel. The weather was fine but, a week later, she foundered. How or why this happened is simply not clear. Accounts are so confused that it is useless to speculate on the matter. Somehow, somewhere, she made water. Her running gear became washed off the pins into a tangled mess as she settled, so that, when it was desired to take in the topgallants, they had to be cut away. It seems that the boats were not swung out in preparation, and there were only few survivors, picked up by Bordes' four-master *Dunkerque*.

If this account seems bare, it is consciously so, since the reasons for the loss are simply not known. However, in view of a possible hypothesis I shall advance for the ultimate loss of her successor, it should be recorded that she did have water-ballast, deep tanks and a pump room.

However, the Association Maritime Belge, so far from wilting under this early disaster, immediately bought Thos. Law's full-rigger *Linlithgowshire* ex-*Jeanie Landles,* to be used as a stationary training vessel, and at the same time they placed the order for the *L'Avenir,* whilst arranging that, in the period before she was ready, their cadets might get sea-time in Rickmers' auxiliary five-master *R. C. Rickmers*.

When built, the vessel was not quite like her appearance in the pictures, for she had a double spanker and a conventionally proportioned foc's'le head, whilst her wheel was right aft. In fact, the vessel was subject to various alterations throughout her career. In her Belgian days she was normally painted white with red boot-topping, except during the years of the first war when she was painted black with mast-coloured spars, and when she ceased to carry cadets but was run as a regular merchantman. At the end of the war, she was brought home from San Francisco by Devitt &

73. *Unusually, the L'AVENIR's hawsepipes were set vertically, the one above the other. Like most later square-riggers, she had a catting davit at the fore-end of her foc's'le head, in contrast to the catfall of the MOUNT STEWART (Pl. 228).*

Moore cadets before resuming her training function under the Belgians. She was never on any particular run, and appeared with various cargoes in various ports. In the meantime her main wheel had been brought amidships and the after one became an auxiliary, while her foc's'le head was elongated to come well abaft the foremast, creating a very small well deck which was prone to fill with water and only clear with difficulty in heavy weather.

The *L'Avenir* kept running throughout the slump years, and received a Government subsidy as an educational establishment. With the low freight rates ruling during most of that time, and with her big complement, including 80 cadets and instructors, a padre and the like, she could

74. Like all vessels, but especially those with long shelter decks, the L'AVENIR looked better deep-loaded. Here she is arriving in the Mersey in 1937 prior to being sold to the Hamburg–Amerika Line.

never have been viable otherwise. Moreover, although a smart vessel, her tonnage was only 2,074 net, which was about 1,000 tons less than the bigger four-masters of the time which were proving to be the most successful in terms of financial return. Moreover, her long shelter deck precluded the carriage of deck cargoes of timber when available.*

When, in the early 1930s, the Belgian Government were persuaded to build and run their own training ship – which proved to be the barquentine-rigged school-ship *Mercator* – the subsidy for the *L'Avenir* was withdrawn and she was sold to Captain Gustaf Erikson of Mariehamn in 1932, while the Association Maritime Belge went into voluntary liquidation. That the *Mercator* was one of the more enterprising school-ships

* Nor was her deep-tank an advantage in this respect.

75. *The L'AVENIR, light ship in the Kattegat. She is setting two triangular courses. Note the very short well-deck.*

is beyond doubt, but whether a barquentine is the most suitable rig for such a vessel might be open to question on the one hand, whilst on the other it could be argued that a sail-training vessel provides better all-round training than any school-ship, albeit the latter can determine their schedules to a greater degree.

The vessel was very prone to set triangular courses – sometimes all three, and sometimes just on main and mizzen. Obviously, these are easier to work, with no sheets or tacks, but the lack of driving power, with the three largest sails virtually halved in area, is quite considerable, and it may seem odd that, on the whole, they seemed the most popular in sail-training ships with big crews. She did have square courses in her locker, and set different combinations, but there is no doubt that her raised wheel amidships restricted the helmsman's view, and no man can steer well by staring into the binnacle – he *must* be able to see ahead and sense the swing of the ship. Perhaps this had something to do with it, since a triangular foresail and mainsail would have facilitated the helmsman's view.

76. *Looking down from the mizzen lower t'gallant yard. The tack of the gaff topsail is very properly led down to the weather rail – something often overlooked in sailing ships afloat today. The safety netting in her tops was a relic of her cadetship days. Note the harness casks at the base of her jigger mast.*

77. *The highly placed wheel of the L'AVENIR. There used to be two steering compasses, one each side, but one of them was carried away in 1935 and the remaining one was positioned amidships. Originally she had had six compasses, which was almost unique – contemporary passenger liners having only three!*

Erikson kept the ship in the Australian grain trade, but much water had flowed since the situation which obtained in the case of the *Mount Stewart* in 1923 (see p. 214) and ten years later all sorts of people were clamouring to sail in square-riggers, whether as passengers or crew. The former were useful to the owner economically (though an infernal nuisance to the ships' companies!), and some merely sailed from British discharging ports up to the Baltic and fewer to or from Australia. Erikson therefore used the *L'Avenir,* when she was home in time, to cruise round the Baltic with a lot of passengers, for which she had ample accommodation. A band; a grand piano and stewards, etc were put aboard, while the vessel was accompanied by Erikson's wood-burning tug – the *Johanna*

74

78. *The L'AVENIR anchored in Stockholm during one of her summer Baltic cruises, with Erikson's wood-burning tug JOHANNA alongside. At night the yards were illuminated with electric light bulbs. It was all a little spurious.*

— which is seen alongside her in Stockholm from the P & O *Viceroy of India* which was also cruising — if in a rather different manner. At night the *L'Avenir's* yards were illuminated with lights in port, and at sea every effort was made to keep her on the one tack in the first watch when dancing was taking place. No doubt it was all very 'romantic' but, despite these bizarre interludes, she was an extremely functional square-rigger for most of her life.

In fact, insufficient people had enough leisure time in those days to make the cruising ventures a great success and, in 1937, Erikson decided to sell her. She was almost bought by the Nord Deutscher Lloyd, who had long been without a sail-training ship, and had, of course, previously

79. Looking aft, the loss of driving power of the triangular courses is evident, as is the better view afforded to the helmsman amidships, especially when so high above the deck.

owned the *Herzogin Cecilie* which had preceded her in the Rickmers yard by five years and, in some sense, the *L'Avenir* was a smaller version of this ship as originally built. Finally, she was sold to the Hamburg Amerika Line and re-named *Admiral Karpfanger,* painted black, and sent out to load wheat in Australia with a full complement of cadets. On her homeward trip she went missing. When built and Belgian, she had had radio which, until alterations were made, set the rigging electrically 'alive' when transmitting, these being rather early days and she one of the first sailing ships with wireless. Erikson never carried radio transmitters in his ships, but the Hamburg Amerika Line re-installed it, yet no clue was received of any trouble from this source. Subsequently some wreckage identified as coming from her was washed up on Tierra del Fuego. In her

80. The cutwater, with the anchors still shackled on to their cables. The upper hawsepipe is out of the picture.

Belgian and Erikson days, when white, with white masts and yards, she tended to look bigger than she really was, since white has this effect, and when seen near other contemporary four-masters, she looked to be lightly rigged. In truth, she was more lightly rigged than the bigger ships, but not for a vessel of her size.

Like her predecessor, the first *Comte de Smet de Naeyer,* she had deep tanks, double-bottom tanks and pumping arrangements which were comparable in their complexity to those in a steamer of similar size. An erroneous manipulation of the valves could have caused flooding and a loss of stability which might not have been discovered until it was too late, and could have caused her to founder, particularly in the sort of heavy weather to be found so frequently in those latitudes. It would not be the

81. *L'AVENIR, showing the sheer-pole which prevents movement of the bottle-screws and the rigging seizings (see page 106). Note, too, in connection with cutting away steel rigging, the steel battens and the dangers inherent in such loose gear.*

first time that valves had been opened in error. There is no more evidence for this theory than for any other, but it is one which provides food for speculation, and perhaps the more so since it is one which equally might fit the foundering of the *Comte de Smet de Naeyer,* which has generally been regarded as being inexplicable.

82. The L'AVENIR off Dover. Under the Belgians each of her royals was decorated with a coat of arms. These survived for some years. Note the effect on the various sails when the wind is right aft.

The Maritime traditions of the Makassarese, who occupy the south-western tip of Sulawesi (Celebes), and of the Buginese, their neighbours to the north, reach back before the period of western exploration. The Bugis were trading as far as the Straits of Malacca when the Portuguese arrived there around A.D. 1500 and at that time they had a reputation for being dangerous to other ships. In those early days there were separate cultures on the islands east of Asia with traditional techniques of building boats up to 100 feet long with hand carved planks. A slightly curved tree was split and one plank cut from each half. In Java, and perhaps also in Sulawesi, there had been a long tradition of building even larger trading ships of up to 300 tons for trade with China and, possibly, as far as India.

The characteristic of the Sulawesi traditional rig was the unstayed tripod mast with a tilted rectangular sail of matting that revolved or tilted in any position around the mast, controlled by braces. By rotations of the sail across the bows and tilting it forward, the boat turns downwind: by rotating it fore and aft and sheeting it down towards the stern, the boat sails well into the wind, with little load on the tiller. This is a totally different tradition from another in Indonesia that used the boomed triangular sails of the Indo-Pacific. The largest of the Bugis cargo boats, for centuries called *padewakangs,* had up to three of the tripod masts each with one huge mat sail. They all retain the ancient quarter-rudders even today.

The same rig persisted on the Makassarese canoes until a few years ago but, at Ujung Pandang (Makassar), it has now been replaced on the canoes by a triangular leg-of-mutton sail, often of black plastic. Ordinary Makassarese sailing canoes have double outriggers and often, nowadays, a single mast. The flying proas illustrated in Pls. 66-73 of Volume 1 were dugout hulls with a special outrigger on one side only, for racing on a southwards course during the east monsoon in Makassar harbour. They were creatures of a day and supported by wealthy sponsors solely for the race. The rig, however, does illustrate the tilted rectangular sail. That rig, with tripod mast, is still seen on fishing canoes in isolated Buginese colonies in other islands, such as Flores, where change has not caught up with them.

The next size of boat larger than the outrigger canoe in South Sulawesi

83. *Prahu besian in Makassar Harbour in 1978. The square sail and tripod mast is man's most primitive rig, which can be traced back to ancient Egypt. The two side rudders are equally old, and went out of use in Europe less than 1,000 years ago.*

is a *bisean* (Makassarese) or *lopi* (Buginese) which still retains the old rig (Pl. 83). It has a keel which characteristically runs in one smooth curve into the stem and stern posts. Nowadays there are floors and ribs, but once these craft were held together by rotan lashings through eyed-lugs that were carved in situ when the planks were adzed from the solid trunks.

All the Indonesian boats have planks carved to the appropriate shape. Therefore every plank is different, and has its own name. The planks are held together edge to edge by hidden dowels every 10 cm or so. To do this, the plank is first roughly shaped; the standing part of the hull is bored, and dowels of a special hardwood are left projecting for about 5 cm. The new plank is then bored to match and fitted roughly. A special tool with a lip and small spike is run along the edge of the hull, transferring its exact shape to the new plank with the dowels in place, so that there is a perfect fit when everything outside this line is cut away. This technique is entirely pre-western and may well go back to the Bronze Age cultures of 2,000 years ago. Plank by plank, the master craftsman builds up a smooth shell and fits the ribs and floors afterwards (Pl. 84). The individual plank shapes and lengths are so well learnt by apprenticeship without plans or drawings that exactly the same plank patterns are still in force as on an early nineteenth century *padewakang* model in the museum at Rotterdam.

The *bisean* bringing a load of Nipa palm leaves into Ujung Pandang is a very typical single-sailed Makassarese prahu of medium size, with all the traditional features. There are hundreds still sailing.

The prahu *patorani* (Pl. 85) with two tilted triangular sails on tripod masts is a specialised fishing boat for carrying the traps for the flying fish and its eggs. The female likes to lay her eggs adhering to the floating baskets, and then both she and the male are caught inside during their courtship dance. The eggs fetch as high a price as caviar. It is a pleasure to find that these boats, which appear to have sailed out of an earlier century, are actually on the increase to meet the demands of the Japanese market for fish eggs.

The largest and best-known sailing prahus of South Sulawesi are the Bugis trading and transport prahus called *pinisi* (P. 89) with the same rounded hull (Pl. 91). The present rig of seven fore-and-aft sails evolved from the rig of its predecessors, the *padewakangs,* during the late nineteenth century. It is a very convenient one for these waters: the

84. *The floors are added when the plank shell is well up. The largest prahus are still being built from grown timbers cut to shape by adze and finished without power tools.*

85. *Prahu patorani about to weigh anchor.*

86. *A bugis pinisi. The poop is built up on a sharp-ended stern.*

topsails catch every breath but can be rapidly closed and furled: the large sails running on a rail on the gaff so that they can be closed like curtains. They often run downwind wing and wing, and the three jibs are able to balance the tiller on every point of sailing.

For centuries the rudders have been long, narrow blades on the quarters, supported on strong transverse thwarts that also form the basis of the poop (Pl. 86). These apparently antiquated rudders are preferred because they lift over reefs; they are readily repaired at sea, and they stress the whole stern rather than the sternpost. In the traditional boats of Asia, it is of interest to look over the whole ship with an eye to where the places of high stress have been eliminated. Fore-and-aft rig tends to stress the rudder stock to the limit and this, with the problem of corrosion of pintle and gudgeon, is avoided by the quarter rudder.

Photographs of Bugi prahus and old models can be dated approximately by the following features: The rig of seven sails means 20th century: jibs plus tilted rectangular sails were found throughout the nineteenth century: no jib means early nineteenth century. For a period from about 1830 to 1860 there were bizarre experiments afloat with fore-and-aft gaff sails together with the huge tilted rectangular mats which were the characteristic of the *padewakang*. The deck, which is not a traditional Indonesian feature, grew slowly from the bows during the nineteenth century, becoming complete with hatches by about 1890. From then on, the freeboard was progressively lowered, because it was no longer necessary to be well above the waves.

Until 1940, Bugis prahus had a marked step in the bows with a short, little low deck right forward but, from 1940 – 1950, this was changed to a schooner bow. Nowadays, flush decks are sealed with watertight hatches and a prahu heavily loaded, with timber piled on deck, can make its whole passage across the Java Sea with decks awash and one side under water for the whole way. The bowsprit is still a huge structure of heavy beams with side boards that reach back as far as the mast.

The numbers and size of the Bugis prahus are astonishing at the present time. They are the largest fleet of wooden sailing ships in the world. At Sunda Kelapa one can find more than a hundred for most of the year. About nine hundred of them are afloat, mainly transporting timber from Borneo and Sumatra into Java for house building. Most of these have

87. The hull shape of the modern Bugis prahus with a schooner bow.

88. Standing gaffs and high topmasts of Bugis prahus in harbour.

been hand-built without power tools on isolated beaches far from a town by teams of dedicated men who carve every plank individually in the old way.

In the nineteenth century and again for a short period during the unsettled times of 1945–1955, the Bugis prahus were mainly distribution ships for manufactured goods to small ports throughout the Archipelago. The annual run from Singapore to the Aru Islands or north to Ternate led to the development of larger ships of up to 400 tons for economies of scale when the monsoons limited the skippers to one trip a

89. *Bugis pinisi at Sunda Kelapa (Jakarta) in 1979.*

year. They would return loaded with trepang, sandalwood, resin, wax, pearl shell, edible birds-nests, birds of paradise, ironwood, pepper, spices and dried sharks fins to trade with the Chinese merchants for another load of manufactured goods. That trade was largely destroyed by the Dutch customs regulations, which were seriously enforced as the independent Sultanates from Lombok eastwards and from Bone (Makassar) northwards slowly came under Dutch control. The Bugis traders were driven into the local distribution trade at smaller ports where the Dutch steamships did not visit.

As a consequence, there was a rapid reduction in hull size, and the next generation of Bugis prahus, often called *Palari,* were only 25–55 tons through the first half of the 20th century. The craft in Pl 76 of Vol 1 is such a one. Copra became a rare item, and the trepang trade continued until the importation was banned by the Chinese government after 1945. For a few years free trade with Singapore was again possible, but this has now ceased.

Fortunately for the prahus, there came just at the right time after 1960 the exploitation of immense timber reserves in Borneo and Sumatra due to a shortage of timber for houses in Java. The prahus are able to carry timber at a lower rate than motor vessels and, in the 1960s and 1970s, a new generation of them, of 100–200 tons with schooner bows and sealed decks, was built from sawn planks in Borneo, and these were cheaply maintained with no need for imported engines or spare parts. In a labour-intensive situation where time matters little and wages are low, the prahus form a cheap transport system, because of the small amount of capital involved in the long turn-round times. All the sailing prahus of this region continue to be built because they are often all that *can* be used when the local economy will not support a technology based on metal, plastics, engines or the interest payments that would accompany modernisation. (Pl. 90)

To meet the need for a handy, small transport, the same hull style, marked by the stem, stern and keel in one continuous curve, has been adapted to a fore-and-aft rig. The trailer boards beside the bowsprit still run back to the mast, and the two lateral rudders have exactly the same supporting beams on the *pinisi,* but we now have a small cutter with plenty of light sail (Pl. 92). The foresail is boomed: the mainsail is on a gunter lug, called *layar nadé* in Indonesia, and the mast is a single pole. Such boats, called *bago,* or west Sulawesi *lambo,* have been operating for most of this century as small traders making overnight passages in and out of Ujung Pandang (Makassar). Until a few years ago, all of them had a long gaff and a topsail, but that now persists only in out-of-the-way eastern islands. Apart from replacing sails thåt blow away, there is little expense in maintaining these craft, but they are not easy to sail because all the gear is weak and the sail must be kept luffing in a strong wind.

90. *Working the prahu is still almost entirely by hand. Note the bowsprit structure.*

91. *A rather lightly laden Bugis pinisi entering Jakarta Bay in 1979.*

92. *A pajala hull with fore-and-aft rig is often called a 'bago', or a West Sulawesi 'lambo'.*

Well within the last century, anybody who visited the seaside had seen sailing ships of most rigs manoeuvring in one way or another and, probably, took such things as a matter of course. Generally they would have seen the smaller, coastal craft – the many brigs, brigantines, small barques and schooners, besides a variety of ketches and the like – and, when all is said and done, the principles involved in a large square-rigger were precisely the same.

Now the tradition has been lost and the subject has become one to which a certain *mystique* has become attached. Some, becoming used to a 'push-button' world, blandly assume that these ships came into the same category, and this was never more clearly demonstrated to me than when sitting on a committee with, amongst others, some eminent yachtsmen to discuss the start of a race for square-rigged school-ships. The suggestion was made that they should start from anchor about half a mile off shore and, when I pointed out that if (as was most likely) the wind should be in the sou'westerly quadrant, the ships would promptly all go aground stern first, it was obvious that the assembled company thought me un-cooperative, to understate the case! Explanations were met with polite disbelief and it was only when one of the captains confirmed my view next day that this absurd scheme was abandoned – albeit unwillingly!

In considering any manoeuvre, or even the normal progress of a big sailing ship, she must be considered as a see-saw in the water, acting in a horizontal plane. There are forces – mainly the sails – acting about the fulcrum, or pivotal point, which is her turning centre. Ideally, this point is a foot or so forward of the mainmast in the case of a four-masted barque, although it can vary slightly according to her trim. In theory, the centre of effort of the sail plan should be coincidental with the pivotal point but, all too often, it is slightly abaft of it, with the result that the ship has a tendency to gripe and edge up into the wind with the rudder amidships, and thus requires weather helm to the detriment of her speed, especially with a beam wind or when the wind is forward of the beam. Moreover, the more a ship heels, the greater will be the tendency to force her bow up into the wind.

Sails can be regarded as levers about the fulcrum, or turning centre, and it is therefore evident that a small sail at one end of the ship – say, a jib or the spanker – will exert a greater relative turning effect than a

93. In the days of sail people frequently saw sailing ships and had a good idea of their working. Here promenaders watch the main skysail-yarder MacCALLUM MORE, one of the most peerless ships of her generation, entering Ostend. Built in 1875 and owned in London by J. C. Campbell, she passed to Carl Flugge of Hamburg to become the ANENOME and, later, into the fine fleet of Carl Brech of Tvedestrand, when she was named HERO.

bigger one nearer amidships. The primary object of sails is, of course, to provide motive power, but some do have other functions, either by accident or design, as the case may be.

To describe all types of manoeuvres for all types of sailing vessels would be beyond the scope of this volume. Since such vessels as the *Lawhill* and *Abraham Rydberg* are considered in section 15 in relation to iron-work aloft, it may be useful to think about such a vessel when getting under weigh, heaving to and going about.

A vessel at anchor which wishes to make sail without the aid of tugs is generally in best case when she is tide-rode (lying head to tide) for, if the wind is more or less aft, she can simply set her sails and, as the anchor is tripped, sail off with her yards braced to the wind. More commonly, the vessel is wind-rode and lying head to wind. The principles remain the same, whatever the point of sailing once she is under way, but let us assume that she wishes to start on the starboard tack. In that case, the fore yards are checked well in to starboard and the after yards the other way, as they will be when she finally starts *forwards*. As the anchor is hove up, sail is set. The amount of sail will depend on the strength of wind and, in light weather, all sail can be set though, in hard winds, perhaps only upper topsails. These are often chosen because they are the slowest sails to set, whether by halliard winch or not and, once set, the job is over and other canvas can be set more quickly. The yardstick is to have enough sail to be able to manoeuvre when under way, but not so much as to make an excessive sternboard or to drag the anchor, which is first hove short. The headsails will be sheeted to starboard.

Thus, whilst all the sails set are aback when heaving up, those on the fore and the headsails are casting her bow to port as she gathers sternway and starts a semi-circular sternboard (which is why the school-ships would have gone aground) whilst the sails on the aftermasts have the opposite effect. The rudder is amidships and the spanker set and hauled over to port to provide additional 'push round'. As she swings, the after sails start to shiver and finally to fill with wind. At this point, when the ship should lose her sternway and be virtually hove to (see *infra),* the fore-yards are braced round to the starboard tack and the headsails taken over, whereupon the ship picks up speed on the desired starboard tack. This principle exemplifies the use of sails as levers about the turning centre.

It will be obvious that, if a ship has rather a lot of sail set for the wind, not only will she be in danger of dragging before her anchor is tripped, but far more strain is placed on the cable (and far more work involved, if heaving up by hand capstan), but she will also make a much longer sternboard which is often, at the best of times, three-quarters of a mile or a mile in distance. The time taken for the whole operation and the efficiency of its execution much depends on the number of hands available and whether the anchor is hove up by steam or not. Heaving in by capstan or, in smaller craft, by the old 'up-and-down' Armstrong's Patent, was a very slow job. I once saw a big four-masted barque lying tide-rode in a

94. The French barque REVEL setting sail as she get under way from anchor. The sails on the main are just starting to fill. The picture was taken in the 1914–18 War and her gun aft will be noted.

95. With a favourable off-shore breeze, a ship could sometimes single up and sail straight off from a jetty, as the PAMIR is doing here from Wallaroo, in Spencer Gulf.

very hard wind, which was remarkable in itself. She hove up by steam from the donkey boiler with her topsails set, which kept the cable virtually up and down and then, as she made way, she simply sailed off in the direction in which she had been heading when at anchor, piling sail upon sail until she was over the horizon. No steamship could have done better. I had sailed in her a year or so previously and she made a magnificent sight for what was to be my last memory of her, since I never saw her again. Now the poor ship is preserved in a commercial sort of way, but I shall never go and see her. It is better to remember that splendid departure, with the sun shining on those lofty, sail-crowded masts as her power and the hard wind came together in sheer harmony of motion.

Methods of getting under weigh on a close lee shore, or with obstructions astern, are rather more complex and involve the sacrifice of an anchor (which can be buoyed for future recovery), but a ship can get away in less space by resorting to 'club-hauling', as described a little later on. However, having got our vessel away on the starboard tack and, having a foul wind for her desired course, she will in due course wish to go about on to the port tack. Assuming that she is in a position to 'tack' (or 'stay' – that is: to go about head to wind) as opposed to 'wear', which entails running right off before the wind, the first order will be *'Clear to go about'*.

On this, all the lee brace coils will be thrown from their belaying pins and coiled down on deck clear for running, while the weather sheets of the jibs and staysails will be hauled to windward, and the clews of the mainsail and crossjack will be hauled up – the sheets and tacks for all three courses being thrown off their hooks on shrouds and backstays. Normally, when steering 'by the wind' (or 'close-hauled') the weather leech of the royal, or topmost sail set, is kept just lifting, but now the helmsman will be told to keep her clean full, or 'full and by', to increase speed a little since the greater the speed when tacking the better. Then, with the spanker boom being hauled amidships, the next order comes *'A-lee',* whereupon the wheel is put hard over to starboard, or nearly so, since too much rudder acts as a brake (which can be fatal to success) and, at the same time, the head sheets are slacked right off, as the ship is turned up into the eye of the wind. Once again, levers are operating: the spanker forcing the stern to port, while the headsails, slacked off, are exerting no

96. *Tacking ship, the POMMERN is almost round. The main and mizzen sails are drawing on the new tack and the watch haul in the fore-sheet as the fore yards swing. The main staysail is still aback and the lee sheet (above the boat) will be hauled over directly. The fore upper t'gallant halliard winch is alongside the deck-house; the two tanks before it are used for rain — and thus washing — water and, next to them, just visible, is the pig-stye.*

counterbalancing influence. All the square sails will quickly come aback, which is why the ship was kept clean full in order to provide sufficient way to carry her through the manoeuvre and, when the wind is about two points on the port bow, the order comes: *'Mainsail Haul!'*

If everything has been timed properly, the main (and mizzen) yards will swing right round almost of their own accord once the lee braces are cast off their pins. In fact, they swing so fast that it is essential that they run clear and do not foul (which is why they are coiled on deck in preparation) and this is true whether a ship has brace winches or not*. If she has them, little work is required except for the man on the brake whilst, if there are long braces, it is a matter of running up the deck on the starboard side to take in the slack. One man can deal with the royal and t'gallant braces on each mast. If, on the other hand, the timing has been wrong, or the ship loses way, it is extremely hard work (or if, with winches, the lee hand braces are insufficiently slacked off). Once the wind has passed over to the port bow, the spanker sheets are slacked off a little on to the new tack and the headsheets hauled to port. Lest there be any misunderstanding about these sheets, it should be noted that the topmast staysails and jibs (except the jib topsail, if carried) have both a port and starboard sheet shackled into the clew, each of which consists of a pendant spliced round a block, through which is rove a whip, the working part of which is the hauling part of the sheet. When a ship is under sail, the weather block is eased over the stay abaft its sail since, due to its weight, it would affect the set of the sail if left on the windward side.

The ship should still be swinging, though probably with little enough way left and, as soon as the after square sails start to draw, the fore braces (or fore brace winch) are manned and, on the command: *'Let go and haul!'* the yards are hauled right round on to the new tack – by main muscle power this time! Now the ship is gathering way on her new tack: the braces are sweated up: the tacks and sheets of the mainsail and crossjack hauled in, and then the weather sheets must be taken over, braces coiled up and the decks generally cleared up. Then is the manoeuvre complete.

In the unhappy eventuality that the ship misses stays and is caught 'in irons' – that she loses her way too early and will not come round, then she must be worn round as described below. If there is no room to wear, as in

*A fouled brace can buckle or break a yard.

97. Square sails were normally sent aloft or down on a gantline, but the courses were always sent up and down in their gear. The KILLORAN is here lying in the Orwell on arrival from Australia, and the rovings of the mainsail are being cut away from the jackstay. The head earing is cast off, the clewline remaining shackled to the spectacle together with the sheet and tack. The horizontal lines aft are cranelines, between the mizzen swifters, which were the means of access to the (brailing) spanker to make it fast or to cast off the gaskets.

narrow or congested waters, then she must be box-hauled by keeping the helm down and hauling the foreyards right round to box her off, while keeping the after sails lifting as she swings, having them braced for the new tack by the time the wind is aft. In other words, a sternboard is made in much the same way as when getting under way. Had the *Favell* not succeeded in her dramatic passage inside the Runnelstone (page 34) she might have had to resort to box-hauling although, in all conscience, there was little enough room for anything! It will have been noted, however, that Captain Lille was doubtful if she would stay in her light trim and in all the circumstances.

Under normal conditions, a ship should stay (tack), and it is always preferable to do so, since she loses no distance by this method. If she is very light and there is much sea, or is badly trimmed and down by the head, it is then unlikely that she will succeed. If a vessel loses headway and fails to come round, it is often because the order *'Mainsail Haul!'* is given too early. If given too late, the yards do not swing easily. Generally, the correct moment is when the sails on the main (which are aback) start to be blanketed by those on the fore. Equally, a ship under short canvas in a head sea can lose her way and miss stays. I was once in a large auxiliary four-masted schooner which would not stay in any circumstances, and this was attributed to the drag of the propeller stopping her.

Further, in hard weather, tacking can be an unwise manoeuvre, because the major part of the staying of the masts leads aft and, in general terms, the whole structure and fabric of a square-rigger (or any other sailing ship) presumes the wind to be striking the after side of the sails. To bring a vessel aback in strong winds can cause damage, and this is no less true when it is done intentionally, (as when tacking).

In such cases there is no option but to wear ship – something which is always resisted because it loses a lot of ground, especially if a ship is beating with relatively short boards in such an area of sea as the Skaggerak or English Channel. Whether the ship is under all sail but in poor trim, or whether under short sail in hard weather, the basic principles are the same. First of all the weather braces are cleared for running, as before, and, if set, the mainsail and crossjack clews raised. All is made clear. Next, the jigger canvas is brailed in, or a full-rigged ship would brail in (or lower, if a hoisting sail) her spanker, and the after staysails will be

98. Here the KILLORAN's foresail is cut away and the sail is being lowered in its buntlines and clewlines. It will be seen that there are double-geared capstans on the foredeck. The tug in attendance is readily identifiable as Watkins' famous old ARCADIA by the holes in her section.

run down. Since we left our ship on the starboard tack initially, we again assume that she is to be put on to the port tack, so the wheel (and rudder) are turned hard a-port to turn *away* from the wind. As she commences to do so, the after yards are squared up, those on the main rather ahead of those on the mizzen, whose sails should be kept just lifting initially. Soon the ship will have the wind right aft and be running right before it, losing hard-won ground, at which moment the after yards should be braced up on to the new tack. As soon as they fill, the fore yards are braced right round, whilst the headsail and staysail sheets have been hauled over. Then the spanker, mainsail and crossjack are all set and, once more, the ship is cleared up on deck. In bad weather, however, when under short sail – say lower topsails – the main and mizzen yards will be squared up when the wind is right aft, and then the foreyards are braced right round and, when the fore lower topsail fills on the new tack, the after yards are hauled round too.

When a deep-loaded vessel is wearing in very bad weather, the decks can become very dangerous as she ships very heavy seas half way through the operation. As the last, full-built square-riggers could seldom lie higher up to the wind than five or six points, and usually lost at least a point of leeway besides, there was little to be gained from tacking in a dead muzzler when the wind was coming from the very direction towards which one wanted to steer, and wearing ship lost a lot of the ground which might have been made. There were occasions – usually unpremeditated – when there was no room to wear.

In practice, there is little that a big sailing ship can do if she can neither tack nor wear, since it presumes a situation which was not anticipated and when there is little time to act. It could happen if suddenly encountering ice, or making an unexpected landfall. Few sailing ships had anything except Admiralty pattern anchors which were secured and lashed down on the foc's'le head at sea, with the cables unshackled and down in the chain locker, so anchoring was hardly practicable in emergency and, even if the anchors *were* over the side and shackled on to their cables (after departure or prior to landfall), the presumption was that a lee shore was involved and there was not always shallow enough water to anchor anyway. However, providing that the lee shore is not steep to, a smaller vessel, preferably with a large and experienced crew, can club-haul the

99. The Norwegian barque NOVO heaves to against the sun by backing her mainyards. Originally the smart British full-rigger KNIGHT OF THE THISTLE, she passed to Sweden to become the HOPPET, and then to Benix J. Grefstade of Arendal in 1907, but was re-named NOVO when sold to Lillesund in 1913. Condemned the following year, she passed successively to Argentina, Chile and Bolivia (which has no sea-board) and, after a long lie-up in Buenos Aires, sailed for Nantes in 1927. After being quoted on the re-insurance market, she reached Madeira and, finally, Nantes when 195 days out, being broken up the following year.

vessel if the lee anchor is outboard. This entails passing a hawser from the lee quarter outside of everything and making it fast to the lee anchor. The cable is unshackled abaft the windlass, leaving sufficient to bring the ship up. (Just imagine this, probably in a full gale, with all the implications of a sailing ship's chain locker!) It is extremely time-consuming in a time of great emergency and it can be said with truth that, if there were time to do all this, there would have been time to avoid the situation!

However, assuming that all this *is* accomplished, the ship is thrown up into the wind as for tacking (with all hands presumably praying, in a gale, that the masts will not collapse on them like those of a ship before being put into a bottle!) and, when she loses way, the anchor is let go – the cable having been stopped off – and the after yards are swung round. Then, as she loses headway, the hawser is hauled taut aft, whereupon the cable is let go forward, so that the anchor is held by the hawser from the quarter, pivoting the ship. Once round, the head yards are braced round and the hawser let go, sacrificing the anchor but saving the ship. It is one of those operations which sounds so fine when given as a *viva voce* answer to an examiner in a seamanship examination, to an examiner who has never seen it done and whose mind is probably boggling at the very thought! But it is a very different matter in practice, at all events for a large ship. For smaller vessels, or for naval vessels with large crews, it was possible, but the principle *could* be used to get away from anchorage on a lee shore, since there was then probably more time to play.

Indeed, those who write seamanship books must have great faith in mankind. In the days of wood and hemp, it was relatively easy to cut away the rigging, since it was no great matter to cast off or cut the lanyards, but when it comes to cutting away steel rigging, the correct answer in the examination room is to strike the bottle-screws hard with a maul! An examination is far removed from a ship, which is likely enough to be almost on her beam ends, when feet have become useless encumbrances and when any sort of balance is preserved by hands: when the wind force will be well in excess of the normally accepted 12, and possibly well over 100 m.p.h. when a man is flattened against the rigging and the simplest action seems to be devoid of normality. How *can* a man swing a maul at bottle screw after bottle screw in these conditions? I have been in a four-master under such circumstances and, although there was no question of cutting away the masts and rigging, I know that it was utterly impossible to do so. After the *Pamir* foundered in 1958, an old sailing ship master wrote to me that he considered that bad seamanhip was involved and that the masts should have been cut away. I asked him: 'How?' and have received no reply to this day!

When the *Glenard* was dismasted (page 23) the situation was somewhat different, since the masts had already come down and the ship was not listing unconscionably. The strain was off the standing rigging in large

100. *The bottle screws and rigging seizings can be seen clearly in this photo of the ABRAHAM RYDBERG. Note the difference between her sheer-poles and those of the L'AVENIR (Pl. 81).*

measure but, if the spars are over the side and still attached to the ship, they can knock holes in her hull with disastrous results. In this case the use of mauls on the rigging screws had absolutely no effect at all (the strain was off them, on the whole) and axes were then used to try to cut the rigging, but the only result of this was to blunt every axe in the ship!

The lower end of each shroud and backstay is turned round a thimble at the top of its rigging screw and, after being wormed, parcelled and served, is seized back on its own part — usually with four seizings of galvanized, annealed steel wire. It was found that these could be cut quite easily with ordinary chipping hammers, and thus the rigging released.

In the last, powerful four-masters, there were about 116 of these seizings in the swifters, shrouds and backstays, before considering the fore-and-aft stays, so that the job could not be accomplished in a moment, but at least it *could* be done. Oddly, this does not appear, to my knowledge, in any seamanship books, which only recommend methods which can *not* be accomplished by any means! It could be argued that the big, steel square-riggers were so strong and cohesive in their whole as to represent a hazard when they were in real trouble.

Until, for better or worse, men started building super-tankers and very large cargo carriers, a screw-driven ship could be stopped in a relatively short distance, but this was seldom true of a sailing vessel, except when making slow speeds. Stopping such a vessel is termed 'heaving to' — an expression which is also used in a different context when, in unusually bad weather, she is laid up as close to the wind and sea as she can ride out the gale most comfortably. This is a different matter altogether and involves bringing the vessel up close to the wind, perhaps under lower topsails: perhaps under a goose-winged lower topsail or, in extreme (examination room) cases, with a weather cloth in her lower mizzen or jigger rigging. Many an examinee has blithely answered this question successfully in the still air of Board of Trade examination rooms, but I warrant that neither he nor his examiner have the slightest idea how the weather cloth is to be spread or secured! If a ship is running before heavy seas and has to be brought up to a 'hove to' position, it can be extremely dangerous, since it is then that she can broach to as the wind and sea are brought abeam, and she can be overwhelmed. Decks must be cleared of men and the master will probably wait, hopefully, for a slight lull before coming round.

As to the more conventional 'heaving to' — to come to a stop — it is certain that no sailing ship ever had hydraulic brakes! She could only be brought to a standstill by arranging the sails in opposition to each other, some being full and some aback. Much depended on the force of the weather for, in really bad conditions, heaving to was simply not

101. The HIPPALOS was originally built by Connell's of Glasgow for B. Wencke Sohne, who owned the MNEME (later POMMERN) in their great Hamburg fleet, as the ARETHUSA. She was absorbed into the Rhed, Ges, Act von 1896 on the death of Friedrich Wencke in 1906, but sold to Lillesund, in Norway, in 1913. Three years later she was sold to Chile, and wrecked soon after the 1914–18 War was over. Here she has altered course slightly and backed her mainyards to heave to.

practicable and, if a man went overboard, there could be no question of picking him up – the master usually consulting the crew before reaching this unpalatable decision, though, of course, considerations of the safety of the boat and her crew were equally, if not more, cogent. When it was possible, the *modus operandi* depended on the direction of the wind in relation to the ship's course.

If the vessel was reaching or with her yards braced sharp up, the common practice was to lower the lighter sails (though not necessarily so in very light weather) and back the mainyards, whilst hauling in the spanker. The mainsails will counter the forward motion imparted by the fore and mizzen, which is not so great, as they are braced sharp up.

102. Reaching, with her tacks bowsed down, the POMMERN flies 'G' (I require a pilot) in the International Code and lowers her upper topgallants. (Being bald-headed, she has no royals above them.) Then, approaching the pilot vessel . . .

Moreover, the trim of the ship, as always, enters into the question: most vessels being about a foot by the stern, and this affects the fulcrum, or turning centre. If, on the other hand, the ship is running, the method of heaving to is to run the fore yards forward whilst putting the wheel up so that, as she comes up into the wind, the foresails are still full, but those on the main and mizzen are aback (Pls. 104 and 105). Generally, these methods will keep a ship relatively static so far as forward motion is concerned, either while a boat is sent away: a pilot boards, or for whatever reason. If this is not the case, adjustments can be made by clewing up or

103. . . . after hauling up her mainsail and crossjack, she backs her mainyards, thus effectively heaving to for the pilot to come alongside. The fore and mizzen sails are full at an angle to the wind: the mainyards backed squarely to it.

lowering relevant sails to maintain the balance. Examination of old photographs will often show a variety of ways in which a ship is hove to – sometimes the mizzen yards being backed, but it must be remembered that there are a number of possible reasons for heaving to, some of which called for a complete loss of way, and others which did not. For example, many pictures exist of vessels which were hove to when stopped for examination or by U-boats in the 1914–18 war and, in this context, it is worth recording that, on those occasions when a ship was taken into port as a prize or for further examination, the naval boarding party involved

104. On the other hand, the LAWHILL, which had run up Channel with a following wind in light weather, has brailed in her jigger canvas and, putting her wheel up, run her fore yards forward and, again with 'G' at the fore, the pilot puts out from the cutter as the ship loses way.

105. The Danish VIKING, with neutrality flags painted on her sides, and with the wind on her starboard side, had done precisely the same things as the LAWHILL in Pl. 104 when stopped for examination in the First World War. Later bought by Gustaf Erikson, the ship is still preserved in Göteborg.

106. The OLIVEBANK in process of heaving to. There is little enough wind and, as she swings to starboard, her mainyards are coming aback while her mizzen sails will do so at any moment. She has not bothered to brail in the jigger canvas in so light a wind.

107. The principles of opposite forces on the sails when heaving to are exactly the same whether in a square-rigger or a fore-and-after: whether in a large vessel or a small one. Here the Lowestoft trawler BOY CLIFFORD is hove to for the warp to be hauled in by steam capstan. The foresail is aback with the sheet hauled to windward. It will be seen that the lanyards are spliced to the deadeyes, and not stopped with a Mathew Walker knot, as was more usual.

often learnt some rude lessons when the crew were unco-operative! Naval Reserve officers, who had had experience in sail, were thus invaluable for these duties, but usually, when they could, had boats' crews of peace-time fishermen (since their boat work was so excellent) but these men had little idea of the handling of a big square-rigger! In essence, the principle of levers about the fulcrum holds as good for heaving a ship to, as it does for getting under weigh and for going about.

108. *Japanese junk off Kuchinotsu in Kyushu in 1921.*

109. *General trading Japanese junks of this sort were very common in the Inland Sea and other sheltered waters of Honshu, though latterly they became motorised. Note the crane arrangement below the fore truck to allow the jib stays to clear the square lugsail. The Japanese junks had a higher aspect ratio to those of China and showed more Western influence – particularly in their headsails.*

110. Fukien pole-junk.

Apart from her bow, which does not conform to the normal Fukien junks of the Foochow – or any other – area, and to which must be ascribed a European influence, this junk is very typical of her trade, which consisted of the carriage of fir and pine from the interior of Fukien province. The woods were floated down the Min river as rafts to Foochow, where they were loaded, some bundles being lashed to the sides, with the lashings taken right round the hull, a number being made fast to the mainmast. The bundles overside provided additional buoyancy and stability.

Apart from the square sails of some river types, the lugsails of junks were controlled by a system of multiple crowsfeet. Another common feature of all junks was the vertical luff, and the halliard was generally attached a third of the way along the yard, while anything from a third to a sixth of the sail, according to type, was before the mast.

111. In the Whangpoo River, in 1921, a typical Hangchow trader, once common around the southern Yangtse estuary.

112. A Chinese fishing junk of the Darien/Chefoo area in the Gulf of Pee-Chi-Li has her trawl down and fish strung up to dry.

113.   A typical Fukien junk.

Pl. 113 shows a Fukien junk of a type common along the China coast, and in the Shanghai area. Her bow is of a more conventional type. Having virtually flat bottoms and little draft, junks perform badly to windward, but all have large rudders which lower well below the keel and act as a sort of centre-board*. Some types – and there are innumerable variations of the junk – can be identified by which side of the masts their balanced lugs are set, there being varying combinations.

Most coastal junks had a series of mast-head devices carried on a small bamboo pole above the main which not only fulfilled the function of a weather-vane but, in the more complicated ones, denoted by symbols the area from which the junk hailed, the owner and the Association within which he operated. Sometimes there were further devices or ornamentations designed to ward off evil spirits, although marine historians have never been able to determine the efficacy of these, presumably because it is impossible to discover what the effect would have been had they not been carried! Moreover, although Western peoples devoted much time and effort to the frustration of evil spirits in past centuries, it is not now a

---

* Junks can point very high into the wind but, due to the absence of keel, generally make a lot of leeway.

114. *A lorcha of the Amoy area silhouetted against the sun.*

115.   Masthead device of a junk.

subject on which Occidental historians – particularly the marine variety – have anything but a profound ignorance, and they are thus incapable of making reasoned comment on these practices of the Chinese junkmen who retained beliefs in the fundamental issues of life. Oddly, there is little standardization in the use of the *oculus* in Chinese junks, since it is to be found in some areas and not in others.

   With their masts raking different ways, the various junks have their own individuality but, whatever criticisms may sometimes be levelled at them, the fact remains that they have served, virtually unchanged, throughout the entire span of maritime history, to the full satisfaction of the Chinese.

116. Outrigger fishing canoes on a beach near Colombo.

When presenting A Camera Record of the age of sail, it must obviously be confined to those last decades when the camera was operative and, in Western nations, this restricts the subjects to the latter developments of the sailing ship. Anyone who has made the briefest study of Occidental vessels will know that there were many developments over the centuries and that many types and rigs, apart from preceding the camera by hundreds of years, were only recorded very cursorily in any form.

In Oriental countries – practically all of those east of Suez – it is broadly true to say that seamen were far more advanced than their counterparts in the west in the first flush of navigation, but that they retained their forms and rigs through the ages to a much greater extent and, in some instances, virtually no change was made at all until the relatively recent addition of the auxiliary diesel engine made its appearance.

If junks had changed very little over the years, so there was certainly an innate conservatism amongst the fishermen of Colombo, as seen in their outrigger canoes photographed in 1938 (Pl. 116). The most primitive craft must be held to be a mere log. The hollowing of a log, simple as it may seem today, represented a great advance, and these fishing boats were neither more nor less than this, with the sides (or bulwarks, if they deserve the term) stitched to them. They did have a rather crude outrigger but, crude or not, an outrigger when first fitted must have seemed a complete revolution in seagoing.

Nevertheless, if it came early in maritime history, the craft must have come to be regarded as being 'primitive' by any standards as the years rolled by, but they never altered their form thereafter. Carrying two men, one of whom could often be seen splashing water on to the sail in light winds, they steered with a paddle amidships. Contrary to a widely-held belief, the outrigger was always on the windward side, and the sail in effect was a spritsail with its tack bowsed down to the bow. To all intents and purposes, they could only sail down wind, when these craft were extremely fast. Ironically, if fibre glass be substituted for the Cingalese materials, they have a distinct resemblance to small 'fun' craft adopted by some of the more impecunious yachtsmen today!

There were never as many types of dhow as there were of junks, but nevertheless the variety was enough to cause confusion: a confusion which was often confounded because different terms were used in different regions. There seems to be very little question that the Western cutter rig, with its fore-and-aft mainsail and headsail, derived from the lateen and settee sails of the Indian Ocean which became common in the Mediterranean, simply by cutting the big sail vertically at the mast and altering the means of setting. Over the years, some dhows adopted the triangular headsail in addition to their lateens, as in the *baghla* in Pl. 117. This particular craft is Indian, though the *baghla* was essentially Arabian in origin and named from the Arabic word *baghl,* meaning 'mule'. Indeed, these craft were the work-horses of their own seas.

Dhow masts always raked well forward, in order to enable the big yard to be raised vertically and swung round before it when wearing ship — for these craft do not stay. When going about, all the shrouds and halliards were shifted over to the (new) weather side, and they did require a large

117. A baghla near the Vengurla rocks on the west coast of India in 1936.

crew for their size. All drew more water aft than forward to a very marked degree, and it is perhaps significant that their hulls were formed on the 'wave-line' principle, claimed to have been invented by the marine architect, J. Scott Russell, in Victorian times, though it did not prove successful when applied to Western ships of the period. He may have rationalised the theory, but it was known for centuries before he was conceived! Given a large crew of cheap labour (which was both needed and available); no great need for hurry and the constant winds, within the monsoon periods, of their theatres of operation, the dhow proved to be ideal and thus preserved its form for so long.

Smaller native craft in the Indian rivers, such as the Hooghly, had a plank, like a stage, slung over the quarter for the relief of nature, corresponding with the old 'heads' in the true sense of the word. Sometimes, at the onset of the sou'west monsoon, a crew member would be seen

118. The topsail, set on a short yard with the clews brought down to the yardarms of the settee, has just been dropped before the settee. Kotias are a bigger form of baghla and always set settees (with a square luff) and never triangular lateens. The steamer is the Japanese BUENOS AIRES MARU leaving Colombo in 1938.

119. When a dhow wished to bring the wind from one side to the other, or to go about by wearing, the lateen sheets and tacks were slacked off and the yard brought to a vertical position against the mast, when it was swung round to the opposite side – one of the reasons for their big crews.

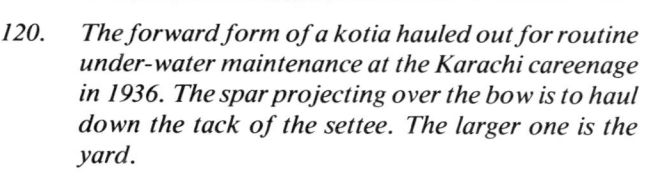

120. The forward form of a kotia hauled out for routine under-water maintenance at the Karachi careenage in 1936. The spar projecting over the bow is to haul down the tack of the settee. The larger one is the yard.

121. The under-water form of a Persian Gulf dhow at Karachi careenage. Note the form of yoke steering and the 'thunder-box' on the port quarter.

122. A smartly turned out kotia.

squatting on the plank and holding an open umbrella over his head! Dhows had a box, usually on the port quarter and irreverently known to Western seamen as a 'thunder-box' for this purpose. As will be seen, the trim *kotia* in Pl. 122, with her ensign smartened by a stiffener in the upper part of the hoist, has a thunder-box on *each* quarter*. Luxury indeed! Note that her mizzen is not furled but lightly stopped to the yard, and also the massive purchases, usually of coir rope.

Despite the innate conservatism displayed in Indian craft, there grew up and existed right up to the 1939 war a strange phenomenon in the form of a fleet of small square-rigged ships running down the Bay of Bengal from Rangoon and Akyab to Jaffna and Colombo with rice, aiming to make three rice cargoes each season, which started when the sou'-west monsoon cleared up at the end of September, for the sailing season

*The native word for this was *choli*.

123. Some of the 13 crew of this kotia of 82 feet in length.

124. In these two pictures, note the heavy four-fold purchase to the main lateen yard: the capstan on the poop, the fishing of the yards and the crutch arrangement aft.

125. *Aboard the kotia KARIMA with her crew of 21. The spar lying fore-and-aft was swung outboard when running free and the tack of the settee was secured to it in the manner of a yacht's spinnaker boom – all on a much heavier scale!*

started with the change of monsoon. The voyage north normally took three or four weeks, usually with the topgallant masts sent down and in ballast. During the sou'west monsoon the craft were usually laid up in Colombo with a number of locally owned dhows, which traded to the Maldive Islands, some 400 hundred miles away, mainly taking out rice, food and general cargo and returning with dried fish (Pl. 128).

These square-riggers varied in size between 200 and 500 tons, and in rig through barques, barquentines, brigs and brigantines. They were all 'Country' craft, built and owned locally, mainly in Jaffna and, owing their form to Western influences, were quite out of keeping with all Indian tradition of sail. Almost all were built of teak, even to the masts

* But the rice traders usually laid up in their home port of Jaffna.

126. Looking aft in the brigantine BRIDGETAMMAL. In the foreground, the arms of the old 'up-and-down' windlass are plainly visible. Unlike the European version, there is a broad handle for the men on the foc's'le head, but also a rope for use by men on the fore-deck, leading down from it.

and spars, because it was freely available locally, although it might be considered that it was too inflexible a wood for their sparring. The sails were of a local cotton and were exceptionally thick, while the rigging was a heavy coir, made from local coconuts at Jaffna except, sometimes, for the deadeye lanyards which were hemp.

Most of these vessels maintained the old style of single topsails, especially the smaller ones, together with outside channels, while they not only carried stunsails but, often enough, more fancy sails than ever occurred to a tea clipper captain. Oddly enough, the local name for 'stunsails' translated to 'steering sails', which is interesting because they had obviously been adopted from European vessels and, although there

127. The BRIDGETAMMAL, looking forward, Again we see the old windlass with the cable awaiting scaling, together with the height of the foc's'le head. This vessel has wire shrouds. The galley is just forward of the hatch.

128. Six dhows and three brigantines lying in Colombo harbour shortly after the onset of the sou'west monsoon in 1935. The photographs were taken in the rain!

129. Captain Mahamedeli of the BRIDGETAMMAL. The accommodation was in a house behind him, sunk three feet into the deck to allow the trysail to be positioned as low as possible. The wheel was immediately abaft this house.

130. A selection of brigantines and dhows lying in Colombo Harbour after the season was over.

131. After laying up in the sou'west monsoon, the ships took on sand ballast to their next loading port. Here the BRIDGETAMMAL is ballasting. If the method seems slow and antiquated, it must be remembered that many liners were coaled in this manner almost up to that time – and quickly at that!

has always been doubt and controversy over the derivation of the word 'stunsails', a school of thought has always existed which maintains that it was a corruption of 'steering sails', to provide steerage way in very light weather.

Although a compass was carried and the noon latitude shot, longitude was still determined by dead reckoning, and few of the rice fleet carried a chronometer. The captains were all Hindus, as were most of the crews (which, in a barque, numbered about 20) and they lived under the 3 feet high foc's'le head which was open, but in bad weather all hands congregated under the poop, which was not sub-divided and also used as both sail-locker and bos'n's locker. There were no unions, and everyone was

132. The BRIDGETAMMAL of Tuticorin herself, lying by another brigantine in Colombo in April 1938. A feature of these craft was that few of them had any ratlines, for the crew went aloft with the facility of monkeys and had no need of them. Both vessels are, of course, high out of the water.

perfectly happy.

To the student of ships without any knowledge of Hindustani, the names of these vessels posed difficulties, since they could contain two dozen or more letters, and were usually composite words with some religious connotation. However, even in the nor'east monsoon, the Bay of Bengal is no picnic area, and it sometimes happened that these vessels were caught in one of the cyclones that beset the area and became dismasted or, sometimes, they simply went missing. As a rule, they were not rattled down, since the crew could go aloft with the facility of monkeys, though there was often a batten spaced at intervals of some 12 feet in the shrouds. The brig in Pl. 133 is unusual in being rattled down.

133. *Coming up to anchorage under her two single topsails and a jib, this brig has a sharply steeved bowsprit and jibboom, which was common, but unusually she is rattled down.*

134. *This brigantine has a barge-type hull and is here beating into Colombo Harbour from Tuticorin in 1938. Vessels of this sort were confined to the Gulf of Mannar and the south coast of India, and were not involved in the rice trade to the Coromandel coast.*

135. *With her two skysails, the NITHYAKALYANI also set a sort of supplementary spanker on a portable mast right aft on her taffrail. The object of this was to make her quicker in stays and, when at anchor or running free, no-one would suspect its existence.*

136. *The barquentine PARVATHAVARTHANIAMMA. Oddly, her spanker is boomed, but the mainsail loose-footed. The odd cut of her main staysails is worthy of attention, as is her long jibboom.*

137. Brigs like the BHYALKSHMY were being built right up to the 1939 War.

138. Clearing the land with a cargo of rice for the run down the Bay of Bengal to Palk Strait, which might take a little over a week, or three weeks, the barque SIVASUPRAMANIAPURAVNY makes sail. Her main skysail is set and it will be seen that her courses clew up to the quarters. Proving the rule, she is rigged with double topsails, which was less usual amongst these vessels.

139. The GROSSHERZOGIN ELISABETH was a beautifully proportioned fullrigger. Her decks are crowded with cadets. The wireless aerials enhance her height.

The school-ships are now in such demand for publicity purposes and are so much in the news today that it might be interesting to pinpoint the first of them. This is not really possible, the more especially when one considers that, although the term was generally used of 'merchant' training, it was sometimes used of 'naval' vessels, and that occasionally the two overlapped whilst, at the same time, different countries have at times used different terminologies. Equally, it would be invidious to claim that any specific vessel is, or was, better than any other, but it is possible to state unequivocally that the ships of the German School-ship Association (Deutscher Schulschiff Verein) were not only the finest to be built up to that time, but that they really set the style of most of the larger conventional school-ships which came after them.

140. *The PRINZESS EITEL FRIEDRICH drying her sails (and a good deal of washing forward) while in Kiel. The iron cross in her ensign denotes that her captain was naval reserve.*

Certainly they were the first vessels built for their purpose in Germany and owed much of their inception and existence to the enthusiasm of the Grand Duke of Oldenburg: the first of them, the *Grossherzogin Elisabeth*, named for the Grand Duchess, being a beautiful vessel, as the photographs demonstrate.

Built in 1901 by Tecklenborgs at Geestemunde, she was of 1260 tons and carried 150–200 cadets and, with nice lines and rather deep topgallants for her size, with a jibboom outside her bowsprit, she always attracted favourable comment, first making a 'shakedown' cruise in the Baltic and then going on, as a rule, to the Caribbean. Part of her cadets were intended for officer rank and the bulk of them to be seamen, although most of the latter subsequently took their 'tickets'. She

141. *In contrast to so many of the modern school-ships, the line of the GROSS-HERZOGIN ELISABETH's sheer was not spoiled by rafts, deck-erections, radar and the like.*

performed with great success until 1932 when, as a result of the effects of the world shipping crisis, she was sold to the German Seamen's School at Hamburg-Finkenwerder as a stationary vessel.

In 1939 she was provided with a brand new suit of sails with the idea of sending her to sea again, but the war intervened and the project was stillborn. In 1944 she was transferred to Wismar before the Red Army occupied the port, and escaped thence to Neustadt in tow of a coaster but, on the conclusion of the war, she was allocated to France as reparations, and rigged down to be a floating barracks at Brest. Now there is talk of restoring her to join the great fleet of preserved ships which are taking shape in reality or upon imaginative drawing boards, but whether there is much to be gained in restoring so old a hull might be open to question.

The next vessel built by the Association was the *Prinzess Eitel Friedrich,* launched by Blohm & Voss in 1909 as a rather larger version of her predecessor at 1566 tons, and she was equally successful but was

142. *The PRINZESS EITEL FRIEDRICH under sail. The pictures demonstrate that these vessels had a certain style about them.*

taken over by the French after the first World War and, although they re-named her *Colbert* after some years and intended to use her for training, in point of fact she lay idle as the subject of various abortive schemes until she was sold to Poland in 1929 to replace their sail-training barque *Lwow* and, re-named *Dar Pomorza,* she still survives as an example of a splendidly designed training ship.

 The next vessel, the *Grossherzog Friedrich August*, was, for some reason, barque-rigged and also provided with an auxiliary engine of 600 h.p., but she was bigger still, at 1700 tons, and launched by Tecklenborgs in 1914. Once again, the proportions and design were such as to excite admiration and, although a barque may be more functional, economical and even practical for trade, it could be argued that the square mizzen sails of a full-rigger provide more work for a large complement – and this ship carried some 200 boys in a crew of 240 – but unlike her predecessors, was not primarily training an officer *cadre*. (The German navy – the

143. A piece of demonstration sailing, with accommodation ladders still outboard. The GROSSHERZOGIN ELISABETH (left) and the SCHULSCHIFF DEUTSCHLAND.

Kriegsmarine – never had any control over the vessels, nor were their boys or cadets intended for the navy, though the *Kriegsmarine* were always pleased enough to have young men who had trained in the DSV vessels). However, at the end of the war in 1918, the *Grossherzog Friedrich August* was also lost to Germany and, after being allocated to Great Britain, was sold to the Bergen Schoolship Association in 1923 to replace their old brig *Alfen* and, re-named *Statsraad Lemkuhl,* is still afloat and often in commission, despite the exigencies of a foundation depreciated in value in an age of monetary inflation.

Having lost their two bigger vessels, the Association placed an order in 1927 for another vessel with Tecklenborgs at Wesermunde, and the result was another full-rigger of almost the same size as the one ship they had managed to retain – their original one, the *Grossherzogin Elisabeth* – since the new vessel, the *Schulschiff Deutschland,* was of 1257 tons and also of fine appearance: the rather deep topgallants of the previous ships being replaced by double topgallant yards. She was a school-ship of rather individual appearance, always seeming to be lofty for her size and with a somewhat 'jaunty' look about her, which generally cruised to the Caribbean and South America. When the war came, she continued to

144. The GROSSHERZOG FRIEDRICH AUGUST *hove to for boat drill. The boat from the empty falls can be seen away on the port quarter.*

145. The ELFRIEDA, showing the squareness of her sail plan, entering Falmouth prior to her purchase by the German Schoolship Association.

train boys for the mercantile marine in the Baltic, and is now preserved in Bremen as a stationary vessel and painted black, although the DSV vessels were always painted white in service, with cream foc's'le heads and half-rounds to their poops.

   The last essay of the Association into a deep-sea training ship was a somewhat extraordinary one, since it bought an old merchant barque. This was doubtless dictated by the economic climate of the day but, at a time when many ships were up for sale due to the depression, the choice of vessel might seem odd. Perhaps it was just too late to make the most of the market, as many square-riggers had been sent to the breakers immediately before the purchase was made.

   In the event, they bought the 1637-ton barque *Elfrieda* from Vinnen Gebr. of Hamburg in 1928. Although not really any bigger than their

146. A fine view of the SCHULSCHIFF DEUTSCHLAND making sail. Not all the buntlines are yet overhauled.

147. Dismasted, the SCHULSCHIFFE POMMERN wallows in the aftermath of the gale while ships stand by her. Note the buckled spars lying over the starboard side.

Grossherzog Friedrich August, she was a heavily built, bald-headed barque which was very squarely and heavily rigged. She had originally been built by Russell's of Port Glasgow for the Glasgow owners D. McGillivray as the *Saxon,* and had been employed in general trade until sold in 1910 to Sorenson's of Arendal, who sold her in turn to H. Borge of the same port in 1916 when she was re-named *Amasis,* which name she retained under Sandefjord registry until sold to Vinnen's in 1924 when she became the *Elfrieda.*

The reason that the word *Schulschiff(e)* preceded both the *Deutschland* and the *Pommern* was that there were already vessels of these names and, if somewhat ponderous, the word 'schoolship' was thus incorporated into their names. The cargo-carrying days of the new ship were over but, on her maiden voyage, after running down to Las Palmas,

148. Boatwork in the GROSSHERZOGIN ELISABETH.

149. Plenty of hands make light work of raising the anchor by capstan in the SCHULSCHIFF DEUTSCHLAND off Bremerhaven in about 1927.

150. *Hammocks saved a lot of space but had none of the curtained privacy of a bunk in the foc's'le of a merchantman. Note the boots suspended from the nettles against rolling or possible ingress of water. This is the SCHULSCHIFF DEUTSCHLAND.*

she was dismasted off the Channel Islands on her way home and abandoned: her crew, who had reacted splendidly, being rescued by the German tug *Heros*. Although towed into St Malo by a French trawler which found her two days later, the cost of re-rigging her was prohibitive and she was soon broken up. Thus her life as a school-ship was exceptionally short.

The charge is often laid against the school-ships that they seldom venture into high latitudes and have far too many cadets for their size – often with some reason. This charge could not be levelled at the Deutscher Schulshiff Verein, since the original object was to train the cadets for *going* into deep-water sailing ships, and they therefore concentrated on certain basic principles: sail-handling, boat-work (to an intense degree) and schooling of various sorts, while discipline was very

151. The SCHULSCHIFF DEUTSCHLAND's cadets man the lower rigging as she passes the homeward-bound, under-manned Finnish barque WINTERHUDE: a vessel which was seldom a happy one – a fact reflected in her general aura of lack of smartness which was by no means true of the majority of merchantmen.

strict and the vessels were all very smartly run. It was not the object to provide an all-round training in sail, but a preparation for it, together with general 'character-building'. In this they were almost unique amongst vessels of their size.

Until about 1920, a cadet spent a year in the ships, but this became extended to two years and, in some instances, to three years. Obviously, after the 1914–18 war, the objects changed somewhat. Germany lost most of her deep-water tonnage as reparations to the Allies and, although she quickly built up a fleet again, it was quickly overtaken by world slump conditions. Concurrently, the German government – which latterly meant Hitler's regime – took a progressively increased hand in matters and, although the German Navy built its own training barques (which were extremely practical and functional, but which never had the style and

152. The SCHULSCHIFF DEUTSCHLAND passing Dover in 1933.

looks of the Oldenburg vessels), the influences of the times found their way into the *Grossherzogin Elisabeth* and the *Schulschiff Deutschland*.

If a relatively small ship, with no cargo, is to be run efficiently with a great number of cadets, discipline must be strict. (To run such a vessel with a small number of cadets is simply not economically viable.) Perhaps the contrast is drawn in Pl. 151 showing the *Schulschiff Deutschland* passing the Finnish barque *Winterhude* at sea, with the *Winterhude's*

153. In latter years, the GROSSHERZOG FRIEDRICH AUGUST has become better known as the Norwegian STATSRAAD LEMKUHL, seen here in the North Sea in 1960.

seaman in the foreground, shirtless and probably wearing patched dungaree trousers (which may, or may not, have been clean!) while the cadets of the training ship, crowding her lower rigging, are all dressed as smartly as though they were on parade. It was all a very different lifestyle, but the fact remains that, apart from the traumatic period after two wars when men had to take jobs wherever they could, almost all the cadets in these vessels did, in the event, follow the sea as a career.

Torreira is a village fifty miles south of Porto, in Portugal. It faces west, out over the Atlantic, and east, across three hundred square miles of the shallow, placid water of the Aveiro lagoon. Being mostly wind-blown sand with little humus to bind it, the land is poor with a sparse natural vegetation of pine trees and scrub, with the result that the farmers have turned to the sea for their major source of sustenance and, in doing so, have evolved a way of life that is centred round their beautiful oxen and two exquisite boats, marvellously adapted for their roles, of which one is the *Xavega* (pronounced *shuv(e)ga*), named after its seine net, but also known as a *Barco do Mar*, possibly to distinguish it from its neighbour on the other side of the village – the *Moliciero* – whose lowlier role is the raking up of seaweed (*molice*) from the shallow bottom of the lagoon. (Pl. 372 *et seq*)

Apart from their greatly exaggerated sheers and their similar stem-heads, the only apparent connection between them is the men who work them and their tireless beasts, for the boats themselves have never met, although their distant ancestors may have been the same, and appear to have been so, judging by their bones.

Although beautiful in its way, the *Xavega* is a monster of a boat compared witht the graceful seaweed dredger. It has power and majesty and its life can be exciting and violent, for its work takes it to sea in the Atlantic from its home on the beach, and the surf between the two can be fickle and vicious.

The coast, south of Porto for sixty miles or so, is low-lying with sandy beaches which are steep as sandy beaches go, but not as steep as shingle. There can be three of four broken waves making their way ashore, wherein lies the problem, for out beyond those breakers swim millions of teeming fish.

The breakers are old hands – they have come a long way and, regardless of the local wind, which may be off-shore for many days, their tireless advance goes on: sometimes fiercely; sometimes less so, depending on the pattern of weather down towards the Azores. They are the enemy: nothing will stop them and they will roll a boat as they might a cork should it give them half a chance.

Experience must have taught the fishermen of Torreira, if, indeed they ever needed the teaching, that to land a fish-laden boat through that surf

154.   The bows of a xavega on the beach.

is to court disaster. Equally unprofitable would it be to moor the boat beyond the breakers, for an Atlantic storm and a lee shore make a boisterous combination. Thus there is no alternative but to keep the boat ashore above the high tide mark and to go to sea only when the weather allows, and to retreat again to safety as quickly as may be. This situation calls for judgement but . . . families must be fed and risks may have to be taken, and so the scene is set.

The drama is a quiet one. The Portuguese must be the quietest of the Latins. They are purposeful, steady and practical and are used to hard work for small returns. Many, on their unhurried way to the boat − for only one will be used, will have paused for a moment at a road-side shrine for a quiet word with the Holy Virgin Mary and, perhaps, a gentle request for a catch to beat all catches.

The day of the *Xavega* begins, as it ends, with a fish basket. The evening one is full, but that in the morning is empty and hangs from the top of a tall pole close to the beach. This may be a tradition but, like so much to do with boats and this one in particular, there is a sound and good reason for the basket since the onshore breeze has not started to blow and a flag, however large, will lie close to the pole and be invisible to those who are awaiting its message: the message being that the sea has dropped its guard and is ready for the fishing. Its recipients are the fishermen and farmers: the supernumeries and hangers-on: the merchants who will need lorries to take the fish away; the simpletons of Torreira who will toil all day and stagger home with nothing but their happiness, and all the idle and busy of the village who will bring to the beach lunch for themselves and their men.

The farmers, who hire themselves and their oxen to the owners of the boat, will be the first to arrive, for theirs is the business of hauling the *Xavega* down to the sea and launching it through the surf. They have done it many times before; they need no orders, they have a long, hot day ahead and the tide is coming in.

The boat was loaded the day before, or the last time it was used. Four miles of rope, seven hundred and fifty yards of net and another four miles of rope — eight tons in all — are stowed, mostly in the stern and the rope handler is tying one end to a stake in the sand.

No-one is in the boat yet but the oars, each 45 feet long, lie horizontal across the gunwales and the looms lashed down to the opposite rail. She is 52 feet long and 15 feet wide, and her bows tower up in a magnificent sweep to a stemhead 16 feet above the sand, to the top of which is fastened a mascot or charm in the form of a crucifix, a lifebelt or laurels. The stern, too, curves upwards, so that the impression given is one of a giant segment of melon.

The four oars are flattened as they cross the gunwale, which is iron shod to prevent chafe, and through the flattened part, which is two feet wide, passes the steel thole pin. The loom of the oar has a thin bar along the top, for only the last foot is small enough to be held in the hand. On each oar there are a number of short ropes with loops, the purpose of

155. The lead oxen have broken off: others prepare to take out the port check rope, and the crutch of the pushing pole is set in position.

156. With the bow checks led each side, the 'pusher' oxen take over and shove the xavega over the rollers and . . . .

157. . . . continue to push as she leaves the rollers and becomes water-borne, when . . .

which becomes obvious as the boat approaches the water and more and more crew climb on board and take up their appointed positions at their oars until each is manned by eleven men: some holding the hand bar; some ready to pull on the ropes, some sitting and some standing.

The launching is not a headlong rush, for the beach is not steep enough. It is a slow haul with the flat bottom of the boat resting on rollers which are themselves resting and rolling on a collection of long, thin pine logs at right angles to the rollers.

As the boat moves down towards the water, pulled by eight oxen fastened to iron loops on the topsides, so the pine tree carpet and the rollers are moved into position ahead of her.

As the bows reach the water, the four teams of oxen withdraw and four others take up positions at the ends of four long ropes, which lead ashore from bows and stern and which will be used to keep the bows head on to the sea as the craft passes through the surf.

Soon the bows of the boat are in the surf and each wave lifts it, but is not man enough to float her free. One final thrust is required, and this is provided by yet another pair of oxen, or sometimes two, who are attached to a 60-foot pole reaching out to the stern of the boat where the crutch on its end clasps the stern and is held there with a short rope.

This, and the return to the beach, are the dangerous times for the *Xavega* for, if things go wrong in the next two minutes, the judgement of the skipper and his lineage will come under immediate attack, while his

158. . . . the great oars take over and the xavega is away.

ability as a seaman will be tested to the full, as will the reaction of the farmers and the strength of their beasts for, if the bows should fall away before the waves' great power, precision timing will be needed to get her back on course, since to swing broadside on to the beach is the prelude to disaster.

Should the worst happen and the great boat be capsized in the surf, then – and not until then – will her most unusual feature, her crescent shape, play its part for, although the crew will be thrown out into the shallow water or onto the sand, the *Xavega* will remain on its side and will not roll onto the crew struggling to get ashore. Since, by now, the boat will be half full of water, there is a good chance that it will only move again as the tide comes in and, although the stem head will probably have been smashed and, very likely, the stern as well, the damage will be appreciably less than had she rolled to and fro in the pounding surf. Moreover, salvage will be easier when the tide recedes.

It must be confessed that this theory is conjectural because, if one asks a member of the crew to explain the shape of his boat, he will have little idea beyond saying that it has always been that way, or more so, and that, anyway, he has never seen one go over. It would also be conjectural to say that a hundred, or even fifty, years ago more risks were taken. The people were poorer: food was scarcer; the economy of the village was less diverse and life itself was, perhaps, cheaper, so that greater risks were taken and boats *did* capsize. It is significant that, although the *Xavega* has not changed its shape in the last thirty years, the *Meia Luas* of Caparica and the *Nettinhas* of Nazare have lost their elongated stem heads and are now appreciably flatter in profile. Could it be that they, too, have benefited from the better times and are no longer required to perform in seas that are too strong for them?

To return to the beach at Torreira, where the *Xavega* is just coming clear of the sand, it is worth noting that the bollards on which the steadying ropes are made fast are as far forward as they could reasonably be without tearing out under stress, while the flat bottom and wide beam not only facilitate the rolling of a heavily laden boat down the beach, but also provide less resistance to the desperate heaves of the oxen in trying to keep her straight. There is more to be said of that flat, wide bottom.

Now the oars have begun to bite, the boat is moving under her own

159. While the boat is away, the scene ashore is somewhat odd, but not particularly nautical, until . . .

power and the steadying ropes are cast off. (Pl. 158) There has been no shouting and no crisis, and the crew settle down to a long, steady row. The stroke of the oar is short. It could hardly be otherwise with eleven men working at it, but one wonders about the enormous length. Surely many small oars would do as well, or better? Like that flat, wide bottom, their significance has yet to be seen.

The *Xavega* now rows directly away from the shore, steered by the rope-minder in the stern sheets who will check the rope as it crosses the gunwale in order to keep it and the boat in a straight line, and this continues for four miles until a white float fixed to the line signifies that the net has been reached, whereupon the boat turns 90° to starboard.

For the next 750 yards the net, a seine with mesh running down from twelve inches to about half-an-inch, is shot until a second white float goes overboard and the boat turns once more to starboard and sets off on its run back to the beach, lowering the second four-mile rope as it goes.

Shortly after this, five pairs of oxen will start the long and laborious business of hauling the first line ashore as the *Xavega*, while paying out the second four-mile rope, returns to the beach.

160.   ... *the returning xavega, after spinning like a top through 180°, comes in stern first. (Note the hauling fitments on the stern.)*

Throughout its eight and a half mile journey, the *Xavega* will have lost eight tons in weight of rope and net and, as it does this, so its waterline length will have shortened appreciably but its beam (since the sides of the boat are almost vertical) will have remained much the same. The craft, now high in the water, will be displaying a strong desire to spin; a desire that is encouraged by the enormous length – and therefore leverage – of the oars, but which is prevented by the rope-minder and his checking.

The time has now arrived for the second, more fascinating and, perhaps, more dangerous of the *Xavega's* manoeuvres, for the boat was launched bows first and must again be launched in this manner on her next trip. Thus it must turn before it enters the breaking surf, in order to present its stern to the reception party who are waiting ashore.

For perhaps eight strokes, or possibly ten, the crew step up the rate to get the boat moving as fast as possible. Then the two port oars stop. The rope-minder lets go. Then the port side back paddles for two strokes. The boat's rush towards the shore is almost unchecked, but she spins like a saucer and, in a moment, her stern is ashore; two hooks are in the hauling rings; the oxen are already moving and the crisis is over.

161. Then, harnessed to the xavega, the oxen haul her up the beach, over the rollers, to be ready for the next launching.

162.   Soon she will be ready in position for the next launch.

There are many ways of beaching a boat. There are many different beaches all making their special demands upon the boats that use them, and the *Xavega* of Torreiro is but one example, yet, surely, a good one to demonstrate how the study of a boat in action can give the clue to so many of its features: the crescent shape to minimize the effects of a capsize; the wide, flat bottom and 45-foot oars, not only to facilitate the launch, but also to provide the skidding spin that shortens by minutes the time that might be spent struggling in the dangerous surf. The *Xavega* may be Phoenician or Greek in origin, or both or neither, but there is no doubt that it has remained unchanged for many centuries and, to that extent, owes its features to tradition, but to suggest that this is the only reason for its shape is to say that its builder, its owner and its seamen are not only fools but the sons and grandsons of fools. No-one, who has seen a *Xavega* at work, could countenance such a suggestion for an instant.

163. The LADYE DORIS in her fitting out basin at Port Glasgow in 1901.

In 1901 Wm. Montgomery's of London built two splendid sister ships, the *Ladye Doris* and the *Eva Montgomery*, and followed them with a third, the *Fitzjames,* the following year. Of 1650 tons, their vital statistics were 267.4 × 40.1 × 23.6′ and, although making no really noteworthy passages, they were regarded as being amongst the finest vessels of their generation. The *Eva Montgomery* was featured in the first volume of this work and, like her, the *Ladye Doris* passed to the von 1896 company of Hamburg in 1910 to be re-named *Oliva*, later being sold to Chile as the *Dharma.* These facts are mentioned, since most of the immediately succeeding pictures were taken aboard or from the *Ladye Doris* between 1904 and 1907, when there were still plenty of square-riggers in trade and real sailors to man them. Captain Wood was master for almost all of this time, leaving her in the Falkland Islands in bad health when she had put in there after a terrible dusting outward bound

164. *Group aboard the LADYE DORIS. Captain Frazer, marine superintendent, standing second on left next to Captain Wood who is next to Mr A. Montgomery, the owner. The Second Mate, Mr Shippen*, is third from the left, sitting, on the left of the apprentice Hay who took these pictures. Mr Wells, the Mate, is holding the dog and, on his left, is Mr Hamilton, the Third Mate. Above them is the ship's motto: 'Dulcis Felixque Domus' – a sweet and happy home.*

off the Horn during which her cargo had shifted. This was shortly before she was sold to Germany.

The name of Wm. Montgomery is perhaps better known as the owners of the *Grace Harwar,* which preceded the three sisters mentioned above by some twelve years, having been built in 1889 and, oddly enough, she was a much more full-built vessel than the ships which came after her, but she did outlast them and, after passing to Finland, survived until broken up in 1935 – the last European full-rigger in trade.

Captain John Hay, now a nonagenarian with a fascinating memory,

*He was master of the GARTHNEILL (Pls. 517/8) in 1919 when, bound the 1,000 miles from Melbourne to Bunbury, he encountered furious westerly gales and put into Sydney. Making a second attempt, the same thing happened, and he then sailed the ship eastabout, round the Horn, sailing 14,500 miles in 76 days! He had had a bad time adrift in a boat in the War and later shot himself.

165. *'Dulcis Felixque Domus' forsooth! The motto did not always hold true. Here the LADYE DORIS is shipping a solid, ice-cold sea off the Horn. The view is from the fore deckhouse, the top of which can be seen in the foreground above the fore-and-aft life-line along the deck.*

was an apprentice and took many of these pictures. He married the elder of Captain Wood's daughters, both of whom figure in Pl. 172 and their house is redolent of the *Ladye Doris*. Indeed, it is a comment on the times that Mrs Hay has rounded the Horn more often than he – although his service in sail was not confined to the *Ladye Doris*, since he was also in the four-masted barque *Chiltonford*.

The pictures were taken on several voyages and no attempt is made to arrange them in sequence as though they all belonged to one. They were taken long before the age of the Leica or Hasselblad by young men with

166. A rare picture of apprentices in the half-deck, navigation books spread on the table. John Hay is under the hanging towel, not only sporting a tie but a tie-clip — equally unusual at sea in such a ship.

167. At Iquique, the Missions to Seamen held a service each Sunday aboard the RIVER INDUS which was permanently moored off the port. This composite picture shows apprentices, captains, their wives and children and some officers aboard her.

168. The fore-all men swigging down on the fore upper topsail halliard.

cheap cameras and, if a few suffer from defects, their inclusion is more than justified by their interest. Surely it was nothing short of a triumph to obtain a picture, in these circumstances, of the interior of the half-deck? Some may ponder how, in all the conditions of a working full-rigger and in the cramped living in that half-deck, it came about that apprentices *did* manage to go ashore in port still looking relatively smart in their brassbound uniforms, for mildew was no less an enemy in the half-deck as in the foc's'le where clothes were concerned. Yet the wearing of ties at sea is perhaps a reflection of the 'style' maintained in the ship, although she had no pretensions as a 'sail-training' vessel, as defined elsewhere in this book. The *Ladye Doris* was no more than a workaday 'windjammer', albeit a rather superior one.

Many photographs have appeared of the last square-riggers preceding the 1939–45 war, mainly in the Finns and taken by young men who only made the odd voyage. Some are of exceedingly high photographic

169. *Yard at mast-head, the halliard is almost two blocks. It is a reflection on the size of the crew that the sail can be hoisted by hand while the foresail sheet has been hauled in simultaneously (see Pl. 168) – presumably with the aid of the cook whose galley was adjacent to it. The upper topsail halliards (with the royals) lay to port for the fore and mizzen masts: to starboard for the main.*

quality, but there were no apprentices as understood in the British ships: it was seldom, if ever, that there was an incidental backcloth of tiers of anchored square-riggers in port; older men, whether in the afterguard, as 'idlers' or in the foc's'le, were a rarity and I doubt if a middle-aged man, wearing a cloth cap and waistcoat, would be seen in them pulling fore-hand, as in Pls. 168 and 169. In principle, it was the same old haul – Around the Horn and Home again – and, if some of the later ships sported brace and halliard winches, they were worked in much the same way.

The Finnish ships rotated their watches differently, and did not know dog watches, since they simply did not exist in them. Pl. 172, with the old

170. *A sailmaker of the old school was a tremendous boon to a master. Here, in the LADYE DORIS, old 'Sails' sits on his bench on deck repairing a sail, with his fids, wax, twine, needles, palm and all the paraphanalia of his trade.*

Edison Bell gramophone, must be one of the most evocative dog watch photographs ever taken and, if a blown out sail, a boarding sea or the work of changing sail might belong as well to one generation as another, old 'Sails': even 'Chips': the clipper-bowed steamer with the forest of masts and spars beyond her: the nitrate lorcha with the Montgomery houseflag – the white 'M' on a blue field: these things were over before the last Finnish crews were born.

Pl. 171 shows the 'tween deck, clear of cargo. It may not rank with the work of modern industrial photographers, but it is no mean effort from an apprentice's camera, and demonstrates how a sailing ship, devoid of

171.   The 'tween-deck.

transverse bulkheads from the fore to after peaks, was really just one big shell – for it was long before IMCO* and all its regulations. It shows, too, the basic construction of such a ship: the upper deck beams secured to the frames (ribs) by beam knees: the central line of pillars and the wood decking on the lower beams. One section has been removed – possibly for use as a shifting board in the lower hold. This could be dangerous, and many men have fallen through into the lower hold, sometimes on to the keelson itself.

When a ship arrives in port after a foreign-going voyage she flies the yellow International Code flag 'Q', meaning 'My vessel is healthy: I require free pratique'. (NOT, as many think, that the reverse is the case and that she is in quarantine!) No-one may go ashore or come aboard until she is cleared by the port doctor (or medical officer). The crew are lined up, and he may inspect their (dirty) hands: look cursorily at their eyes and, sometimes, conduct a 'short-arm' inspection of that organ known more familiarly as 'John Thomas'. It seldom amounted to much, but complied with regulations, as shown in Pl. 174.

*International Maritime Consultative Organisation.

172. *In the Dog Watch: one of the most human square-rigger photographs ever taken. The second mate plays his old Edison Bell gramophone on the main hatch to the delight of Captain Wood's younger daughter (in bonnet). Next to him is Captain Wood's elder daughter who later married Hay (centre) – perhaps vindicating the motto!*

173. *The carpenter caulking the deck. To keep the seams watertight, they must be filled solid with oakum with the caulking mallet and chisel in his hands, and then payed with hot pitch. Caulking needs to be renewed periodically. The carpenter was an 'idler', insofar as he was on day-work and did not keep watches.*

174. *The Medical Inspection on arrival in port.*

175. *The LADYE DORIS in Liverpool with a couple of Mersey flats alongside.*

176. Aboard the QUEEN MARGARET, an albatross, magnificent in flight, is ungainly on deck.

177. The Southern Ocean starts coming aboard as seas rear up astern. The LADYE DORIS.

178. Approaching the Horn, life-lines are rigged – a lee side view . . .

179. . . . and looking forward along the weather side as the LADYE DORIS scends to the seas, the heavy sprays working their way down to leeward.

180. Soon the decks are a maelstrom of water as . . .

181. . . . the ship runs on before a freshening gale.

182. *A flash of sunlight may give a certain enchantment to white water on deck in a picture, but it does not alter the working conditions of the crew.*

183. *The running rigging is hitched to the lower shrouds to avoid being washed off the belaying pins. The LADYE DORIS is lucky if her decks are clear before . . .*

184. . . . the next sea boards her, right up to her sheer poles. She has little enough freeboard.

185. *In all the motion and blown spume, the camera catches a man who has jumped up on to a lifeline. If she takes a big sea and catches him in this position, he may spin round and round if he manages to retain his hold. It is clear from the halliard blocks (right) that the main upper topsail is still set.*

186. *The Pintado, or Cape Pigeon, a larger version of the Stormy Petrel, is seldom seen aboard ship. Often flying in droves in her wake, close to the water and sometimes using their legs to hop along its surface even in wild weather, with their apparently dappled appearance, they are attractive to see. Although seeming to be black and white in flight, the black is in reality a sooty-brown.*

187. *A sea is clearing from the decks. Boarding seas were more spectacular, but prone to damage cameras! The three white blocks are those of the main braces – always wet in a deep-loaded ship in high latitudes, being right in her waist. Ahead of them is the fore topmast staysail sheet rising out of the water.*

188. *A great sailing ship cargo was coal from Newcastle, NSW, particularly to the West Coast of South America. It was a dangerous one, being prone to spontaneous combustion. Here large coal hoppers on railway flats are alongside the LADYE DORIS.*

189. *Getting along nicely 'full and by'. Note the chain tack to the foresail.*

190. *The coal hoppers were lifted by crane and deposited on staging on deck. Then . . .*

191. ... with the bottom of the hopper opened, the coal is dumped and the hopper swung ashore. The coal is shovelled below to be trimmed in due course.

192. Getting ready for sea, the mainsail is bent at the Farewell Buoys. Like many older vessels, the clews are led up to the quarters of the yards.

193. *Outside Newcastle, the LADYE DORIS set sail alongside the Finnish barque ISOBEL BROWNE with little wind. This barque was owned by August Troberg of Mariehamn, having been built for Browne & Watson in 1885. She was sunk by the German cruiser PRINZ EITEL FRIEDRICH in 1915.*

194. *When sails are sent down, they are made up neatly into rolls before being stowed in the sail locker. Note the 'rovings' of ropeyarns on deck in the foreground. These are passed through eyelets in the head of the sail and round the jackstay to secure it to the yard. Note, too, the roping round the leech of the sail in the left corner.*

195. Old cameras and slow films in the hands of an apprentice could give excellent results, but had restrictions. Thus a man diving into the water from the accommodation ladder appears to be ectoplasm. A poor picture, but providing an impression of Iquique, with a fine Bordes four-master astern.

196. When the sail is made up, it is carried off like a long, flexible sausage. There is a lot of weight in a big sail, often with wire roping and iron spectacles. Courses in big four-masters could weigh about 1¼ tons.

197. There were sailing ships around wherever one looked off Iquique in those days.

198. Discharging on the West Coast, the coal was loaded into baskets in the hold and hove up with a hired winch (seen on deck).

199. Iquique was one of about a dozen Chilean nitrate ports, lying alongside the desert under the Andes. Note that some ships are well out of trim while loading.

200. When the last basket was filled it was hoisted with some ceremony with a man holding the Pilot Jack.

201. *The point of this poor picture is to show how the poop was tented in an effort – usually in vain – to exclude the coal dust while the LADYE DORIS discharged.*

On the West Coast of South America, the saltpetre was mined some fifty miles inland and brought to the coast – at this period – by rail. (Llama trains had been used formerly.) In Pl. 202 a lorcha sails out with a load for a ship, the smart and distinctive hull paint of one of the French ships of A. D. Bordes et Fils being visible ahead of her. Sometimes the bags were hauled up singly and landed on the sloping plank (Pl. 203) which connected with others to form a slide right down to the lower hold, where one stevedore took it on his shoulders and, in fact, loaded the entire ship. Sometimes a sling of bags would be hauled up and loaded on to a trolley (Pl. 205) which was wheeled to the hatch and then, again, one bag at a time was shot down below to the waiting stevedore.

202. *A lorcha under sail takes a load of nitrate to the anchorage.*

203. *Landing a bag of saltpetre aboard.*

204. *While the apprentices row the 'Old Man' ashore* . . .

205. *. . . the crew carry on with the loading.*

206. Sailing ships loading at Antofagasta, another nitrate port, giving a good idea of the nature of the coast.

207. Passing the bows of the full-rigger SCOTTISH ISLES, a lighter proceeds to the LADYE DORIS with the Montgomery house-flag set atop her bags of saltpetre.

208. The LADYE DORIS in the tiers of ships off Iquique, in the shadow of the Andes.

209. *Iquique jetty.*

210. *A quarter view of the ship at the anchorage. The ship on the right has rigged a wind-sail for ventilation.*

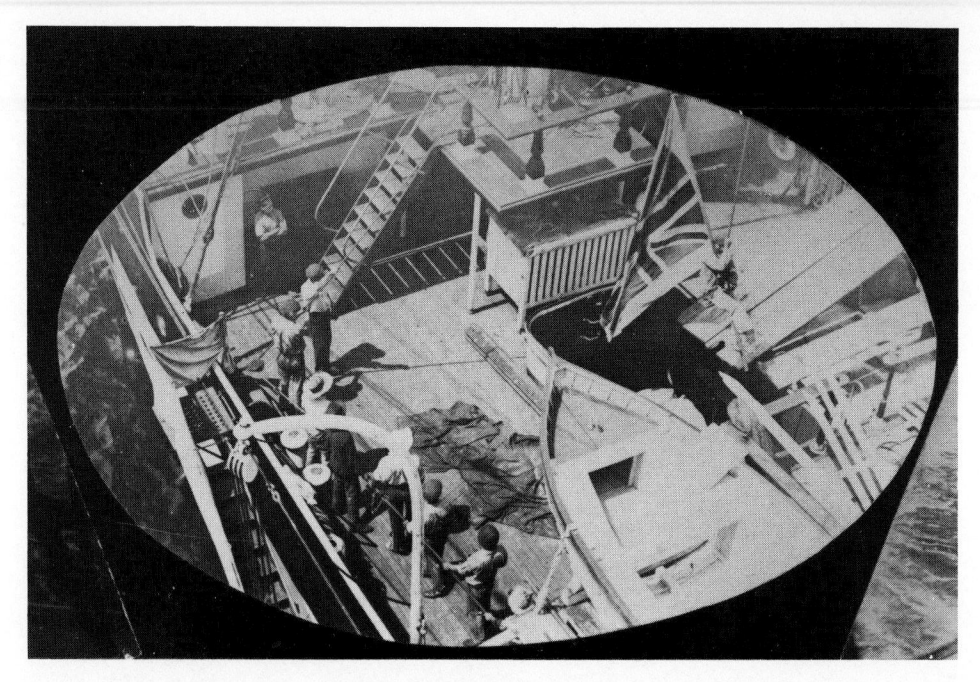

211. *Preparing to chantey the last bag of nitrate aboard.*

212. *Aloft changing sail in the tropics, when the oldest sails are substituted for the storm canvas, was a splendid job. Note the gaskets hanging. These lengths of point-line are made fast to the jackstay. When making them up a man winds the loose end round his elbow and the inside of his thumb into equal bights: then takes a couple of turns round the whole and, with the standing part, passes it through and over one set of bights. Thus they* should *all be neat and of the same length! They can be cast off with one hand when needed to make fast the sail to the yards.*

213. In the second dog watch, one apprentice acts as barber for another. A picture evidently taken soon after Pl. 173 as the decks have evidently just been caulked and payed with pitch.

214. One of the LADYE DORIS' sister ships was the FITZJAMES, which became the PINNAS in the Laeisz Hamburg 'P' Line, as seen here. She was dismasted and abandoned off the Horn in 1929.

215. *Never mind the flaw in the negative! Here most of the lower topsail is blown out: the ship is almost under bare poles; it is blowing like Hell and two men pass more gaskets round the cro'jack. Plenty of work building up for old 'Sails'. These were conditions which separated the sheep from the goats. Note that, like the L'AVENIR, (Pl. 76), the LADYE DORIS has safety netting in her tops.*

    Saltpetre was very heavy and, to ensure that the ship was not too stiff, with her centre of gravity too low, the proportion in the lower holds was built up in pyramids, and more was stowed in the 'tween decks. Due to its weight, there was much spare space left in the holds after a nitrate cargo was loaded. When the last bag came aboard, it was chanteyed up by all hands, usually including the officers, with a man straddling it and holding a Pilot Jack, and each ship in the harbour was cheered, and each, in turn, returned the cheers, while the ship's bell was rung (Pl. 211). Sometimes a wooden framework of the Southern Cross was hoisted aloft. It was all a pleasant enough custom in an age when voyages were of no pre-determined length, and it is difficult to imagine any similar spontaneous

216. The *LADYE DORIS* – *sails full with fair wind*.

demonstration when the last container is loaded aboard a modern container vessel in a computerised port. Life is too real and earnest today for a seaman or docker to deviate one iota from his rule book – or so they think! Had they muzzled a split topsail off the Horn (Pl. 215) they would know how real and earnest life *can* become, and perhaps have more understanding of what really makes men tick. The men of the *Ladye Doris did* tick, and would have felt out of place in modern vessels. As the *Dharma,* she came into collision with the British *s.s. Pear Branch* off San Antonio in Chile early in October, 1925 – more than half a century ago. These pages may resuscitate her memory! Not comparable with the clippers, she had few peers in the age of her building.

Some vessels which might otherwise have gone unrecorded achieved a certain fame due to some peculiar circumstance or because of their association with a well-known person. An instance of the former case was a 775-ton schooner, the *Elizabeth Bandi,* which was laid down in a hurry at the end of the First World War and built of wood at Gulfport, Mass. for the Marine Coal Company of New Orleans. By the time she was ready for sea the shipping boom was over and, on her first voyage, she loaded lumber for Bahia but, running into bad weather, she made a great deal of water and ran back to Bridgetown for shelter. After she had resumed her voyage, her master disappeared overboard in mysterious circumstances, whereupon she was again run back to anchorage, where her officers and crew took one of the boats and went ashore.

History does not relate what happened to them and it was some time before it was realized that the ship was deserted, whereupon a new master and crew were sent out to take her over. When they arrived, it was discovered that her only buoyancy lay in her cargo and that the teredoes had really got to work on the hull. Obviously, a schooner of this size had not the scantlings of the giant schooners discussed on page 256 *et seq.* but, nevertheless, there is a great thickness of timber in a wooden vessel and, although it is true that she was not sheathed, the presumption is that poor, unseasoned wood was used in her construction at that time of crisis and shortage of tonnage.

The holes were plugged as well as possible with the ship still afloat and loaded and, eventually, she proceeded. In due course and after a great deal of pumping, she arrived back in Philadelphia where much of her planking was renewed and her rudder, which was virtually eaten away, was replaced. It was all a poor start to life.

She then loaded coal for the Caribbean, but was soon in the same sorry state: so much pumping being necessary that the crew became mutinous with the master standing over them with a gun! Things did improve a bit after that second voyage, but she was still dogged by the teredo and becoming so expensive to maintain that she was sold to E. Reid of Bath, Me. in 1925, and ran successfully in colder waters until she arrived in the Mersey in 1930 with a cargo of lumber from Pictou, N.S. when the photo that is Pl. 217 was taken.

'Success' is a relative term and used here only of her actual voyaging,

217. The ELIZABETH BANDI. She measured 178.7 × 36.2 × 15 feet.

for she was a long time in the Mersey because the ship and part of her undischarged cargo were placed under restraint in order to pay the crew and other charges, which finally resulted in the sale of the schooner to Raumo owners and, with the word *Elizabeth* dropped from her name, the *Bandi* traded in the Baltic until 1938 when she was bought by J. T. Essberger of Hamburg to be a training ship for his steamer fleet. He renamed her *Seeute Deern,* completely re-rigging her as a three-masted barque with single t'gallants, royals and a double spanker: her foc's'le head being built up and extended and her hull painted black with painted ports. Conversions are not often very successful, but this was not the case in this instance and the ship behaved admirably and must have been unique in having steel masts and spars on a wooden hull. She carried a small amount of cargo, mainly in the Baltic, and, trading intermittently during the war, is now preserved and acting as a restaurant in Hamburg. It was a strange career.

The 373-ton steel schooner *Morten Jensen* had been built in 1913 by the Frederikshavns Shipyard for Nykobing owners, being given an auxiliary in the form of a two-cylinder Bolinder engine. In 1916 she was sold to Arendal and became the *Tyholm,* and then to Skien (also in Norway) but was captured by the Germans. After the war, Count Felix von Luckner, who achieved unique fame as commander of the full-rigged raider *See-Adler* (ex-British *Pass of Balmaha),* bought her to make luxury cruises and converted her to a jackass barque, as shown in Pl. 218. Her rig was odd in that era, but it should be noted that, contrary to some expressed opinions, she cannot be described as a schooner since, for practical purposes, a schooner must be deemed to have a boomed fore-and-aft sail abaft her foremast, whereas a square-rigger, in whatever form, will have staysails between main and fore*.

In the event, the luxury cruise project was still-born due to lack of applicants and the vessel was bought by the German government and used as a training ship, still with the name which von Luckner had bestowed on her – *Niobe.* In this role she proved to be extremely satisfactory until one day in July 1932, when sailing off the Fehman Belt, she was hove down by a white squall and capsized with the loss of 69 lives, only those on deck at the time being saved. As a matter of naval routine when a ship is lost, the captain was court-martialled, but exonerated from blame on the grounds that there was no time to do anything. At the time, there was much waterside gossip to the effect that all those on deck had been watching the *Graf Zeppelin* (or some other airship) passing to leeward and had never noticed the squall working up on them. Whether credence can be placed in this story which had common currency at the time, or whether it is gross calumny, it is now difficult to judge and it is included here in the hope that some light may be shed on the matter one way or the other. There is enough evidence elsewhere in this book to demonstrate that the results of enquiries are not always satisfactory.

Subsequently the *Niobe* – perhaps unfortunately named in the event, when one recalls the grief associated with that lady – was towed into Kiel after being raised, but that was the end of her career.

The full-rigger *Vik* seen towing out of the Mersey (Pl. 219) had a number of Norwegian owners from 1909 until she was broken up in 1924, and was an iron, full-built ship built in Southampton in 1882 as the

*In this context I exclude the fore spencer, which was only carried by ships which were incontrovertibly square-rigged.

218. *The true jackass, or hermaphrodite, barque did not normally set a square mainsail. The fact that the NIOBE did so does not alter the fact that she was such a one – witness the proportions of her yards.*

Leicester Castle for J. Coupland. In due course she passed to R. A. Smith & Co. who sold her to Joyce & Co. of Liverpool, under whose house-flag she really came into the news.

In 1902 she was homeward bound from San Francisco and still some 300 miles north of Pitcairn Island when her captain, who was reading in his bunk one evening, was called by an American member of the crew to attend to a sick man. He told the man to tell the second mate to bring the patient into the saloon but, instead, another American came in and the captain was shot in the arm; then clubbed about the head and then shot again. The second mate, hearing the shooting, rushed in and was promptly shot dead.

The mate, unhurt in all this, called the hands aft, but the two Americans, with a third compatriot, failed to muster. It was a dark night with the ship making about 3½ knots and, fearing further attack, all hands remained in the cabin with the intention of staying there until dawn but, in the event, the shape of a raft with three men aboard was seen drifting past. The ship was then hove to, in the hope of catching the murderers, but dawn revealed an empty sea and it was clear that the raft was a most flimsy structure, made up of a few planks lashed together, some 12 × 4 feet in area, with three cork cylinders from the forward boat to give it some buoyancy. The captain, who was horribly injured, survived to bring the ship home and to have five bullets removed on arrival at Queenstown.

The case has always been considered to be odd. In the first place, it has been questioned why the three men did not take one of the ship's boats. The likely answer to this is that they could not have done so without some noise and exposing themselves, since they probably did not know where the rest of the crew might be, nor whether the mate was armed. Yet the crime was clearly premeditated, and the three men took all their effects with them on the raft together with some stores. Their revolver had been stolen from the second mate's cabin. It seems that some vital aspect of their plan, whatever it may have been, had miscarried.

It is also cited as being extraordinary insofar as it appeared to have been motiveless. This, too, may be queried, since the ship had had to pay the crimps 'blood money' in San Francisco, and these were shanghaied men. Much has been written about the crimps in various ports: about some masters who came at odds with them, and about the few Missions to Seamen padres who matched themselves against the practice, which has taken on a somewhat romantic aspect of 'goodies' and 'baddies', all of which makes good lurid (and thus popular) reading. It is true that a ship would not get away from many ports unless blood money *was* paid and crews, usually drugged or dead-drunk, 'purchased' from the so-called boarding house masters – the crimps.

It is also true that most of the men so traded were sailors; that one ship was much like another in the final analysis (though some were indubitably worse than others) and that they came to view their situation with a certain philosophy. Yet not all shanghaied men were sailors, and the fact is that a number of men who had no connection with the sea found

220. The hull of the CHARLES RACINE, rotting at Beira, shows her underwater lines.

219. The VIK towing down the Mersey.

themselves 'coming to' in an outward-bounder, making sail for a long voyage round the Horn. In common terms, these men had been kidnapped – no more and no less, and forced to a work and way of life that was probably utterly repugnant to them.

The three Americans in the *Leicester Castle* had been shipped aboard by the local crimp, and it is reasonable to suppose that they resented their lot bitterly. Were I to be kidnapped, whether by a Sicilian bandit, a terrorist or by a ship-master, I would not hesitate to take any possible opportunity of liquidating my captors and effecting an escape. The legality of such action I am not competent to judge, but the equity is clear. It is my view that these men had every motive for doing what they did, and can only express surprise that there were not more incidents of like nature from men who were, in effect, kidnapped. That the real villain of the piece was the crimp is immaterial. The men found themselves aboard a ship against their will and, whatever the odds stacked against shipmasters in certain ports, it is undeniable that they were party – whether willingly or not – to the transactions.

A man who signs articles voluntarily is strictly bound by them, and mutiny is one of the most heinous of crimes at sea. In any case, the legal dice were generally loaded against the seaman. The three Americans in the *Leicester Castle* had either not thought their plan of campaign right through, or it failed in some aspect. The foremast hand was in no case to take over a ship and, in any case, 'murder' is always murder while, apart from that, the officers were generally armed or had arms available, whereas the crew had not. Yet, when one reflects on the matter, there was motive a-plenty, and one must remain astonished that, if shanghaied men seldom resorted to such extreme measures, there was not a great deal more sabotage to the ships concerned. So might one comment on the impressment in the old British Navy. The fact was probably that a good ship quickly bred some sort of camaradie and, for somewhat different reasons, a bad ship had the same effect, since all, whether signed on voluntarily or not, felt themselves to be, literally, in the 'same boat'.

In the Norwegian seaport town of Stavanger is a statue of a rather broad, squat man, brimfull of determination, looking towards the harbour. He is Sigval Bergesen; one of so many shipowners in that country who were building its maritime power at the end of the nineteenth

221. The CHARLES RACINE off Havre in July 1904.

and beginning of the twentieth centuries. By the harbour itself is a large, modern office block, housing the present vast Bergesen interests and, in its foyer, is a magnificent model of a barque – the *Charles Racine*.

In 1891, Bergesen had decided to build a new vessel – a steamer, and offered the command and supervision of her building to Captain Gustav Waage, who had made a great reputation for fast passages in the Stavanger full-rigger *Birmah*. Waage regarded steamers with near loathing and looked down on them as vessels *'which boiled themselves across the sea',* and wrote to Bergesen: *'I will sail so long as the wind blows'.* Strange to relate, Bergesen acceded, and the steamer became the three-masted barque *Charles Racine!* Even when the Sunderland builders submitted the plans, Waage's influence was apparent, since he persuaded the owner to have them altered to give her finer lines and thus more speed but less cargo space. This was asking rather a lot in that last flush of sailing ship building, especially from a shipmaster still in his thirties.

Launched in 1892, the barque achieved a world-wide reputation for good passages, but Waage was not so conservative as the foregoing comments might lead one to suppose. The ship had, for example, a messroom for the crew, which was certainly unusual in a sailing ship. Waage himself was a religious man in a pantheistic sort of way, and believed in God. He held a service each Sunday morning in the saloon, at which there would first be some religious story, followed by hymns, which he would accompany on the piano or organ. The crew would all dress in their best clothes on these occasions and, after the service, would be treated to cigars and canned fruit, while any seaman who could sing or play a musical instrument was encouraged to do so. This enlightened and extremely unusual treatment was not actuated so much by piety as by a desire to provide a break in the monotony of the life of the men.

It need hardly be said that she was a popular ship in which to sail. Once, when her old sailmaker, named Hansen, who was well on into his sixties, was robbed of two years' pay in Antwerp, he hurried back aboard to sign on again as fast as he could, rather than face the prospect of having to join any other vessel.

On 21 October, 1894, she was in the English Channel, four days out of Shields with a cargo of coal bound towards Iquique, when she fell in with the brand new Italian barque *Giuseppina Accame* which was still on her maiden voyage and proceeding from Queenstown towards Antwerp, with a pilot aboard, to discharge a cargo of grain from Buenos Aires. On the second day from the Irish coast she encountered a very strong sou'westerly and the pilot hove the ship to, considering that there was insufficient sea-room to run before the gale. By the time she was sighted by the *Charles Racine* her cargo had shifted, she was listing dangerously and was flying distress signals. The Norwegian manoeuvred as close as she could and a volunteer boat's crew got away but, within five minutes and before they could reach her, the Italian had capsized and disappeared. From the wreck of a lifeboat and some spars, the Norwegians succeeded in rescuing eleven men, including the master and owner, who were all landed at Portland.

In 1910 the *Charles Racine* narrowly escaped damage in the bad fire at Mystic Dock, when flames were shooting 100 feet into the air only a ship's

222. The CHARLES RACINE partially dressed in Durban.

length away from her, destroying the sheds of the lumber company and five railway cars, but, luckily, there was an off-shore breeze and the barque was able to get away from the quay. When she left she carried as a super-cargo for $75 Eugene O'Neill, who travelled with a friend and worked in the day-time. Later he was to become famous as a Nobel prize-winner for literature, besides collecting three Pulitzer prizes. At this time he was still in his roistering period, and his marriage was not a success. He had recently returned from an unsuccessful trip to Honduras prospecting for gold and, indeed, his son had been born only a month before he joined the *Charles Racine* – an action which seems to have been actuated partly to escape his domestic duties and partly because sailing ships were exerting a fascination over him. Perhaps few people familiar with his verses appreciate that the lines at the beginning of this book relate to his time in the barque, as do passages in *The Long Days Journey; The Hairy Ape; Bound East to Cardiff; Anna Christie* and other works.

By this time, Captain Waage, a well-built man with silver hair and moustache and with a calm authority, was still somewhat in advance of his times (although, in these days, when even the display of a golliwog in a toy shop is held to have racial 'overtones', perhaps some people would say that he was behind them!). At all events, black and white men did not always get on well in Norwegian ships and, on this voyage at any rate, they were berthed apart and the fact was that everyone was happy. The cook on that voyage was a negro, who rejoiced in the name of Lancelot Silver Garth! The seamen at that time were paid 54 kronor per month, which was the equivalent of about £3, or $13.50. There were 19 crew in all.

After a couple of days anchored off Boston due to headwinds and fog, she made quite a good passage until almost on the parallel of the Plate, when she was struck by a storm which carried away part of her deck-load of lumber. In consequence she made the poor passage, by her standards, of 57 days. (The next voyage, from Bridgewater, N.S. she made Buenos Aires in 45 days.)

O'Neill left in Buenos Aires, and it may be an interesting reflection on the emphasis of the advertising of the times that one brothel tout, from the flourishing 'red light' district, had written on a card: *'Come up to my house: plenty fun, plenty girls, plenty dance, three men killed last night.' Chacun a son gout!* After staying a while in the port, during which he helped to discharge the German full-rigger *Timandra,* O'Neill finally came home in the *s.s. Ikala* which served as the basis for his *s.s. Glencairn* tales.

On 15 January, 1916, the barque achieved the dubious distinction of being the sailing ship which found herself between the battle-cruiser fleets at the Battle of the Dogger Bank, when under Captain Thørvesen, and the next year Bergesen sold her to J. W. Johannesen of Oslo and, five years later, soon after she had left Durban in ballast for the St Lawrence, she encountered a bad storm in which her ballast shifted and much of the rigging was lost. The crew managed to work her back into Durban where she was condemned and lay, disintegrating, for a number of years before being hulked at Beira.

'I have eaten my share of "stock-fish"
On a steel Norwegian barque;

223.   The THOMASINA McCLELLAN.

> *With hands gripped hard to the royal yard*
>   *I have swung through the rain and the dark.*
> *I have hauled upon the braces*
>   *And bawled the chantey song,*
> *And the clutch of the wheel had a friendly feel*
>   *And the Trade Wind's kiss was strong. . . .*
>
> *For it's grand to lie on the hatches*
>   *In the glowing tropic night,*
> *When the sky is clear and the stars seem near*
>   *And the wake is a trail of light,*
> *And the old hulk rolls so softly*
>   *On the swell of the Southern Sea. . . .'*
>
> *The Call* by Eugene O'Neill

One of the finest full-riggers of her generation was the *Thomasina McClellan*, built by MacMillans for Thomson & Gray of Glasgow in 1873. Originally, her 'tween decks were fitted out for the emigrant trade, which reduced her deadweight tonnage to some 2,700. With a main skysail and a long jibboom outside her bowsprit (it became a spike bowsprit in her latter days under British ownership), she never bent a crossjack and set five staysails between her masts – unusual for a British ship. She was sold to E. F. & W. Roberts in 1900 and to J. Nicoll & Co. in 1902 and, three years later, she was bought by August Troberg of Mariehamn and M. Lundquist of Värdö, her skysail yard being removed and her name shortened to *Thomasina*. In 1915 she was torpedoed and sunk south of Queenstown when outward bound.

In the 1880s, the Hooghly pilots regarded themselves as the cream of creation, maintaining great style. They came aboard immaculately dressed, with their apprentice, leadsman, servant and gear, and expected a bath each evening, which was no light matter in a sailing ship! Once the *Thomasina McLellan* arrived off the pilot brig at the Sandheads, to be boarded by a Mr Ancel, who was astonished to find the crew all dressed in top hats, tail coats and striped morning trousers. It is true that, for the sake of ventilation, they had cut square holes in the 'toppers' and that they had neither collars, ties, dress shirts nor shoes to match, but the effect was nevertheless startling, particularly when the pilot ordered the royals and skysail to be set and saw men running aloft dressed in just this manner!

Imperturbably, he remarked to the master, Captain McCulloch: *'You've got a bunch of swells aboard'*. The master agreed, somewhat ruefully. It seemed that there had been an acute shortage of seamen in Melbourne, whence the ship had come, and that, instead of the prevailing rate of £4 per month, he had been obliged to pay £10! The men, feeling that they had done well and would do things in style, had gone in a body to a second-hand clothes dealer and equipped themselves accordingly in this fancy dress. However, they did prove to be an exceptionally smart lot, though they caused even greater surprise when the ship fetched up in Garden Reach. (She had sailed up to Saugor and then towed up to Sister Trees in Royapur Reach the next day. Proceeding up the day afterwards, she did ground momentarily but, fortunately, was pulled off quickly by the tug *Scinde*.)

The Hooghly pilots always maintained that the river was not navigable at night. No-one pretends that, with its shifting sands, it is an easy river, but that myth was exploded once and for all when a Harrison steamer master, who knew the river well, took his ship right up one night and without a pilot!

224.   The NARCISSUS.

One of the most famous and least photographed of ships in literature is the *Narcissus*. Conrad is known as a sea-writer novelist although, apart from his masterpiece, *The Mirror of the Sea* (which is not a novel), few of his full-length books are really sea stories, but rather tales of the seaboard. He used the *Narcissus* as the basis for *The Nigger of the Narcissus**, for he made a long passage of 136 days from Bombay to Dunkirk in her in 1884 as second mate. Like most of Conrad's tales, the story is not factually true, but based on a variety of real experiences. The negro's real name – in the *Narcissus* – was Joseph Barron, and James Wait, the name given in the book, was a negro he had come across when an A.B. in the *Duke of Sutherland*† six years previously in Sydney. Old Singleton was actually Sullivan, and some of the characters *were* in the ship with Conrad. It is one of the (few) great novels of the sea.

*Titled *'A Tale of the Foc's'le'* in the United States.
†Pl. 356.

225. The TORRENS, in which Conrad made two voyages as Mate, is probably the most famous of his ships. Composite-built with teak planking in 1875 for Elder & Co, she was, in her time, the favourite passenger ship to Adelaide. In 1896, soon after Conrad left her, she hit an iceberg and stove in her bows, losing part of the fore rigging, when outward bound. She is here repairing on the slip in Adelaide.

As to the ship herself, she was built of iron in Glasgow in 1876 by R. Duncan for Robert R. Paterson of Greenock for the sugar trade although, mainly, she was running out East. In 1899 she was bought by Captain Vittorio Bertoletto of Camolgi and registered at Genoa, being converted to a barque. She traded to Australia and the Pacific until 1907, when she was forced to put back to Rio after storm damage off the Horn when bound from St Louis (Rhône) towards Talcahuano. She got back to Genoa where she was hulked until, in the grab for tonnage during the 1914–18 war, she was sold to R. Passos of Rio and re-fitted — again as a barque — and named *Isis*. She was sunk in collision in Rio in 1922, but raised and sold to E. G. Pontes of that port, being finally hulked in 1925.

226. Not even the smartest of ships looked her best when high in the water and with her mizzen top and topgallant masts sent down. The MOUNT STEWART preparing to load rock salt in Birkenhead before her last voyage in 1923.

There was such a multiplicity of ships, of all sizes and rigs from all nations, that it is impossible for all to appear in the rolls of fame, and it is usually the more superlative ones; or those which 'made news' in some disaster or other, or those which established themselves statistically as being the 'first' or 'last' in some context, which usually engender the greatest interest. Those which were first of a type are seldom clearly defined, since developments tended to occur gradually and only seldom did a new type appear suddenly, fully fledged and accoutred like Pallas Athene nor, to use a more nautical simile, did they appear from the waves, fully developed, like Venus Anadyomene. Those which were 'last' are not necessarily of any great importance, since the fact that they

227. The MOUNT STEWART.

survived beyond their peers was usually mere accident of chance and not dictated by any merit.

Most people suppose that Noah's *Ark* was the first ship. This belief can certainly be discounted, since she was built to most enlightened proportions which have been repeated in a variety of vessels of varying sorts, ranging from Brunel's *Great Eastern* through the wool clipper *Golden Fleece* (a beautiful vessel) to the big four-masted full-rigger *Palgrave*. Thus it might be tempting to postulate that Noah was as far in advance of his times as Brunel was in his, but it is far safer to presume that he based his design – assuming the very existence of the *Ark* – on an abundance of previous and unrecorded experience.

For the record, some pictures of vessels which were statistically 'last' have been included. It is often said that the *Mount Stewart* and *Cromdale* (Pl. 336) were the last of the wool clippers. This is not strictly true, though they were the last two sailing vessels built specifically for the trade but,

228. *Warping the MOUNT STEWART in by the foc's'le head capstan. The figurehead is replaced by a scroll. The heavy tackle leading down to the eyes of the ship (from the fore topmast head) is the catfall, used for getting the anchor over the side.*

launched in 1891 from Barclay, Curle's yard and of iron construction and with main skysails when new, they were more full-built than the clippers, despite the fact that they did make some good passages. Pl. 227 gives a good idea of the way a square-rigger's yards are braced with a leading wind, in what has been termed 'the screw of the sails', with each yard checked in progressively more than the one below it. This was partly because the wind direction aloft is seldom the same as that on deck and also because, when close-hauled and the weather leech of the topmost sail was just a-shake, the ship would not come aback, as she might easily do in squally or shifty weather if all the yards were parallel to each other.

When one considers modern container terminals, it is interesting to view the space between the ship and the warehouses in Pl. 230 – a situation which prevailed in so many British docks and was a far cry from modern technologies.

There was no rush for berths in the *Mount Stewart* (or any other sailing

229. *The MOUNT STEWART was not broken up until 1924.*

ship) when these pictures were taken in 1923, and a notice at the foot of her gangway proclaimed that she needed a crew, with the qualification that *'Irishmen need not apply'*. No doubt Captain McColm, who was her master for the last fifteen years of her career, was thinking of times in port rather than at sea but, in this year of grace, such a notice would lead to him being hauled before a Race Relations Tribunal! The assumption that statutory legislation will alter peoples' prejudices is one of the clearest symptoms of the *malaise* which affects the world today*, and is part and parcel of the virtual impossibility of dismissing an incompetent man – whether at sea or anywhere else – in Great Britain. Whatever abuses may have existed – and they *did* exist – sailing ships were not run on such nonsensical lines, and it will be a poor prospect for those of the future,

*When a doctor living in the South of England advertised for a Scottish housekeeper – (it should be 'person' now!) – to help in his house, he did so because he wanted his porridge made properly, and because the Scots can do this. He and the newspaper which carried the advertisement were found guilty of contravening the Race Relations Act! Nor was this the mere decision of some petty local bureaucrat, for the decision was supported by the Chairman of the Race Relations Board! If this item has no immediate nautical significance, it is nevertheless interesting in the light of Captain McColm's notice half a century ago. With the Equal Opportunities (for women) Board promulgating similar absurdities, the mind boggles at the sort of crew – and its composition – that a Cape Horn shipmaster might find himself obliged to sign on today, were there such a one . . . but the rub is that, *if* sailing ships *are* built again, *this could well happen*. Some may look back to the Age of Sail to find Romance: others to discover sanity!

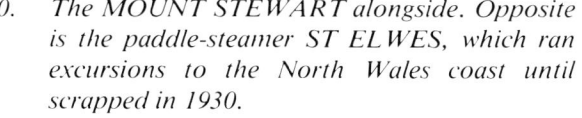

231. The DIEGO drying her sails. Someone forgot to slack the upper topsail downhaul — see the lower topsail yard!

230. The MOUNT STEWART alongside. Opposite is the paddle-steamer ST ELWES, which ran excursions to the North Wales coast until scrapped in 1930.

should they be revived, if they are to be subject to such lunatic legislation.

The last two square-riggers to be built in Great Britain for British owners were the sisters *Sunlight* and *Rendova* for Lever Brothers and were employed in the carriage of palm oil from Rendova Island, in the Pacific, to Port Sunlight for soap-making. Ugly sisters they may have been, but, of some 1,200 tons with stockless anchors and a bald-headed rig, they were inevitably purely functional vessels in that very last flush of building. Both were sunk by U-boats in the First World War, the *Rendova* being by then under Norwegian colours.

The last merchant square-rigger wearing the Red Ensign was the barque *Diego,* owned in Mauritius and wrecked on the Chagos Archipelago in 1935. She had been built in 1865 as the *Charlotte* for the Mediterranean run, but was later in both the Indian and copper ore trades before passing to E. Drago of Genoa to become the *Tomaso Drago.* Later, she was registered in Sweden as the *Janes,* although actually owned by Sir James Bell of Hull, and was employed in the split-wood trade until passing to Mauritian owners in 1924.

Norway, of course, had a vast fleet of square-riggers, of which the bulk of the larger ones were bought in second-hand, but the last square-rigger actually to be built in the country was the barque *Lingard* (Pl. 408) which, after a brief period under the British flag in 1923–4 as the *Wathara,* was bought by Gustaf Erikson of Mariehamn and restored to her original name, being employed in the split-wood trade until she came into collision with, and sank, the *s.s. Gerd* in the Kattegat in 1935 and was condemned. However, the following year she was refitted to be preserved and to act as the club house for the Norsk Seilskute Klubb of Oslo but, as with so many preservation schemes – in the past and probably in the future – the expense proved to be too high (for even a static ship requires much maintenance) and she was scrapped. The last square-rigger in trade under Norwegian colours was another barque – the *Pehr Ugland,* which had been built in 1891 in Grangemouth for J. L. Ugland of Arendal, who sold her to Copenhagen owners in 1910. However, she was bought back to Frederikstad in 1927 and remained registered at that port until broken up in 1935.

Sister ship to the *Beethoven* (illustrated in Volume 1), the *Mozart* was the last big barquentine in deep-sea trade. Built by the Greenock &

232. *The bald-headed barque SUNLIGHT had a steel deck.*

233. *The PEHR UGLAND discharging at Strood, on the River Medway, in September 1925.*

234. The MOZART ghosts past the Dover pilot boat on her way back to Mariehamn after discharging a cargo of grain from Australia.

Grangemouth Dockyard Co in 1903 for A. C. de Freitas of Hamburg, she carried a number of cadets in her voyaging between Germany, the West Coast of South America and Australia before being sold to Schluter & Maack of the same port, who kept her more or less on the same run. After the war, when the German ships were up for allocation to the Allies, she was bought by Hugo Lundquist of Mariehamn and was then mainly in the Australian grain trade until broken up in 1935. She was grossly under-canvassed for her size and, being a heavy ship, woefully slow. This really over-rode the considerations of economy in crew with such a rig. Sailing wing-and-wing in the Westerlies, she was the very devil to steer, and sometimes she ran before them with only her fore square sails set. This was not conducive to making a passage of any note and, with her bald-headed fore, she was certainly lacking in good looks.

235. *The FÖRLIG VIND, last vessel trading purely under sail in Sweden, passing Borgholm Castle on the island of Öland, across the Strait of Kalmar from Pataholm.*

Not all readers will have heard of Pataholm – a small port on the mainland of Sweden opposite Öland, but it scored two rather important statistical 'lasts', for the *Förlig Vind*, owned and registered there, was the last merchant sailing vessel in Sweden to trade without an auxiliary engine. Built a little further north, at Timmernabben, in 1892, she traded until 1952, being rigged on the lines of a Swedish *galeas,* but with a short mizzen similar to a ketch, whilst her gaffs lowered, so that her lowers did not brail in to the mast like a conventional *galeas.*

Pataholm's greater claim to fame lies in the fact that it was the port of registry of the *Gerda,* which was the last European brig in trade. She was not the last brig in the world, since the rig survived, oddly enough, along the Coromandel coast in Country craft*, but she was indeed the very last of that enormous fleet of vessels of this type whose numbers used to be

*See pages 126–136.

236. The GERDA lying in Helsingfors about 1903.

legion in North European ports. Built at Gävle in 1869 by O. A. Brodin, of 234 NRT, she measured 109 ft 2 in × 26 ft 7 in × 11 ft 3 in and continued in trade until 1930, latterly being owned by Per Ohlsson. She was then laid up for six years, at the end of which she was towed to Gävle, the port of her building, to become a museum ship but, in due course and sadly, partly due to the increasing costs of maintenance, she foundered at her moorings*.

As it is absurd to produce useless statistics, so it is a folly to become too pedantic, since various nautical terms have had diverse meanings both in different eras and in different countries. In Volume 1 was a picture of the brig *Aid* of Åbo, which was subsequently reproduced in another book by an author† who contended that she was a snow, and who further stated that a snow always set a loose-footed trysail.

This latter comment is not necessarily true. The origin of the word 'brig' is not in doubt, since it derives from the word 'brigand', and thus a

---

*Those responsible for preserving ships today cannot gauge the future and there is a clear case for those who subscribe to them to think deeply before putting their hands too deeply into their pockets in the first flush of enthusiasm.

†*Square Rigged Sailing Ships*, D. R. MacGregor, Argus Press.

237.   The GERDA taking in her trysail when northward bound in the Kattegat in 1929.

'brigandine' was originally used of a variety of rigs, usually in relatively small craft, which were used by pirates (sea–brigands). In due course, a vessel with two fully square-rigged masts became known as a 'brig' (a contraction of 'brigandine') whilst one which was square-rigged on the fore but fore-and-aft on the main became known as an 'Hermaphrodite brig', but this, by common, if erroneous, usage, became universally known as a 'brigantine'.

In the meantime, a small gunter mast was sometimes stepped abaft the main lower mast to take the trysail and, in some peoples' opinion, this translated her into a 'snow'. The real reason for this trysail mast probably found its origin in older days of seamanship when it was common practice to lower the mainyard altogether when the sail was taken in during heavy weather, and to let it lie athwart the bulwarks, which was what was described as being 'a-port last'. This phrase is now part of dead language, since the practice it describes was discontinued long ago. However, this

238. The GERDA anchored off Pataholm in 1931.

operation could not be carried out so easily if the trysail gear and hoops were in the way, and it is safe to presume that the gunter mast was introduced to facilitate the lowering of the mainyard a-port last.

It is easy to say that a vessel so rigged is a 'snow'. The *Gerda* had such a gunter (trysail) mast, but Herr Martin Ohlsson, who served in her himself and whose father was both master and owner of the brig, describes her as a *snau-brigg* (snow-brig). He regards a loose-footed sail as being too dangerous and unhandy altogether in any sort of wind and the *Gerda* did, as is evident in the pictures, carry a boom. Yet . . . some vessels *did* have a loose-footed trysail.

Some will say that the object of the gunter mast was to provide a larger trysail in order to make the ship spin on her heel more quickly when being tacked, and it is true that some vessels, particularly in Holland, had a much longer lower-mast on the main than on the fore and certainly did

239. The GERDA arriving in Gävle in 1936 to be 'preserved', in which state she foundered.

not bend a square mainsail, but they did, obviously, have a much larger trysail. These were clearly very handy in stays, and should probably be regarded as the true 'snows'.

Those brigs with lower masts of approximately equal height, like the *Gerda,* and which carried a gunter mast, were so rigged because the diameter of the mainmast made the jaws of the gaff and boom very large if taken to the lower mast itself, and the separate mast made the trysail gear smaller and easier to work. In Scandinavia, a true brig usually had a standing gaff and brailing sail to obviate this trouble. Of course, when one considers the gear in much bigger schooners mentioned elsewhere in this book*, this argument might appear to lack validity. However, we are not considering big schooners, but small brigs with small crews, often engaged in short-sea passages. In these circumstances, the case for the gunter mast carried a good deal of weight.

*Pages 254–84 *et seq.*

240.   The MIDDLETON in tow. Note the sheets of the foresail made fast to the ends of the Bentinck boom.

Frenzied reference to old marine dictionaries or seamanship books is not likely to help the reader very much. It is a bit late to try to set definitions today, long after the craft have vanished from the face of the seas, but it cannot be disputed that a true brig had two square-rigged masts with the trysail set from the main lower mast. There is no such term in English as 'snow-brig', but this Swedish term has much to commend it to describe a brig setting a square mainsail and with a separate gunter (or trysail) mast, while the vessel with the longer main lower mast, no square mainsail and a larger trysail set on a gunter mast might properly be described as the true 'snow'.

One thing, however, is certain: No-one sighting a 'brig' or a 'snow-brig' at a distance could say which she was. Nor, in fact, did it matter very much, because those who built and sailed the craft under discussion were not concerned with dictionary definitions, nor with the pedantry and arguments of arm-chair historians who would come long after them!

241. The brig MERMAID, built at Dartmouth in 1844 and owned by W. N. Court, brails her trysail in to the mast, but . . .

    Whether of the one sort or another, and even in the case of many small barques and barquentines, a Bentinck boom was often carried, as in the case of the *Middleton* (Pl. 240). This vessel was typical of the myriad such craft employed in the British East Coast coal trade, having been built by Pearson of Whitby and owned by W. H. Hill of South Shields until she was wrecked in a storm off Whitby in 1893. She was of 204 NRT. The Bentinck boom, which can be seen below the foreyard, had a bridle in its centre, to which was shackled a tackle, the other end of which was shackled to an eyebolt on the deck, acting as the fore-sheet. A rope from each boom-end led half-way along the bowsprit and back to the rail, acting as braces. This arrangement eased the normal working of sheets and tacks and, in view of its name, one is tempted to suppose that it owed its inception to that same Captain Bentinck who introduced triangular courses, and who may be presumed to have had a fixation about sheets and tacks!

225

242.   ... the TERRIER, built by W. Kelly of Dartmouth eleven years later, lowers her trysail gaff which, it will be seen, is a sail of quite different proportions. She is really a 'snow-brig', with a gunter mast abaft her main lower mast.

Apart from the comparison of her trysail working with the *Mermaid*, the *Terrier* is interesting in these days in showing a flying jibboom outside her jibboom; bowlines to her courses and Cunningham's patent reefing topsails. The centre cloth, which was called the 'bonnet', should be noted. In fact, the sail was divided down the middle to a point roughly below the bottom set of reef-points, and the sides of the division were roped so that the roping would pass through travellers. The bonnet was sewn between them, and was drawn up as the yard ascended, or pushed down as it descended. (The word 'bonnet', of course, has other nautical meanings.)

To introduce a full-rigged ship when discussing brigs and their family may be out of order but, in contra-distinction to the Cunningham's gear in the *Terrier*, the *Kagosima* was one of the vessels fitted with the patent reefing topsails invented by Collings and Pinkney of Sunderland, which involved the sail being rolled up, like a blind, on a small spar on the fore

243. *The TERRIER in stays, as she tacks ship off Sandy Hook.*

244. Although slightly out of order here, it may be of interest to view the KAGOSIMA as a new ship in Aberdeen in 1862 with her patent reefing gear.

side of the yard by parbuckles led from the topmast head to the yardarms. The principle was not unlike that of the French roller-topsail schooners discussed on page 45 *et seq*. Moreover, it is often interesting to speculate when certain fitments first appeared. When, for example, did brace pennants first appear? The *Kagosima* certainly has none.

Brigs abounded in the middle of the last century, and could be found in many smaller ports, besides the larger ones. They were so common that they scarcely merited a second glance from passers-by. These pictures have been confined to Wisbech, on the River Nene, the pictures usually being taken at low water, as the exposure was often up to 40 minutes – a far cry from the fast roll-films of today! The ships were usually taking the ground in this period, thus avoiding undue movement. At this date single topsails were still *de rigueur* for these craft, and double yards seldom appeared amongst them until the 1870s. It is interesting to note the hull

245. Schooners were to be found all round the coasts in the last century and, like the brigs and brigantines, up almost every creek and river where there was habitation since they were the mainstay of all transport before the internal combustion engine.

forms. Most are brigs or snow-brigs, but in Pl. 251 the barque *Protector* in the foreground sports a main skysail — a very small yard. The cockbilling of the lower yards (with their Bentinck booms where applicable) was common practice in port.

Pl. 247 shows the *Highland Chieftain* on the slip, a very box-like vessel which may have been the one of that name built in New Brunswick in 1840 and later owned in Maryport. It was a common name, and it is not always easy to be certain precisely which vessel of the same name is depicted in such photographs as these. The snow-brig alongside in this picture is the *Commerce,* built at Blyth in 1826 and of 106 tons O.M. being owned by the local firm of W. Stevens (of Wisbech). In some sense, the date of her building is apparent by the fact that her foremast is stepped so far forward, which was the practice amongst older vessels.

246. *Coasters, mainly colliers, lying in the Nene in September 1861 – the NORA, CAROLINA, ALEXANDER, CAREY OF BLYTH, FREDIQUE and HANNAH AND ELEANOR. All, save the barque in the foreground, are brigs or snow-brigs. There were many QUEENS, and this one was probably built in 1838 and owned by Souter & Co of London, being 157 tons (OM) and often running down to the Mediterranean.*

247. *The snow-brig COMMERCE. On the slip is the HIGHLAND CHIEFTAIN.*

248. *Within the same year, the JOHN AND HELENA, OCEAN and MARIEN-DORFF lie off Wisbech, yards and bentinck booms cock-billed and the odd sail loosened to dry. Note the hull forms. The OCEAN was owned locally by Cooper & Co. of Wisbech and mainly running to Sunderland or the Baltic. There were many snows and brigs of this name.*

249. *The brig LYRA, of 213 tons, was built at Greenock in 1839, but owned at this time by Kirkby & Co. of Whitby, and was mainly coasting and voyaging to France. She has come up the Nene from Kings Lynn to berth at Wisbech.*

250. *Five years earlier, the Portuguese brig AMELIA lies in the foreground, with different lines altogether, ahead of the CRAGGS and VIGILANT.*

251. *The CAROLINA, QUEEN, ALEXANDRA, R. J. HAYES and PROTECTOR – a barque – at Wisbech in 1861. The ALEXANDRA was built in 1828 and owned by D. Slater of Whitby.*

252. *The snow-brig HYLTON of South Shields on the mud in the Nene in 1853. Note the manner in which her trysail is stowed.*

Few students of the sailing ship era, particularly in its closing decades, would associate a blacksmith with the complement of a vessel, but the celebrated Captain F. C. B. Jarvis (widely known as 'Brace Winch' Jarvis), in his valuable *Wrinkles and Suggestions for Sailing Vessels,* recommended shipmasters to 'Occasionally carry a blacksmith' and, indeed, did do so himself when in command of the four-masted barque *Lawhill* during the years 1902–04. When one considers the amount of ironwork used in the outfit of a large sailing vessel, the value of Captain Jarvis' advice can be appreciated the more readily. The blacksmith is the only artisan who cannot work alone in the normal pursuit of his occupation, and is dependant on the services of his assistant, or 'striker'. Today, he is a very rare operator, owing largely to the replacement of wrought iron by mild steel, and the changes inevitably associated with forms of modern transport.

The art of the blacksmith was practiced in wrought iron, a metal which has valuable qualities, but which has given place to steel in general usage owing to the lower costs of the latter in manufacture, to advances in welding techniques and to various other factors. Nevertheless, the metal is still used where the property of being able to withstand sudden and excessive shocks without permanent injury is required, and for this reason it is still chosen for chains; crane hooks, railway couplings and the like.

It does not call for practical experience to imagine the terrific strain put upon the trusses of the lower yards when a sailing ship is rolling and pitching under full sail in a seaway, for those yards each weigh four or five tons in a vessel of above 2,500 NRT. The fibrous nature of wrought iron gives visible warning on the surface of any impending fracture before complete breakdown occurs, whereas, with any other metal, it would in all probability fracture suddenly across its section. In all likelihood, it was the first form of metal to be used by man, and the art of the blacksmith was practiced at least 2,000 years ago, wrought iron being the nearest approach to pure iron.

Examples of this craftsmanship abound, both alow and aloft, in a sailing vessel, and mention need only be made of stanchions, spider bands, yard trusses and parrels, bumkins, chains, shackles, anchor release gear and similar vital equipment to illustrate the value of the

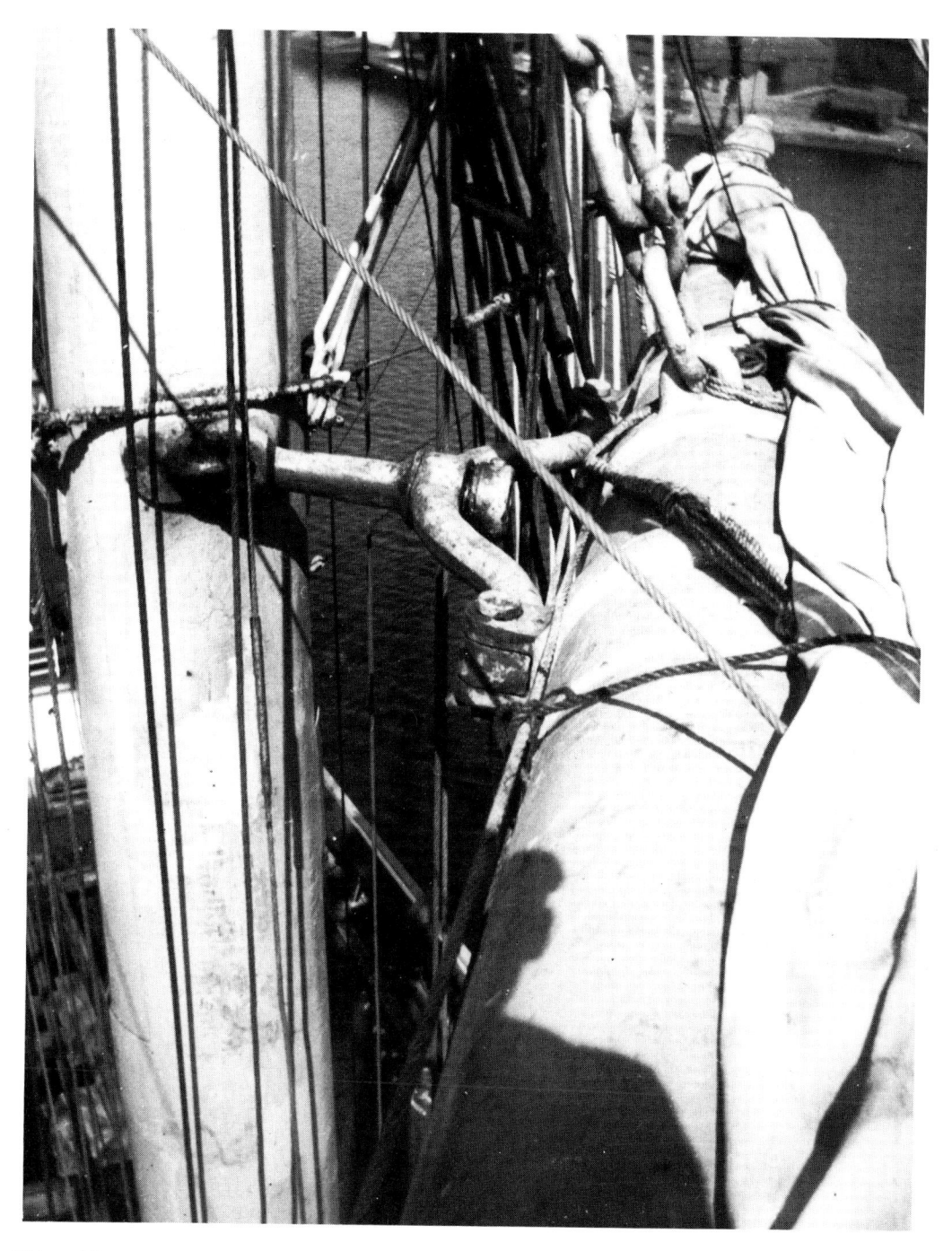

253. *The LAWHILL – the truss of the foreyard.*

blacksmith's contribution. The deep-water sailor of the sailing ship era was noted for his versatility, and the blacksmith at sea would seldom be at a loss for the recruitment of his striker from among his shipmates. Even in the last days of sail, it was not uncommon to see a smith's forge set up on deck and repairs executed to gear, at a great saving in cost to the owner. Today, of course, trade union restrictive practices would ensure that such goings on would soon be outlawed by the nautical equivalent of the shop steward.

Study of logs has shown that very few sailing ships signed on a blacksmith, although a few did. However, although the incorporation of a donkey-engine into a ship's equipment did not mean that a man was necessarily signed on as a donkeyman, it became a more and more common practice, particularly in the larger ships. Like the blacksmith, he was ranked as an idler, which meant that he did not stand watches, but was on day-work, and was only required to help to work the ship in emergencies. The donkeyman usually undertook a certain amount of necessary smithy work, and some of them were fully qualified smiths who wanted a change and managed to get to sea under this guise, for the majority were quite capable of providing and fitting the necessary ironwork to a new spar, fashioned from a spare one, when the occasion arose. Very occasionally, they were referred to as 'smiths'.

Yet another cause of the demise of the blacksmith is the use of modern methods of oxy-acetylene and electric arc welding and cutting which has almost entirely displaced the 'fire' or hand-weld of the blacksmith. Given a billet of wrought iron, a clean fire and the requisite hand tools – not forgetting the striker – the old-time blacksmith would proceed to forge anything from a four-ball stanchion to a spider band intended for half a dozen belaying pins (of iron): the band being made from one piece of metal on the anvil. One of my most interesting experiences in my early days of engineering was the demonstration of welding by a master smith and his apprentice engaged in fire-welding the heads on special bolts used in the shipyard. The mating parts were got up to the critical sizzling heat (when the sparks fly off the hot metal) and were then instantly joined and hammered until no sign of the joint was visible.

One of the finest examples of the blacksmith's art is still to be seen in the beautiful ornamentation of the main gates giving access to

254. The crane of the lower topsail yard.

255. Upper topsail yard truss and shoe. Note the track bar.

256. *The unusual halliard tye arrangement on the LAWHILL's mizzen upper topsail yard.*

Buckingham Palace, but Pls. 253–67 showing ironwork aloft will serve to illustrate the versatility of the smith who provided such an essential part of the equipment of the square-rigged sailing ship. Of course, in the first instance, it was all done in the shipyard, as much as the building of the hull: the making of the masts and even the rigging of the ship, but there was always damage to be made good, or renewals to be made, throughout a ship's life, and the more of this that could be done aboard, obviously the better it was.

As ships – and thus sails – became bigger, single topsails gave way to double ones in the mid-1850s and double topgallant sails came later. Since these changed the essential proportions of the sails, it was no longer

257. *The LAWHILL's topmast, showing the top of the track for the upper topsail shoe and the chain tye passing through the sheave in the mast.*

possible to clew them up to the quarters of the yards, and it was then that they were clewed up to the yardarms. In each case the lower yard was fixed to the mast by its truss but the upper yards were hoisted (Pl. 255) and, when lowered, the downhauls were manned. These were shackled on to the top of the lower topsail (or topgallant) yardarms and led through a sheave below the upper yards, through another at the mast and then, usually with a whip through a block in the eye of the downhaul, down to the deck. Hoisting these sails, when full of wind, was a heavy job and, when rigged with halliard winches, a slow one. The sheets of the upper yards were generally very short and, in later ships, of chain of the right length, so that they were not worked at all. Some vessels did have a little

258. After loosing sail (Pl. 259), the PAMIR sets her topsails as the tug drops astern....

drift on them, so that they could be taken up minimally, but the drift was very small and the working part, if it existed at all, was generally made fast aloft.

A very few ships, probably all of them German, did have conventional sheets, so that the yard could be hoisted with the sail still furled and then the sail could be sheeted home very quickly. (Equally, if need be, the sail could be clewed up to the mast-headed yard.) The famous *Preussen* was so rigged, and the accompanying plates show how quickly the *Pamir* was able to set sail as she dropped her tug. The advantage was so great that it was extraordinary that so few ships had long sheets to their hoisting yards.

Since the *Lawhill* appears throughout this book, she may be taken as being a good example of fittings aloft. Pl. 253 shows the foreyard, with

259. With her upper topsail and t'gallant yards hoisted, the PAMIR starts to set sail and then, in Pl. 258. . . .

260. But by the time the barque is past has two courses and lower t'gallants set — all very quick.

the truss which allows the yard to swivel in a horizontal plane at the mast. In some ships, there was a futtock band right round the lowermast which not only took the base of of the futtock shrouds, but the truss which pivoted on a pin. The horse-shoe like portion is the span, in the centre of which the yard may pivot in a vertical plane. The ends of the span are attached to the truss bands which are visible and which go right round the yard, the weight of which is taken by the chain sling, of which the lower part is seen above its centre. The truss, of course, is not only a form of universal joint, but keeps the yard at its correct distance from the mast.

The later big, steel ships had their lower and topmasts in one piece, like the *Lawhill*. A band is shrunk and riveted to the lower mast head or, where a topmast is fidded, round both masts. On the fore side, it is so fashioned with a lug to take the head of a large pin the lower end of which fits through another lug slightly below the first, as shown in Pl. 254. This pin supports the inner end of the equivalent of the truss which, in the case of the lower topsail yard, is the crane, again allowing horizontal movement. Vertical swing movement is allowed on the outer end (invisible beneath the furled sail) through lugs on the single yard-band. The lower part of the upper topsail yard in its lowered position shows plainly the blocks taking the upper topsail downhauls and lower topgallant sail sheets.

Pl. 255 shows the top of the *Lawhill's* fore upper topsail yard. The truss and truss bands are basically the same as for the lower yard but, like most latter-day square-riggers, she had steel masts, and the vertical pin of the truss is set into a shoe which travels on a vertical track as the yard is hoisted or lowered. Hoisting yards do not have a sling, but a chain tye, the lower part of which is shackled into a stout link passed through a hole in the middle of the tye span at the centre of the yard, and the upper part of which passes through a sheave in the mast near the masthead and is attached to the wire halliard leading down to the halliard winch or, in ships without these winches, to a three-fold purchase down to the pin rail – to port for the fore and mizzen and to starboard for the main and, if applicable, the jigger.

It is never safe to say 'This – or that – was always so', since there were exceptions to prove every rule. The *Lawhill* was not only unusual in having her t'gallant masts stepped *abaft* her topmasts (which were in one

261. *The fore topmast cap of the* ABRAHAM RYDBERG *with the t'gallant mast stepped conventionally – before it. Unusually for a four-master in the 1930s, when this picture was taken in the Millwall Dock, London, this vessel crossed single t'gallant sails.*

262. *Looking in along the* ABRAHAM RYDBERG's *foreyard. The truss and truss band (round the mast) can be seen, while the chain sling passes through the eye of the forestay to the lower masthead. Below the top are blocks through which lead the foresail buntlines to blocks seized to the jackstay, and thence through bulls eyes on the fore side of the sail to its foot.*

piece with the lower masts), having only the upper t'gallant yard crossed on the t'gallant mast, but her mizzen upper topsail yard was also unusually rigged, since it will be seen in Pl. 256 that the tye span (above and between the truss bands) has *two* halyard shackles. The left hand one was the standing part, which led through a block at the masthead and down, through the sheave block (of which the base is visible above the right-hand shackle) and through the sheave in the mast-head to the halliard. This was a relic of Captain Jarvis' command of the ship and, doubtless, originally an experiment. One might wonder why the mizzen rather than the main! However, the principle had been adopted in some of the larger American clippers in which the topsail yards were of great weight, some of which had the tye in the form of a watch tackle with a block shackled on to the yard.

Pl. 266, also aloft in the *Lawhill*, is a-typical because, although it shows the crane of the lower t'gallant yard very well, and just how the yard can swivel in either plane, the fact is that, as stated above, the ship had her t'gallant masts stepped abaft the topmasts, and thus this crane is at the head of the topmast and not, as would normally have been the case, at the base of the t'gallant mast. As may be seen, the upper t'gallant yard is well abaft the lower one, but this unusual arrangement was very useful in the ship's case oil days since, when loading in New York, it was sometimes necessary to lower the t'gallant masts. This was much easier than usual, rigged in this way, with only one yard on the t'gallant mast. (Being bald-headed, the vessel crossed no royals.)

The shoe and track portrayed in Pl. 255 was common enough in the last big square-riggers, but the general run of vessels did not have them, but a parrel which was, in effect, a collar fitted round the mast. In Pl. 265 which shows the *Lawhill's* upper t'gallant yard, it will be observed that the centre of the (wooden) yard is not round, but octagonal which was the general practice in the centre quarters of wooden yards, and that the truss is attached to the parrel.

A parrel was, of course, of a constant diameter, and thus the sections of a mast on which it travelled could not be tapered. Pl. 263 shows the upper topsail parrel aboard the Swedish four-masted barque *Abraham Rydberg* together with the lower part of the sheave shackled to the tye span through which her halliard tye worked. Below is the lower topsail

263. The fore lower topsail crane and upper topsail parrel aboard the ABRAHAM RYDBERG. From the angle of view, the lower topsail yard itself cannot be seen.

crane but, due to the angle of the camera, the yard itself cannot be seen.

Pl. 267 is a view looking down on the *Abraham Rydberg's* foreyard from her fore top, of which the fore edge is the curve at the bottom right. The sling and truss can be seen just clear of the top and above them – doubled as usual – the forestay. It will be seen that the yard is checked well in and why it is necessary to have chafing gear on the forestay to protect the foresail. The ship has only single jackstays, like most vessels, and to this the head of the sail is made fast with robands. Additional handholds are provided by the grommets seized to the jackstay. Sometimes these were beckets, in the form of a 'U', through which, in theory, a man might thrust his arm and use two hands. 'In theory' are the operative words, since movement was much restricted!

264. *The old barrel steering gear of the Finnish schooner NORDEN.*

265. *Close up of the centre of one of the LAWHILL's upper t'gallant yards.*

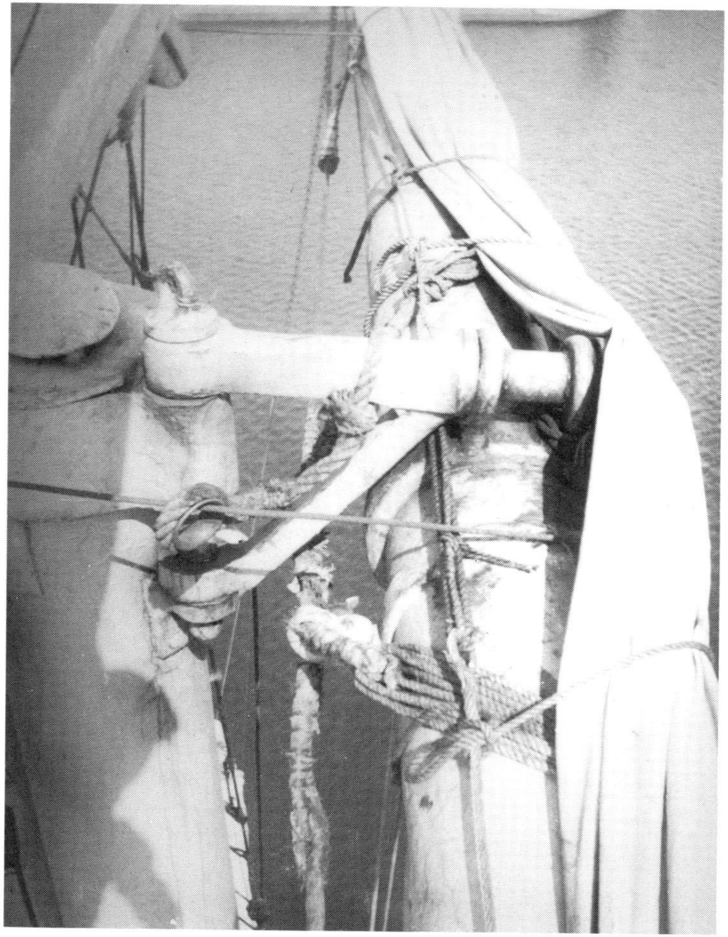

266. The *LAWHILL* – the lower t'gallant yard and crane.

267. Looking down on the *ABRAHAM RYDBERG's* foreyard from the fore top.

It is commonly said that the very big schooners built on the East Coast of the United States, mainly for the coal trade, were not a success, but the yardstick by which this judgement is made may be open to question. Indeed, of the vast literature devoted to the sailing ship in her various forms, very little is concerned with her economics or her profit and loss accounts which, in the final analysis, were the only criteria which mattered to her shareholders.

Yet, in assessing a rig or an individual ship within the perspective of the whole age of sail, it is really necessary to look beyond the purely economic factors, which could be distorted by current terms of trade and freight rates, by competition and even by whether or not the vessel was being used for the purposes for which she was designed.

The whole history of the schooner rigs, in many countries, is a vast one with many facets, and there is no doubt that many small examples of the rig have been as attractive, handy to work and functional as any sailing craft ever built, but it is beyond question that there are strict limits to its size if it is to handle well and to be really successful, save in very exceptional trades.

Like most rigs, the form changed over the years and, although the United States of America certainly made the large schooner something almost (but not quite) peculiar to its own coasts, the first vessels of this rig were to be found in Holland and England in the seventeenth century and, genealogically, they probably took their inspiration from the lateen-rigged vessels of the Middle East and Mediterranean – the fore lateen being split into foresail and headsail.

There is little doubt that the Americans pioneered the first really fast schooners with the famed Baltimore clippers and, soon afterwards, the Marblehead schooners developed further north. These were fine-lined craft with heavily raked masts, used both for commerce and as privateers with great success, the former trading salt fish with the West Indies and then all sorts of general cargo. In 1817 President Monroe – of 'Monroe Doctrine' fame – closed all American coastal traffic to foreign shipping and even to vessels built outside the United States, and this act has never been repealed to this day. It gave a great boost to local building and ship-owning on the East Coast, and the fleet gradually increased in tonnage and in size of individual vessels right up until the American Civil War,

268. *Watching this pretty coasting schooner with her extreme clipper bow as she beats out of New York in the 1850s, no-one would have guessed how the rig would develop. Note her fore topmast. The fore lowermast passes through the fore deckhouse.*

269. *At about the same time, a New York pilot schooner, bound for the outer station, is passed by a big racing yacht of the time – so much better to the eye with her gaff topsail and bowsprit than the marconi-rigged craft of today. Note the four rows of reef-points in the schooner's mainsail and the size of the sail when the fourth reef is in – it passes through the twirls of the '2'.*

which dealt American shipping a blow of such magnitude that it never really recovered from it in the days of sail.

In the 1830s, the coastal tonnage exceeded that trading deep-water, mainly on account of the trade with the Southern States for coal, cotton, grain and other commodities, whilst clothing, ice, and various other goods were carried on the southern leg.

The average size of the schooner of those days was some 75 feet in length with two masts, and it was not until the early 1850s, with its boom in clipper building, that the clipper bow became common in schooners, together with the elliptical stern, though this latter feature was by no means universal. Generally they carried fore and main lowers, two topsails (though the fore topmast was often sent down in winter time), a big 'jumbo' (fore staysail) and a jib but, by about 1885, their size had increased to a degree that two masts were no longer practicable, and by this time all sails were bigger and there were generally four headsails, sometimes on a spike bowsprit, but sometimes there was a jibboom outside the bowsprit.

There had been a number of three-masters built since the turn of the century, but some had been very small – less than 100 tons – and the largest built until 1850 was of 500 tons. In 1855, the *Kate Brigham* was launched. She was of 546 tons and, perhaps, started a trend, since she was the first with masts of equal height: the first, in fact, of the 'tern' schooners, as these craft were called in both the United States and Canada, although the term fell into disuse in the U.S.A.

Although schooners with masts of equal height may have seemed to be common enough latterly, it was a major departure at the time and, when the *Eckford Webb* sailed over to England, her appearance caused much comment and raising of eyebrows.

Until this time, and for some years afterwards, American schooners had been of two basic hull types (and I am speaking now of the period when they had settled down after the extreme Baltimore schooners and the like) and the difference was that some had very shallow hulls with centre-boards, whilst others had more conventional hulls, like the run of deep-watermen. This practice continued as masts were added, and there was no doubt that the centre-boarders, in which the boards were somewhat off-centre, were generally faster and had the advantage of draft,

270. The fame of the schooners from Gloucester, Mass. and similar ports, which fished on the Grand Banks and George's is legendary. Latterly they were built with spoon-bows, but this old-timer, with her dories nested on deck, has a clipper bow and different lines altogether. Nonetheless, she was 'fast and able', as the local expression went. Note the cut of her jumbo (as the big fore staysail was called) and how it is sheeted home.

particularly in the smaller ports and creeks which were often visited, but they were more limited in their cargo capacity than other vessels of comparable dimensions. By 1869 there had been built only 34 three-masters, of which only four had exceeded 500 tons but, in the next decade, centreboards were sometimes combined with deep hulls, and these vessels proved to be most successful. They were well-constructed and stronger craft, *pro rata,* than the multi-masters which were still in the future, and did not lose their sheer, or hog, to the same extent.

One feature of the American schooner which was unique to them — and necessarily so — was the use of power to hoist the big lowers. The first vessel so equipped was the three-master *Charles A. Briggs,* which was built at Bath, Maine, in 1879 and, by the standards of the times, quite big at 750 tons, since most of those being built contemporaneously were of around 350 tons. Some 1,500 of these three-masters were built on the East Coast and in the Gulf ports (to a lesser extent), while there were about half this number built in Canada in the peak building years. Not all were of the same size and, indeed, one may wonder what prompted the 21-ton *Maple Leaf,* obviously of Canadian origin, to be rigged with three masts. However, shortly after the *Charles A. Briggs* was launched, the three-master had reached the practical limit of size, and one or two steamers were converted to sail as four-masted schooners but, unfortunately, they came to violent ends and did not last long. The first vessel specifically built with this rig was the *William L. White,* of 1,450 tons deadweight and measuring 205 on deck $\times$ 40 $\times$ 17' depth of hold, and with 5,017 yards of canvas. Launched by Goss, Sawyer and Packard for the coal merchant Jacob B. Phillips of Taunton, Mass. who already had eight large three-masters, she was employed in the coal trade which became the *raison d'etre* of the big schooners. Within years, schooners not equipped with donkey engines wherewith to hoist the lowers became known as 'hand-pullers' and were shunned by the more experienced coastal seamen. Latterly, such craft had trouble in getting crews and, being mainly old, it was not thought to be worth fitting donkey engines at that stage in their lives. This decision was probably right in some cases: wrong in others.

Most of these new four-masters had centre-boards which certainly were a tremendous help to them when light ship, but the practice became discontinued owing to the higher construction costs; the difficulty in

271. Built at Essex, Mass., in 1865, the M. C. WETHERALL gave little indication of things to come, like . . .

272. . . . Crowell & Thurlow's JACOB B. HASKELL, seen as she beats past, close-hauled. She has the typical deck railings of the New England schooners.

maintenance and the loss of cargo space entailed. In those days there were plenty of tugs in the ports they used, and towage was cheap. In all, there were 450 four-masters launched on the Eastern seaboard of the United States, of which the bulk were built in Bath, Maine in the 1880s, although nearly a third of the total was subsequently built during, or immediately after, the 1914–18 war, when there was a shortage of bottoms and a temporary boom. That Maine came to succeed the great wooden shipbuilding centres of New York and Boston was mainly due to rising labour costs and soaring values of real estate in these ports.

Schooners were being built on the West coast, though they never advanced in size as did those on the East and, whereas a yard on the fore was common there, one of the few East coast schooners to cross one was the *Haroldine* which, having been originally laid down as a square-rigger, did not have the typical schooner hull either. Of 1,361 tons, she was the biggest of her rig afloat when new in 1884 and, after a passage to Melbourne of 104 days, and then coming back via Newcastle, N.S.W. to Hong Kong (with coal) she settled down on the East coast coal trade and lasted in it for 14 years, being lost at sea in 1898 after a profitable career.

It is probably wrong to talk about beauty in ships since, although many fell within this definition, it was largely fortuitous because their objects were invariably functional. Perhaps 'pleasing to the eye' is a better expression, and there can be little doubt that no craft were more pleasing to the eye than the smartest schooners. Perhaps the Banks fishermen were the most peerless of all, though they were a quite different conception, but it can be said that the advent of the tern schooner detracted from the appearance of the rig and that, with each additional mast which became added, the less attractive was the vessel to the eye until, in the ultimate schooners, they could only vie with each other in sheer ugliness, since they had no rivals in this respect in the rest of the world. However, in fairness, it should be commented that one does not send a beauty queen to hump coal!

The biggest of the four-masters, in terms of tonnage, was the *Northland* of 2,047 GRT – one of the few of these vessels which did not have a name like an entry in a telephone directory – but the longest was the *Frank A. Palmer*, of 2,014 gross, which was the first of Nathaniel T. Palmer's fleet to be fitted with rigging screws. (These, of course, were

273. One of the last of the 70 odd vessels owned by Crowell & Thurlow to be built was the ALCAEUS HOOPER, at Stockton Springs, Me. in 1920. Of 1,305 NRT and 207.2 × 41 × 22 feet, she foundered four years later, 300 miles east of Cape Henry.

never in such common use as in Europe, where iron, and then steel, construction was so much more common in larger ships.) She was very heavily built with, for instance, her 'tween-deck planking 14″ square, being fastened with 1¼″ iron. She, too, was a coal-haulier and, in 1901, sold to the J. S. Winslow fleet of Portland, Me. but, the next year, when following the five-master *Arthur Seitz* in bad weather with poor visibility, both schooners stranded on Skiff Island, a few miles to the sou'west of Muskeget Island in Nantucket Sound. The *Seitz* was a total loss, and the *Frank A. Palmer* was brought in leaking and repaired, but was sunk in collision within months.

    The four-masters were similar to the three-masters except for the additional mast, which was named the 'spanker'. This is not to say that the fourth mast was always the spanker – it was the term used for the *aftermost* mast in all Down-East schooners of three masts and more. Most of them had two decks, although the lower one was often purely beams and not decked, but some had three, in which case the lower one was invariably planked. The majority were shelter-decked throughout, though

274.   The four-masted schooner MARJORIE BROWN foundering in the North Atlantic in a winter gale in 1913. She was built in 1889.

some had a well between the foc's'le head and the shelter deck, and it was usual for a boat to be slung over the stern on davits. This passage may require clarification, because terminology is not the same on both sides of the Atlantic, and I am using that used in Europe, where a shelter deck is deemed to be a deck *above* the main deck – as it were, an extension of the poop. A vessel with a continuous shelter deck was called 'flush-decked' in the U.S.A. So she was, insofar as the shelter deck had no break in it, but in Europe a 'flush-decked' vessel is one which has no deck (such as a poop, foc's'le head, etc) built above the main deck. This is a matter which causes confusion to Europeans reading American books and to Americans reading European books.

The Canadian effort, which was quite large in respect of the 'terns', was much less in building of four-masters, and only three dozen were built in all.

275. In contrast to the North American 'tern' schooners was the EUFROZINE, built by A. Rahouix at Boulogne in 1903, of 119 × 29.3 × 13 feet. Here owned in Riga, one might suppose her windmill pump, unusually far forward, to provide motive power!

The first recorded five-master was the *David Dows* which was built for the Great Lakes trade in Toledo, Ohio, in 1881, but the first on the East Coast itself was the *Governor Ames*, of 1,778 tons, launched in 1888 at Waldoboro', Mass. She was named for Oliver Ames, governor of Massachusetts, who was a share-holder in several schooners. Although not as big as the bigger (and later) four-masters, she was really ahead of her times, since it was ten years before another was built. She had a 35′ centre-board, which dropped 14′, and a length of 245.6′. On her maiden trip she was dismasted in a severe gale off George's Shoals because her deadeye and lanyard rigging slackened up and her crew were unable to set it up before disaster overtook her. However, she was towed in and re-rigged and, in 1890, sent round the Horn to San Francisco, making the passage in 140 days, whereupon she spent four years on the West Coast before coming home in 139 days from Port Blakely, after which she was put into the East Coast coal trade. She proved to be very strong and never hogged, although this may have been due to her rather unusual construction in which the hatch coaming structure ran the whole distance along all her hatches. Normally she carried 10 men, on the basis of two men per mast, although she had 11 aboard when she was finally lost off Cape Hatteras in 1910.

The next five-master was the *Nathaniel T. Palmer* – the final addition to that Palmer fleet – in 1898. She was 2,440 tons gross and 295.1' in length, with a conventional hull and no centre-board. With the rest of the fleet, she was sold to J. S. Winslow in 1901, and finally abandoned at sea ten years later. There were 37 five-masters built in all, the majority of them between the years 1899 and 1904 and, generally, each was bigger than her predecessor until the *Jane Palmer,* in the latter year, which measured 3,138 GRT. After her, they tended to become smaller, and the last two to be built – the *Edna Hoyt* and the *Mary H. Diebold* – in 1920 were barely 1,500 GRT. The *Jane Palmer* was originally intended to be a six-masted auxiliary, but this plan did not materialise and she lasted for 16 years, being abandoned some 500 miles east of Cape Hatteras in 1920. She had almost been lost in the 1907 Boston waterfront fire when her rigging, cabins and part of her cargo were burnt before she was towed off and the fire brought under control. The longest of the five-masters was the *Fuller Palmer*, at 309.4', being one of the six over 300' long.

In 1900 the first of the six-masters, the *George W. Wells,* was built for Captain John Crowley and, at the time of her launch, was the biggest sailing ship in the world, with a deadweight tonnage of 5,000 and measuring 319.3' × 48.5' × 23'. Her two anchors were 8,250 and 7,500 pounds respectively, with 9 shackles of 2½ inch chain in each locker. She once made a passage of 518 miles at just over 10 knots, which was considered to be the best performance of any of the coal schooners. In total, there were eleven of these six-masters, and the second down the ways was the *Eleanor A. Percy* which was bigger still. In 1904 these two came into collision near Cape Cod and both made port although, had the *Percy* not been light, she would probably have sunk, being badly holed. The biggest of this brood was the *Wyoming*, built in 1909, for she was just over 6,000 tons deadweight and measured 329.5' × 50.1' × 30.4', being lost off Nantucket Sound in a blizzard in 1924 with all of her 13 crew. She

276. Built in 1904 at Boston, Mass. the JANE PALMER was the largest five-masted schooner ever built (3,128 GRT, 2,823 NRT and 308.6 × 49 × 22.4 feet). With 13 men all told, her crew was roughly half that of a four-masted barque of her size – and so was her sail area. Here seen in the Mersey, she was abandoned at sea in 1920.

277. With all sail set, the GEORGE W. WELLS, built in 1900, has nothing like the sail area of a square-rigger of similar tonnage.

278. *The CORA F. CRESSEY, of 2,089 tons, was one of the five-masters built by Percy & Small at Bath, Mass. (in 1902).*

had been seen at anchor before visibility was lost, and it is not known whether her bow pulled out, or what the final cause of the disaster may have been.

Apart from the *William C. Douglas*, which was built of steel in 1903, and not much smaller than the *Wyoming*, these six-masters, and most of the five-masters, were built of wood. I do not think that the strength of their construction has ever been in question. Their scantlings were enormous, being reinforced inside with huge keelsons six or seven feet high, set in their bottoms over the keel, with sister keelsons each side and diagonal iron strappings over the closely spaced frames in an effort to avoid hogging. It was a very hard trade, the coal being shot into the holds in bulk, and often enough they touched bottom unevenly when loading. They were, initially, competing with barges and were thus big boxes, with no pretensions to fine lines. As their size had increased, the great weights carried had begun to tell even with their heavy scantlings, and most hogged badly, although this might not seem apparent in their pictures since they were all built with heavy sheers, and they still seemed to have a sheer even when hogged. Some builders incorporated a 'rocker', or reverse keel, to try to mitigate this trouble, but nothing was successful and, hogging apart, they very soon leaked badly and could seldom be

279. The five-masted collier schooner DOROTHY PALMER.

sailed hard on this account. Indeed, the *Jane Palmer* worked so much that her deck-house was said to rise and fall some two feet when reaching in a stiff breeze – almost like a Viking ship, except that it was intended in the long ships!

When she was deep-loaded with coal and wanted to cross Nantucket Shoals, she had to anchor off Nobska in order to pump out first – the operation being carried out by the donkey engine which became an absolute necessity to these cumbersome giants. Without them, they would have been impossible. Moreover, with their great size and relatively small sail area, they exposed great wall sides when sailing light, and this detracted from their performance.

In 1911, the four-masted *Samuel L. Groucher,* of 2,547 GRT, touched the shore and hung on a ledge off Portsmouth, New Hampshire, at high water. The weather was calm and it was presumed that she would be floated off in good order but, as the tide receded, her bottom simply fell out, discharging her 4,000 tons of coal faster than any ship has discharged before or since – regrettably in the wrong place! She was seven years old at the time and, needless to say, did not survive this catastrophe.

Owing to this weakness in the wooden hulls – a weakness only apparent because size, weight and treatment were now very close to the limits of this hull form – a few steel schooners were built. They did not suffer from this trouble but, of course, steel was never used for sailing ship building in the United States to any great extent due to it higher cost relative to the wood on its own coasts. In Europe, it was a different matter. Indeed, it was Sewalls, who had built the few big, steel square-riggers in Maine, who built the six-masted steel *Kineo* and, initially, sent her out to the Pacific round the Horn. The fact is, as has been proved in practice, that big schooners are seldom suited for deep-sea passages. They do not have the necessary sail area for their size: they are poor performers down-wind and, above all, they are heavier on their gear than any square-rigger, especially in a calm with a swell, when mast-hoops alone have a very short life, and even ironwork aloft wants renewing after a single voyage. Later, she was converted to be a full-powered tanker. Nevertheless, some of the multi-masted schooners made successful long, ocean passages, but this is not to suggest that they were ideally suited for them, nor that such successful voyages as were made were as much due to good judgement as to good luck.

For all their faults, the big schooners were profitable, perhaps, again, rather as a result of good fortune than anything else because, had the shippers and others got together and started a line of steam colliers, which well *could* have happened, they would have been out of business overnight. Latterly, they *were* squeezed out and seeking cargoes – mainly lumber, though shelter-decked vessels were not suited to deck cargoes. The *Eleanor A. Percy,* despite her narrow escape in 1904, lasted twenty years, the longest of all, and only two lasted two years or less, one being the *Dovrefjeld*, the longest of all at 332.2′, since she was originally a paddle-steamer which had been converted to a barge and, in the 1914–18 war, when bottoms were so scarce, was rigged as a six-masted schooner. She sank shortly afterwards off Staten Island but was raised, and then foundered eighteen months later off Hatteras with a coal cargo. The average life-span of these six-masters was over twelve years and none of them finished their careers laid up but, in fact, all met violent ends. Much the same is true of the five-masters and, initially, they were paying for themselves in their first two years although, as time went by, profits were not so good due to greater steam competition and falling freight rates. Thus it is that the economic success of a ship can only be judged within the

280. The MERTIE B. CROWLEY demonstrates the limited sail area of a huge multi-master.

281. Deep-loaded, the WYOMING leaves Hampton Roads in calm a few days before she was wrecked and lost after being anchored near the Pollock Rip lightship in Nantucket Sound, when bound towards St Johns, N.B. She was the largest wooden sailing ship in terms of deadweight tonnage. Her wreckage was washed up on the north shore.

282.   The WILLIAM C. CARNEGIE, one of the Winslow fleet, became a total loss when she went ashore on Long Island on 1 May, 1909.

times and conditions within which she finds herself. Many of the schooners, of all sizes, would carry ice on the south-bound trip. It is not generally realized that up to 3,000,000 tons of ice could be sailed south in a year, comprising well over 2,000 shiploads of various sizes.

It is true that, if one searches the records, some fast passages can be discovered. One schooner made a round trip from Portsmouth, New Hampshire, to Newport News and back in thirteen days, and the *Eleanor A. Percy* made the same trip from Boston and back in the same time in 1903, when fairly new. Another big six-master, the *Ruth E. Merrill,* once made fourteen round trips in a year, but on the whole they were lucky to achieve eleven. Even at that, it was quite a lot of coal to carry by the standards of the times and, although these vessels figured quite a lot in the casualty reports, they were sailing in all seasons through some of the stormiest waters and past most treacherous coasts. When the steam colliers did start running to Boston and elsewhere, they could not only load and

283. *The building of the big coal schooners was almost a specific aberration, and small and beautiful schooners were still being launched. This is the E. A. WHITMORE, of 1892, built at Millbridge, Me.*

discharge more quickly, but make the passage in a week. Their potential was four or five times that of the schooners and, for all the size of the latter, the steamers were, at that time, of about 7,000 tons deadweight. Taking account of crews, building costs and all else, they were still three or four times more economical to run than the sailers. Latterly, the last of the multi-masters tended to be sold foreign or to disappear under other flags.

The East Coast of the U.S.A. was not the only area where big schooners were built and owned, but in no area were there so many which were so big and, indeed, no other locality or country ever matched the biggest. Those on the West Coast were, generally, smaller (and the run down to the Islands was as ideal for a schooner as could be found), but, at the end of the First World War, about 170 four-, five- and six-masted schooners, including a few barquentines, were built or converted on that coast, the majority being laid down just at the end of, or immediately after, hostilities. Some were built for overseas ownership: some 54 of them, all consisting of four- and five-masters, being ordered in France alone; others went to Canada, Norway, and elsewhere, but many, of course, came under different flags in due course. A great many spent much of their careers laid up in the slump conditions which followed and which overwhelmed them, for very few had useful or profitable lives.

It is interesting to compare the *Forest Dream* with the *City of Orange*, since both were built in 1919 and were of much the same size. The *Forest Dream* was 1,605 tons and built by and for the Grays Harbor Motorship Corporation at Aberdeen, Washington and, with her two sisters, the *Forest Pride* and *Forest Friend*, made a vastly better-looking trio than the Texas-built post-war schooners and barquentines designed by Henry Piaggio, the Gulfport Italian consul, to trade between that area and the Mediterranean*. These vessels achieved very little, simply because they were overtaken by the slump. I joined the *'Dream'* in Port Adelaide after she had discharged a cargo of west coast lumber and we proceeded to Mauritius and then back to Newcastle, N.S.W., but the ship was by then insolvent, and sold to Sweden to be owned in Strömstad, but she spent most of her time under the Swedish flag laid up until she was burnt in 1933. Her two sisters became barges on the West Coast of North America and a third, the *Forest King*, was converted to a steam schooner when on the stocks.

In contrast to the *Forest King*, a number of Ferris steamer hulls were converted to sail on the stocks at the same period. A virtual sister to the *Anne Comyn*, illustrated in Volume 1, was the *Katherine Mackall* which was built by the Ralph J. Chandler Shipbuilding Co at Wilmington, California and owned by the Pacific Freighters Co, measuring 266.5′ × 46′ × 24.1′. There were five of these near-sisters. I myself sailed in the *Mackall* from Portland, Oregon, to Melbourne, Newcastle, N.S.W., over to Antofagasta and back to Seattle. Maybe I should have taken the photo of her when the saloon table-cloth was not set out to dry!* I was in other of these craft too – the *Cecil P. Stewart*, a big barquentine, owned in Rockland, Maine – from New York to Newport News for coal to Bordeaux and back to New York in 1920: the bald-headed barquentine *Molfetta*, which was later dismasted, down the East Coast to Cuba and back again, but these craft, although capable of

*There were 16 auxiliary barquentines alone.
*Pl. 291.

284. The CITY OF ORANGE.

285. The FOREST DREAM.

286. The BIANCA.

earning their keep when freights were fair, had none of the abilities of a square-rigger of similar dimensions, even when beating.

It is worth studying the hull profile of the *Mount Hamilton**, of 1,537 tons, which was built in Seattle in 1918 by the McAteer Shipbuilding Company for Norwegian owners in Haugesund. There is a lack of grace of line. Her sister ship, the *Mount Whitney,* also built for Norway, was wrecked in Carmarthen Bay in 1925, while the *'Hamilton'* was sold to Germany in 1924. The square foresail, which brailed in to the mast, was usually only hauled out on the weather side, and such ships usually passed the gaskets round the sail by lowering two men in bos'n's chairs to do the job.

Very few six-masters were built on the West Coast, but one was the *Fort Laramie* – at North Bend, Oregon, of 2,240 tons. Built on an uncompleted steamer hull, her lines bespeak the fact with her straight bow and only a beak below the bowsprit. She, too, has the brailing foresail,

*Pl. 294

268

287. The FORT LARAMIE.

seldom seen on the East Coast, and it will be noted that all these vessels retained outside channels.

Another of the post-war 'horrors' was the five-masted *Bianca* which crossed a yard high on each of her first four masts, from which she set raffees above and inverted raffees (for want of a better name) below them. Of 2,139 tons, she was built by the Elliott Shipbuilding Co. of Seattle for the Bianca Shipping Corporation, but she went ashore after five years west of Clallam Bay, when bound from Alaska towards Puget Sound with a cargo of canned salmon, and became a total loss. Her inverted raffees must have been almost unique, and the upper ones were cut away to allow the passage of the topmast stays. Really only useful with a fair wind, they could not have been as good as a square-sail of conventional design. When built, her topmasts were taller than in Pl. 286, and the lee part of the raffee would have blanketed the gaff topsail, when set together.

Whether for better or worse, many of these post-First War vessels had departed from the American schooner conventions in design, but the Canadian four-master, *Cumberland Queen*, launched in 1919 into the Diligent River, N.S. for J. N. Pugsley and others of Parrsboro' and which measured 179' × 38' × 13.2', had the East Coast 'look' about her (Pl. 288). The year after this photograph was taken outside the Mersey (whither she had put back after collision with a steamer, the *Slieve Gallion*, off Holyhead), when bound from Turks Island towards New York with a cargo of salt, she went ashore off Hatteras and was abandoned, later being salved and towed in to Norfolk, Va. by the Coastguard cutter *Manning*, to be sold as a wreck to A. P. Vane of Philadelphia, who restored her to sailing condition and re-named her *Emerett*. In 1931, after desultory trading, she left Jacksonville, Fla. with lumber for Puerto Rico, but early in March was sighted dismasted, waterlogged and abandoned. Her crew were never seen again. The Coastguard cutter *Modoe* towed her into Norfolk once more, but she never went to sea again, gradually deteriorating until some picnickers caused her to catch fire in 1942.

The last of the East Coast five-masters to be built was the *Edna Hoyt* in 1920, by Dunn & Elliott at Thomaston, Me. and owned in Boston. Much smaller than some of her big predecessors, she was only 1,512 GRT, and 224 × 41.1 × 20.8'. In Pl. 289 she is seen in New York, preparing for sea,

288. The CUMBERLAND QUEEN.

289. The last of the American East Coast five-masters to be built was the EDNA HOYT.

290. *Seen trading on the East Coast of the U.S.A, the brailing fore square-sail provides one clue that the ROSE MAHONEY was built on the West Coast. Launched at Benicia, California in 1918 and of 2,051 GRT and with a crew (unusually) of 13, she was owned in San Francisco but went ashore at Miami in a hurricane in 1926 and was scrapped where she lay.*

with a banner in her fore rigging advertising her voyage to Coro, in Venezuela. In 1937, registered at Rockland, Me. she was towed into Lisbon in distress and, condemned as unseaworthy, sold as a hulk in that port.

For those who choose to pursue the East Coast schooners in greater detail, it should be mentioned that confusion can easily arise due to the fact that there were two distinct companies of 'Palmer' schooners, all named after members of the respective Palmer families, and that the two were quite unconnected. Nathaniel T. Palmer built five four-masters and the five-master named after himself, the fleet passing to the firm of J. S. Winslow after his death in 1904. William F. Palmer's fleet came later and was rather remarkable since he himself had been a school-master, but had determined to enter the shipping business. He not only found backers, including Benjamin B. Crowninshield, the designer, and the owner of the

291. The KATHERINE MACKALL, looking forward. She was broken up in Puget Sound about 1930, after a long lay up.

292. The bald-headed five-master NANCY was built in 1918 at Portland, Or. being 2,117 GRT, but was owned in Philadelphia, Penn., by Miss Clema Collins — a one-ship concern. In February 1927 she dragged her anchors and went ashore on Nantasket Beach, Mass. as seen above, remaining there some years before being broken up.

Thomas W. Lawson and others, but he taught himself the art of naval architecture and designed all but two of the vessels in his fleet, which consisted of two four-masters and thirteen five-masters. He died in 1909, and this fleet also passed to J. S. Winslow, but in the case of neither company were the names of the various 'Palmer' schooners changed — hence the confusion! In 1906, which was possibly the last peak year of the collier schooners, William Palmer's fleet paid a dividend of 14%.

Other big fleets were those of Crowell and Thurlow who later went into steam: there were some builders, like Percy and Small of Bath, Me., who built on their own account on occasions, and there was also John G. Crowley, who had under his control five five-masters and the six-masters *George W. Wells*, *William C. Douglas* and the *Mertie B. Crowley* which was originally being built at Camden, Maine, by Holly & Bean when they got into financial trouble, whereupon her frames, which were standing, were dismantled from her keel and all were taken to another yard at Rockland, Maine, where they were set up again and the vessel was completed — an unusual situation. Crowley was a man of very big ideas and it was he who owned the *Thomas W. Lawson* which may be considered justly to be the ugliest sailing ship ever built, but certainly unique in being the only seven-master and the biggest of any rig built anywhere.

She was Crowley's conception and designed, as stated, by B. B. Crowninshield, being built by the Fore River Ship & Engine Co. of Quincey, Mass. and named after a financier who had an interest in her. She was launched in 1902 and, built of steel, had some extraordinary vital statistics for a sailing vessel. Having a deadweight of over 8,000 tons on a GRT of 5,218, she measured 375.6 × 50 × 32.9′. She had two decks with a raised poop and t'gallant foc's'le and, apart from her pine topmasts, was steel throughout. She could load 1,070 tons of water ballast in a double bottom four feet deep. Her seven lower masts each weighed 20 tons apiece, being 135′ long and 38″ in diameter, while her topmasts were 58′ long and her spike bowsprit 85′ but, although these dimensions were considerably in excess of any square-rigger ever built, her sail area was only 44,000 square feet. She drew 12′ of water in ballast, but 29½′ when loaded, and this meant that, in the coal trade, Newport News was the only port where she could be afloat when deep-loaded and, indeed, she went aground on the coast several times.

293. In 1919 the BRADFORD E. JONES – a four-master of 1,647 GRT – was being built, as seen here, at Boothbay Harbour, Me. She was owned in Boston.

294. The MOUNT HAMILTON. (See page 268.)

295. The THOMAS W. LAWSON. *Not much sail for so big a ship.*

    Light, she presented an enormous surface of hull – more than 40–45′ from the waterline to her foc's'le head and, with her sail area so small in relation to her size, she was a crank sailer light ship and would never stay in these circumstances, always having to be worn round. It is said that she was sometimes club-hauled*, but in view of the fact that each of her two stockless anchors weighed in excess of 10,000 lbs, one must presume that this only happened in the direst emergencies – if, indeed, it ever

*See page 104.

296. *A picture giving a good idea of the big, wall-sides of the THOMAS W. LAWSON.*

happened at all. Unusually, at that time, she had steam steering gear, electricity and a telephone system, while the crew's quarters were steam-heated and, of course, the lowers were hoisted by winches. Incidentally, the donkey boiler of these schooners, and often the winches, were installed while they were building on the stocks and used to expedite the work.

Initially, she was painted a light grey above red boot-topping but, like other schooners in the coal trade before her, it was found that black was a more practicable colour for the hull. Her houses and rails were white, with green tops to the deckhouses and varnished decks and topmasts. However, her unhandiness did not help her in the coal trade which invariably demanded a good deal of beating and this, combined with the lowered freights in the middle of the first decade of the century, caused her to be withdrawn and chartered to the Sun Oil Co. for five years, during which, with her topmasts sent down, she was towed for most of the time between Port Arthur, in Texas, and Marcus Hook, Penn., having been converted to a bulk tanker in the interim. On one occasion, in Sabine Pass, Texas, she suddenly rolled over and was only righted with some difficulty: this being attributed to poor ballasting.

Then, in 1907, she was chartered to The Standard Oil Co. for a trip across the Atlantic in an effort to compete with the steam tankers, and duly left with 2,003,063 gallons of oil and, for the ocean passage, a crew of eighteen. She cast off her tug outside the Delaware Capes and all went well until she ran into headwinds of hurricane force off Newfoundland, when she had almost all her canvas blown out and simply ran before the gale. No sights could be taken, and the wind remained. She was soon down to bare poles, heading east as nearly as she could, virtually out of control. However, on 12 December she made soundings and, the next day, sighted land. Captain Dow had hoped to make his landfall off the Bishops, but had had no fix for 48 hours and anchored in Broad Sound, off the Scillies and well to the north of his estimated position, with 75 fathoms of cable in what was then a light nor'westerly wind, bringing up very near to Annet Island — one of the Scillies.

This was no place to be, and a lifeboat came out from St Agnes, but her assistance was refused, though a pilot was put aboard the big schooner, which was rolling a lot. The other cable was paid out to 90 fathoms and, when the St Mary's lifeboat arrived, only to lose her mast against the side of the *Lawson*, she was requested to send for a tug, but it was all too late. By midnight it was blowing great guns, with jagged rocks only half a mile astern of the helpless giant. The crew donned lifejackets and took to the rigging but, at 1.15 a.m., the port cable parted. She tried to send up rockets, but they were wet and, at 2.30 a.m. the other cable carried away. Within minutes, the world's biggest sailing ship was hurled onto

297. *This picture breaks the rules of this book because it is not a photograph, but an extraordinarily accurate painting by the celebrated Swedish artist Carl Friberg. Not even so talented an artist can make her an object of admiration. Sailing ships were not built to be beauty queens (though some were), but to show healthy balance sheets. If the LAWSON did so, it was because she was towed for much of her life.*

Hellweather Reef and, splitting in two between her sixth and seventh masts, she rolled over and sank.

The pilot and sixteen of the crew were lost, and only the master and engineer, both injured by the rocks, survived. The cargo was insured but the schooner, which had cost $250,000 and was then valued at $150,000, was not. Whether she paid for herself in her working life of five years is very doubtful. She would not have earned much profit in her period in the coal trade at that time, and there were all the costs of her conversion to a tanker to be taken into account. Had she continued to be towed down south she might have proved to be profitable to her owner but, even if this had been the case, it was by no means the purpose for which she was built. As a freak – for she was no less – and as a unique vessel in both rig and size, she cannot fail to interest, but she must be accounted a failure and, although this covers but the barest bones of her short career, she should be a warning to all those who extol the huge schooner as the ship of the future when we can no longer use oil for motive power. Add to this the inability of a big schooner to take the best advantage of the wind on ocean passages: her poorer performance down wind, her inevitable under-canvassing and the unbelievable wear and tear to her gear, and it will be apparent that there is, in general terms, a strict limit to her size and that the advantage of the multi-masters was theoretical rather than practical.

The editor of this book told me that, in the 1930s, when he was in a four-masted schooner of a mere 1,688 GRT and fitting out, the crew were highly diverted because an American multi-master had been towed into port as a salvage case because she had run out of fuel wherewith to hoist her lowers. Indeed, he said, they laughed immoderately! Then, with at least three times the crew of the American, the British schooner towed to sea, with no winches or even capstans on deck and, as they passed through the Downs, commenced to hoist the big lowers, 75′ on the leeches and 60′ on the luffs – big sails, but nothing like the American's. Each throat halliard was two three-fold purchases, one on each side of the mast and made fast to the two ends of a whip rove through the block to which the halliard was spliced. No-one laughed about the American schooner again after that! The crew were all square-rigger men and, for his part, he had just come out of the largest afloat, but I know that no such vessel could produce any hauling job to approach those lowers! Had

298. The American schooner BERTHA L. DOWNES as the Finnish ATLAS.

299. Lying in Marseilles in 1933, few people would suppose that the steel schooner NINA PODESTA of Genoa, owned by Luigi Getelli & Co, was built in Svendborg, since she does not conform to type. She **was** built there, as the DROGDEN, in 1919. Of 395 NRT, she was 138.8 × 29.7 × 11.1′.

300. *Down to her marks in Boston Harbour before her last passage, the THOMAS W. LAWSON looks slightly better, but even the ugliest square-rigger had greater aesthetic appeal.*

that schooner been manned to the tune of two men to a mast they could never have done it. Once the lowers *are* set, the working of a schooner is virtually a rest-cure as compared with a square-rigger, but the spanker of that British schooner brailed, and was thus easy to work although, in consequence, it could not be reefed. The answer to any further essay in this direction in the future, however ill-advised it may be, is surely to have split brailing sails with two or more gaffs.

The evergreen question is: *'How were the Lawson's masts named?'* There is no answer, as no nomenclature was ever standardized aboard. Even in her short life, there were variations. In the case of the six-masters, it was Fore, Main, Mizzen, Jigger, Driver and Spanker, and the five-masters dropped the 'Driver'. Simply rigged, with four shrouds and two topmast backstays, with small crews and stoutly, if functionally, built (figureheads, for example, were rare in the Down-East collier fleet), they sailed dangerous and tricky waters, often crowded with traffic, all the year round. There were a number of collisions, many strandings and, as stated, all their ends were violent but, if we except the *Thomas W. Lawson* as a freak ship, it can be said that, for all their imperfections, they did, in broad terms, achieve what they set out to do and, when one sets out to think about it, that is no bad epitaph!

There are very strong temptations which urge people to opt for the schooner rig on very big hulls, whether on purchase, when building or, more particularly, when converting or re-rigging. The arguments include reduced capital outlay: ease of working; reduced wage bills, the ability to sail with less skilled men and much else. Only the first of these is really valid and, in general, the other advantages prove to be mythical. Much the same can be said, to a lesser degree, of very big barquentines. A square-rigger can be scaled up successfully to a certain tonnage, though there is reason to believe that conventional vessels of this type had, in the more exceptional instances, verged on the limits of size with which they could be handled safely. At the time of writing, there are plans afoot to build a square-rigger half as big again as the *France (2)** in terms of deadweight tonnage and, if she comes to fruition, she will test the truth of this assertion.

Much seems possible on a drawing board, but such plans do not take account of the human factor. That man has not advanced at the same pace as his technical inventions is borne out by the losses and collisions which still take place with monotonous regularity in the case of supertankers, ultra-large carriers and the like, of several hundred thousand tons deadweight. The same arguments are the more cogent in the case of a square-rigger, but for purposes of ocean voyages, and neglecting all human factors, there are clear limits on the size of a schooner.

At first sight it may be difficult to believe that the *Cidad de Porto* (Pl. 302) was the same vessel as the *Hans* (Pl. 301) and sister to the great *Moshulu* (Pls. 303/5), but this was the case. The *Moshulu* had originally been the *Kurt* and, with the *Hans,* had been owned by G. J. H. Siemers of Hamburg, running mainly in the Chilean nitrate trade alongside the Laeisz vessels until the first war, when both became interned: the *Kurt* in Astoria and the *Hans* in Santa Rosalia. These two big four-masted barques, with painted ports, midship islands and double spankers, passed to the United States, the *Kurt* being first re-named *Dreadnought* and then *Moshulu,* making about five voyages with lumber and enduring years of being laid up before being sold to Captain Gustaf Erikson in 1935, when she entered the Australian grain trade.

The *Hans* was towed up to San Francisco after the first war and re-named *Mary Dollar,* but she never went to sea again as a square-rigged

---
*The largest square-rigger ever built — see Pl. 10.

283

301. The HANS loading coal at Port Talbot in her German days, and . . .

302. . . . the same ship as the CIDAD DE PORTO leaving Lourenco Marques in 1945 — quite a transformation from the HANS! The funnels are the tugs on her port side.

ship. The Dollar Company held on to her, hoping that freights would improve. Initially, they had got four of the ex-German ships to sea, very temporarily, but freights never seemed to pick up and, finally, having offered her to the State of California as a training ship without success, since no funds were available, the *Hans* was sold and towed down to Los Angeles where she was stripped of all her top-hamper and her big midship section, while a roof (rather than a shelter deck) was built from foc's'le head to poop. Then, re-named *Tango,* she suffered the ultimate degradation of becoming a gambling hulk, moored off the port, until this activity was closed down.

In the Second World War there was, once again, a need for anything which would float, and the ship was stripped down, dry-docked and converted to a six-masted schooner. With a deadweight tonnage of around 5,393, it was clear that the old temptations, coupled with a measure of expediency, were in operation! There was initially some doubt whether or not she should be rigged as a barquentine since, although it is commonly said that a schooner can sail closer to the wind, this is not necessarily true of very big ones in which the large booms cannot always be hauled amidships so easily when close-hauled. However, despite the wear and tear to gear aloft endemic in so rigging the ship, the old, misconceived arguments prevailed and the six-masted *Tango* was cleared for Cape Town with a cargo of lumber and, proceeding via Cape Horn, arrived in 103 days. The *Star of Scotland,* once the famous *Kenilworth,* another fine four-masted barque, had also been in the gambling hulk row as the *Rex* and, named *Star of Scotland* again, was given the same six-masted schooner rig and sent to Cape Town where I boarded her — not recognizing the vessel till I saw her bell! Certainly she engendered no desire to sail in her in her converted form.

However, the *Tango* had recovered her costs on that first voyage, thanks to the high war-time freight rates, and she then made one or two trips between South Africa and South America before being sold to Portugal. Her crew was not much less than it would have been as a four-masted barque under the Finns (though no American ship would have sailed with so small a crew as them) and her wage bill was very high.

As the *Tango,* she had been painted white, but her new owner, one Julio Ribiero, had her painted black and re-named *Cidad de Porto,* and she left Durban (where the sale took place) for Lourenço Marques where she was acquired by the Regulating Commission of the Cotton-Wool Trade, of Portugal, in February 1943, with the intention that she should carry cotton from Mozambique (then Portuguese) to Portugal. For some reason, this never came about and, after lying idle for a further year, she loaded a full cargo of coal for Lobito, in Angola, and was on the point of leaving when Pl. 302 was taken, with neutrality flags painted on her sides. She left on 24 August, 1945, but was towed into Durban in distress with storm damage on 19 September, and did not proceed again for two months, when she encountered another storm and more damage, being towed into Cape Town on 30 December. Here she remained until 7 April, 1946, when she was towed to her destination by the *s.s. Pungue.* Subsequently this steamer towed her to Lisbon where, after a further lay up, she was broken up in 1948.

It was not a happy resuscitation. Whether it be deemed to be an argument against big schooners might be debatable. She was bald-headed and, although she is said to have handled reasonably well during her voyage to Cape Town, it will be noted that, unlike the multi-masted colliers of New England, her masts were not spaced apart equidistantly. It is, indeed, rather an odd sail plan. In terms of size, she ranked amongst the biggest of the schooners, only seven ever having been bigger than her. She was, in her short life as a fore-and-after, employed deep-water, and this has never been the *forte* of very large vessels of this rig, though it is true that some of the Palmer schooners and others did make the odd trans-Atlantic passage successfully. The truth is that much more depends on the weather encountered for large vessels of this rig than for square-riggers of similar size.

By the end of the Second World War the *Moshulu,* her twin, was a hulk. The subject of various abortive schemes, and after many years, she was finally restored *(sic)* in Philadelphia with a *restaurant* aboard her! Despite having served in the ship myself when each meal was as unpalatable as the last, I am not tempted by her menus, whatever they may be. If it is desired to preserve an historic building – perhaps a famous old restaurant – there would be an outcry if it were to be converted to look like a square-rigger, if that were possible. However loathsome the food was when I knew the *Moshulu,* I respected her then, as I respect her

303. The MOSHULU when new, as the KURT, towing into the Elbe, high out of the water and very different from her appearance in Pl. 304.

now, as a powerful and staunch Cape Horner and, if she is to be preserved, she should not only maintain her image, but even all those smells so redolent of her kind: the Stockholm tar, the red lead, the tang of rust about her anchor cables below the foc's'le head and so much else.

It may be of interest to see pictures of the ship at different stages of her career, and, of course, they make a salutary comparison with the *Hans*, when she became the *Tango*. Which ship suffered the worse fate, it is difficult to say. I think that that of the *Moshulu* was the more opprobious. The *Hans* is broken up, after being re-rigged in a manner which, to her, was much as an old lady hobbling on crutches, but at least she was giving some semblance of service in trade. Preserving ships is a vexed matter, however high the ideals and motives of the entrepreneurs, on which the vessels themselves are never consulted. When, in 1967, the splendid old auxiliary barquentine *Bear* was being towed to New York to become a restaurant-cum-museum ship, she saw fit to founder en route. I remember the *Bear,* and wonder whether she had some vision of her intended future which led to her voluntary euthanasia.

The counter arguments are cogent ones which revolve around finance. The vast army of fee-paying sightseers want more for their money than a bare, functional ship, bereft of sails and life, which, when in dock, is never, in any case, more than a shadow of the sight she presented swinging on her way under full sail with a great, white bone in her teeth.

304. Here the MOSHULU is deep-loaded and, unusually, painted white.

When in port, only the expert can appreciate her finer points. Thus it is that something must be done to raise money to make the ship viable as a continuing exhibit but, whatever that may be, it must be done *ashore* and adjacent to the vessel. It *can* be done, as exemplified in the splendid preservation efforts at the Exeter Museum and elsewhere, albeit the craft are generally smaller.

When the ex-Laeisz vessel *Peking* was taken to South Street, New York, to be restored – though the connection between this vessel and New York is obscure, to say the least – a wealthy business man underwrote the project . . . and called the tune! Now the wretched ship is lying there with some sort of tubular spars which have no relation to her appearance when she was in trade, and those of the *Moshulu* are only marginally better. In the case of the *Peking,* the iron-work aloft is so wrong that her lower yards can no longer be braced round, as though she

305. Down to her marks with the biggest grain cargo loaded by a sailing ship in Port Adelaide, the MOSHULU tows down the river, her low freeboard accentuated by her very short poop. Her cargo gin is still slung between fore and main.

were half-paralysed after a stroke. I remember her well when she was in trade: a blustery day when she was winging her way down Channel; the days when she lay in the Thames and Medway before she was raped and, moreover, her last master became a good friend of mine. He is now dead, and it is as well that *he* cannot see this caricature of a ship, this mummified Cape Horner, lying in shame in a port so strange to her.

There is so much to be said for the preservation of the maritime heritage of the world, and no-one supports the ideal more than I do, but it must be preserved properly. If the *Moshulu's* sightseers must be fed to make her viable, than they should be fed ashore. If there are to be exhibits – and how interesting those can be! – they, too, should be ashore and close by the ship. If these things cannot be, or are not, done, then one is minded of the words Tennyson put into the mouth of Sir Richard Greenfield (Grenville) towards the end of his great fight in the *Revenge:*

306. After being laid up in Lake Union during the slump in the 1920s, the MOSHULU was only towed out in the nick of time as the bridge was being completed.

'Sink me the ship, master gunner, sink her, split her in twain,
  Better to fall in the hands of God than into the hands of Spain.'
For 'Spain' may be substituted whatever word my readers wish, whether it scans or not! No ship looks her best in a wet or dry-dock, nor when she is in ballast and high out of the water. The *Moshulu,* like the

307. Siemers' SUSANNA and KURT (on her maiden voyage) loading coal in Port Talbot. Note how the headsails and staysails are made up on their stays. The Siemers house-flag was an odd one, being three points of a star backing on to a quarter moon complete with face, in yellow on a red field.

Peking, represented the quintessence of square-rigger building. They were demanding ships, but they found their real *métier* in the Westerlies of the high latitudes. For my part, I believe that a series of very large scale models, showing the construction; the loading, and the ship under various states of sail in differing conditions of wind and weather would give a far better idea of what a sailing ship was all about than the real ship, permanently in the one condition – far from her best – and with her decks crowded with trippers and their inevitable progeny. Have they any idea of the reality of furling a frozen topsail in high gale? Do they go home believing that the clippers and big carriers had great, safe staircases down to their lower holds? Yet . . . old ladies cannot manage vertical ladders. So their must be *some* compromise, but . . . compromise does not mean a restaurant! *'Sink me the ship, master gunner. . . !'*

308. The PISAGUA taking steam after collision.

The *Pisagua's* collision was described in Volume 1, and she was shown in Dover. Here she is, with her bow and all her headgear gone, in tow of Watkins famous *Arcadia* – (the *Conqueror* is astern). The P & O liner *Oceana,* which was at fault, was sunk with a lot of specie and ivory aboard, though this was subsequently salved. The *Pisagua* was, in a sense, a transition vessel in the Laeisz company, since she had been built with a midship section but had not yet adopted the double spankers which came to be a hallmark of the fleet later. Note her very short poop. Two black balls, signifying 'Not under command' are hoisted in the fore rigging.

The Laeisz ships were plagued with Channel collisions, probably because their big, powerful ships were making much better speed, with very little fuss, than was anticipated by the steamer officers who crossed their bows. The *Passat* had been in collision with the French *s.s. Daphne* in March 1928, and had hit the British *s.s. British Governor* the following year when Pls. 309–10 were taken.

309. The PASSAT in floating dock at Rotterdam after collision in June 1929. She is not afloat, but resting on blocks. The double frames, which extended the greater part of her lower length, will be observed. The right-hand picture gives a fair idea of the bow structure of the latter steel sailing ships.

310.

311. Wooden barque after collision.

In contrast to the *Passat*, the little wooden barque in Pl. 311 has suffered most of her damage above the water-line. Her bowsprit has snapped off, and it will be seen that her fore shrouds, taken down to outside channels, have been slacked off to permit the removal of a couple of strakes.

The effects of collision, even of the most glancing nature, were unpredictable for a sailing ship since, as another vessel scraped down her side, rigging could be carried away with the result that gear aloft could be damaged or lost. The British *s.s. Koranton* struck the Swedish four-masted barque *Abraham Rydberg* a relatively glancing blow in the Channel in 1936, carrying away the main t'gallant backstays (after first hitting the barque at the after end of the foc's'le head) and buckling the t'gallant and royal yards, while carrying away the topgallant mast (Pl. 312).

The *Loch Carron* was one of the few four-masted Loch liners, and is

312. The ABRAHAM RYDBERG's mainmast after collision in 1936.

seen in Pl. 363 after collision with the barque *Inverkip*, owned by Walker's of Greenock. The accident occurred in thick weather and a heavy sea south of the Fastnet, the other barque sinking fast. Being on the port tack, the *Loch Carron* was held to be to blame and had to pay large compensation, although the weather was such that there was not even time to shift the helm when the *Inverkip's* port light was sighted close aboard. Long before the days of radar, this raises a nice point. Should a sailing ship heave to, in such circumstances? Should she do so, she is precluded from any quick manoeuvre. If *all* ships were to heave to in thick weather, that would be one thing, but if one does and another does not, then the ship hove to is a sitting target if she is in the path of a running vessel. In regions of ice, there is normally also fog when the warmer air condenses. Every sailing ship wants to make the most of fair wind and around – say – Tristan da Cunha may be making 12 or 13 knots, *with ice*

295

313. *The LOCH CARRON in Queenstown after collision with the INVERKIP in 1904.*

around. It is asking a lot to heave to in such circumstances and, not knowing precisely where the bergs may be, she may drop down on one. It is so easy to sit in judgement and say that no sailing ship should proceed in inadequate visibility but, if she is out of soundings and safe anchorage, just what would the judges do, were they in command? . . .

Only two men were saved from the *Inverkip*, which was homeward bound*, while the *Loch Carron* was doing around 7 knots close-hauled. By an unhappy chance, the two masters and their wives were exceptionally good friends. The *Loch Carron,* with her sister, the *Loch Broom*, were built of iron in 1885 and peculiar in that they had single topgallants on the fore, but double yards on main and mizzen. Both were sold to S. O. Stray of Kristianssand in 1912, the *Loch Carron* being re-named *Seileren* and the *Loch Broom* the *Songdal,* the latter being sunk by a U-boat in 1917 when bound from Beunos Aires towards Queenstown.

As was so often the case in the days of sail, there was an untold saga of the sea as the 826-ton barque *Anirac,* owned by C. Schiaffino of Genoa,

---

* 146 days out of Geelong, she had just hove to and her hands were aloft stowing the foresail: the two men saved falling from the port yardarm to the *Loch Carron's* foc's'le head. The four-master suffered superficial damage and started a lot of rivets in her hull but, as she was carrying locomotives in her lower hold, it was possible to get at the shell-plating and plug the rivet holes with wood. Otherwise she would probably have foundered too.

296

314. The two-masted schooner MADBY ANN of 102 tons, owned by William Caisley of Goole and built in 1865, lying in Dover with her foremast almost gone; her main spreaders broken and sundry other damage. In 1920/21 she was owned in Falmouth.

315. The ANIRAC towing into Newhaven in distress.

316. The THORSTEN capsized in Egersund.

was towed into Newhaven with the local lifeboat alongside after she had had her sails blown out in a Channel gale, and with dire trouble to her fore and t'gallant rigging. This was in 1912, but she had been built by W. H. Potter in 1876 as the *Letterewe,* when owned by Irvin, Dixon of Liverpool. Continuing her 1912 voyage, she arrived in Buenos Aires with more damage and was sold. In 1920 she became the *Vittoria,* then the *Henriette,* but in 1924 she was sold to Bilbao and became the *Sanita,* then the *Frexas* of Barcelona and, later still, to Gijon to become the *Astur.* Her hull was still around in 1954, in use as a pontoon.

Of course, ships should not capsize in port, but there have always been instances in both small and large vessels and invariably, in the final analysis, they were brought about by human error. Pl. 316 shows the small barque *Thorsten* capsized in Egersund. She was owned by B. Govansen and built in 1876. Like the two vessels beyond her – the barque *Actie* of 1860 and the *Ungdoms Venner* of 1869 – she was one of that vast concourse of sailing vessels which seem to have been lost in the annals of time and not to have been recorded in the history books. The *Ungdoms Venner,* of 534 tons, had been built in Mossglen, N.S., by Wentmore & Merritt and was owned by Th. Nordeas of Egersund, having been originally named the *Carrier Dove.* She was found derelict in 1890.

The brig *Duen,* on the other hand, is no trouble at all in Pl. 317, but 'hove down' in order to clean and treat her bottom – a method to which resort was frequently made with smaller vessels when a dry-dock was not

317. The DUEN hove down and the brig PATRIE.

318. The ARDENCRAIG sinking on 8 January, 1911. (See page 300.)

319. The TARAPACA blocking the lock at La Pallice.

available. It was an arduous business, since it had to be done twice – once for each side. This brig had been built in Arendal for H. H. Petterson of that port, being 262 tons and measuring 92.8′ × 26.8′ × 25.4′. To the right is the *Patrie* of 1848.

The *Ardencraig,* a steel full-rigger of 1,969 tons, was built in 1886 by Russell's for Edmiston & Mitchell of Glasgow, but passed to Crawford & Rowat's 'Port' Line, though she was not re-named to conform with their standard nomenclature. It was she which rammed and sank the bald-headed four-masted barque *Norma* off the Semaphore Anchorage outside Adelaide in 1907. In Pl. 318 she is sinking herself, after striking the Crim Rocks, in the Scillies, on 8 January, 1911, when bound from Queenstown, where she had called for orders, towards Calais after a voyage from Melbourne. It was always the custom to head the log-book, or speak of a ship, as being bound from one port *towards* another – never *to*. This section provides the reason for this. The word 'to' is tempting fate!

'. . . and the old, long-since loved ESMERALDA, long since sold.'

320.   The ESMERALDA in Rio after collision with the s.s. CADIZ.

Masefield wrote of this vessel in his famous poem *Ships*. Built of iron in 1866, of 735 tons, for T. H. Ismay's management by Thos. Vernon of Liverpool, she was sold to Paolo Olivari of Genoa in 1906 and was under his ownership when she came into collision with the Spanish *s.s. Cadiz* off the River Plate in 1911 and arrived in Montevideo in the sorry state shown in Pl. 320, after which she was sold. Sailing ships only had two transverse bulkheads — the fore and after peak ones — between which they were just one big, empty shell. The *Esmeralda* must have been very close to fracturing her fore-peak bulkhead on this occasion.

A. D. Bordes' fine four-masted full-rigger *Tarapaca* made an unhappy homecoming in 1902 when she arrived at La Pallice from Tocopilla, as she hit the pier, holing herself, and sank in the lock with a heavy list, blocking it for five days (Pl. 319). The Bordes fleet was always bigger than the 'P' Line of Hamburg and every whit as smart in appearance and in passages. The *Tarapaca* was ultimately torpedoed south and west of Oleron in 1917, her crew getting ashore in the boats.

Ships in trouble sometimes did reach their destination by one means or

321.

322. *The ZEALANDIC towing the GARTHSNAID into Melbourne after dismasting in 1922.*

another. The *Garthsnaid* had been Milne's *Inversnaid,* but had not been long under her new owners when, in 1922, bound from Iquique towards Melbourne, she was dismasted in bad weather to the south'ard of Gabo Island. The Shaw, Savill liner *Zealandic* found her with her boats stove in and her decks a terrible mess of fallen spars and rigging and, after four abortive attempts to tow her in, due to the bad weather, finally brought her into Melbourne, as seen in Pls. 321–2. She was condemned and hulked after discharging.

Built in 1897 for J. Hardie of Glasgow, and not dissimilar to the *Archibald Russell* (Pls. 411/20) the *Hougomont* was in the casualty lists on a

323.   The HOUGOMONT limping into St. Vincent Gulf under jury rig.

number of occasions. Sold to Gustaf Erikson in 1925, she was finally dismasted south of Cape Borda in 1932 and succeeded in limping into St Vincent's Gulf under jury rig. On arrival the next year, the *Herzogin Cecilie* was sent round to go alongside the *Hougomont* and to salve and bring back as much of her gear as possible. The *Herzogin* had been built as a Nord Deutscher Lloyd training ship and was a magnificent vessel, bigger and more powerful than the *Herzogin Sophie Charlotte* (Pls. 368–71). Erikson had bought her on the recommendation of Captain Reuben de Cloux who achieved a great reputation for successful passages when master of both the *Lawhill* and this ship, but left to command the *Parma,* in which he had an interest. He was succeeded by Sven Erikson who was, in a sense, lucky to obtain command because de Cloux had never forgiven his mate, Harald Lindfors, for his part in smuggling a girl stowaway (in whom he had more than a passing interest)

324. The HOUGOMONT sunk as a breakwater in Stenhouse Bay.

aboard the ship in 1928, and had stipulated to the owner than *in no circumstances* should he succeed him. Consequently Sven Erikson joined as mate and was promoted to be master when de Cloux left to take over the *Parma*. (Lindfors nevertheless obtained command of the barque *Carmen*, in the Baltic trade, and then the *Archibald Russell,* of which he was master when Pls. 415–6 were taken.)

On the one hand, Sven Erikson was an extremely daring master, although it must be said that dare-devilry and courage are not necessarily to be equated with good seamanship. Certainly I have never met anyone who sailed with him who had a good word to say for the man. On the occasion that he brought the *Herzogin* alongside the *Hougomont,* he came up the Gulf in a fairly stiff wind, sailing right past the pilot cutter and then, reducing to lower topsails, with all other sails clewed up in their gear, dropped both anchors without luffing up, when close to the hulk of the *Hougomont*. The cables carried away and then, quite out of control, the ship fell down on the hulk and the remarkable picture in Pl. 325 shows the bowsprit of the latter ship aboard the *Herzogin*, having 'speared' the jigger middle staysail and forced it round and away from its gear as the

325. The HOUGOMONT's bowsprit spearing the HERZOGIN CECILIE's mizzen middle staysail as she falls down on the dismasted hulk.

326. *The HERZOGIN CECILIE racing the OLIVEBANK, whose performance was the better since she had lost her fore topgallant mast, and was thus without her fore t'gallants and royal and flying jib for the passage since before she spoke the HERZOGIN.*

Herzogin swung on her. It was a very lucky thing that the *Herzogin's* rigging was not carried away in its entirety, and it cannot be denied that it was a risky and unseamanlike manoeuvre. Had it come off, it might have achieved cheap acclaim, but it failed and brought the ship within an ace of disaster. Note will be doubtless be taken of the similarity of situation in Pls. 39 and 325, if brought about for quite different reasons.

Still under the command of Sven Erikson, the ship was wrecked, quite unnecessarily, inside Start Point in 1936: all the indications being that the magnetic variation was not applied to her compass course after leaving Falmouth a few hours earlier.

Pl. 326 was taken from the *Olivebank* of the *Herzogin* on her homeward trip after she had taken the *Hougomont's* gear and loaded grain.

327. The HERZOGIN CECILIE alongside the hulk of the HOUGOMONT to salve her gear.

328. An undignified way of foundering was to sit on an anchor. The SONGVAAR was lying to two cables off Port Victoria, one short and one long, when the wind shifted and she was pierced by one of her anchors. She was never salved.

329. Deck view of the SONGVAAR foundering off Wardung Island off Port Victoria. Built of iron at Stockton as the BARCORE in 1884 for Eyre, Evans & Co, she was sold to S. O. Stray of Kristianssand in 1909, being lost in 1912.

The two ships were racing hard with all the wind they could stand under all plain sail. Some fine pictures were taken from the *Olivebank* on this occasion, but there seems to be a dearth of any taken from the *Herzogin*. The reason for this is that, when the *Olivebank* was first sighted just the other side of the Horn, Sven Erikson presumed her to be the fine Laeisz four-master *Priwall*, which had sailed a week before him, and he was as pleased as Punch to have caught up so much time on her. When, however, he discovered the other ship to be the old *Olivebank,* which had sailed a week *after* him, his mood changed utterly and he kept his crew so working up the ship that there was no chance to use cameras at the crucial moments. Later, the two ships were again in company near the line, and the *Olivebank* finally arrived four days before the 'crack' *Herzogin Cecilie,* thus not only destroying that ship's reputation for invincibility (at that time) but, under Captain Mattson, repairing her own image

330. Severe gales around the coasts still take their toll, and always did so. Here, despite the shelter often afforded by the Downs, the brig STAR OF THE OCEAN belies her name as she lies ashore facing an unidentified white schooner a century ago.

331. The smart little barque ETHEL, owned by Stobart, Fenwick which became France, Fenwick, the well-known North-East Coast collier owners, was running regularly out to Hobart until sold to Norwegian owners and registered at Flekkefjord . . .

332.   . . . but at 10.0pm on 2 January, 1904 she ran ashore on Cape Spencer at the entrance to Spencer gulf in a strong gale with heavy seas and thick weather . . .

which had declined as a passage-maker over some years when under Captain Troberg, who had never pushed her.

Sister to the *Mount Stewart**, the *Cromdale* was making up to the Cornish coast in fog in 1913, 126 days out of Taltal with a cargo of saltpetre, when she checked her position with a passing steamer and was advised to alter course, which she did . . . and went ashore on Bass Rock, near the treacherous Lizard. Pl. 336 was taken soon after the wreck, and the after davits can be seen swung out with the boats gone. It was not long before she broke up.

Sailing ships running into the coast after long voyages, often with no sights for days on end and working on dead reckoning, were not always certain of their position. Those of the future, equipped with modern

*Pls. 226/30.

333. . . . and it was not long before her masts were gone and her forefoot badly twisted. It was not found possible to get her off and . . .

334. . . . in the event, the ETHEL became a landmark for years although, latterly, she disintegrated until only the frames of the stern section and a few plates remained.

335. *The hulks ADA and ISABEL LLUSA in Malaga in 1933.*

navigational aids and the ability to obtain radio 'fixes' almost anywhere and at any time, should thus have a great advantage, but this can be said of modern power-driven vessels which do not seem to avoid the casualty lists, for, as Joseph Conrad said: *'Ships are all right: it's the men in them'*. Designers and others can produce splendid vessels and improve them enormously, but they *cannot* improve the men who sail them, for the factor of human fallibility is a constant.

Many sailing ships eked out years of service as hulks after their voyaging days were over. It was sad to see them in this state, but it was incredible how so many of them managed to demonstrate their pedigrees even when rigged down and grimy with coal dust. When the famous Aberdeen White Star wool clipper *Samuel Plimsoll* served as a coal hulk in Fremantle and was moved from one berth or ship to another in tow, her hull barely left a ripple in the water.

If one looked, there were old sailing vessels to be seen in ports all over the world. In Pl. 335, taken in Malaga in 1933, the *Ada,* built in 1895 as the *East African,* later to become the Norwegian *Risor* and Stray's *Skomedal* until hulked in 1918 after storm damage, lies outside the *Isabel Llusa,* one of the Spanish Llusa fleet and built as the Italian barque *Oriente.* Some hulks were interesting in themselves, particularly very old

336.   'And now from the darkness of water the CROMDALE outcried
         "O beautiful passer, I once was the CROMDALE, a queen
       Most lofty, most lovely, most delicate stag of the sea,
         Now nothing but jaggings of iron encrusted with shells'. . . ."
                                    (The Wanderer, by John Masefield.)

337. The JAVA was old before the first clipper was launched.

ones, like the *Edwin Fox* in Picton and the *Java* off Gibraltar, since it was fascinating to view the old stern windows: the massiveness of their construction, and so on, but I suspect that, for those who gave them more than a second glance and who went aboard, there was some atavistic longing to touch the memories of the past. If ships had memories and could speak, what tales could have been told!

The *Java* was old before the Malaga hulks were conceived, for she had been built in 1811 of prime Burmese teak, and commissioned in 1813 for the Hon. East India Company, with 30 guns. She was their last ship, trading to India and China, and also being chartered to the British Government for trooping and the carriage of ordnance. Finally, after 77 years as a hulk, she was broken up, but in that long period alone she had seen innumerable changes in all sorts and shapes of ships. Perhaps it was a pity she did not live a few years longer, when the ship preservers might have got their hands on her, for not only was she of enormous historic interest but, with her teak hull, would have needed much less maintenance than many of the unsuitable vessels which *are* being preserved and which

338. The FORTUNA, ex-MACQUARRIE ex-MELBOURNE passing Gravesend in 1906.

must inevitably fail for lack of funds on this score, unless purism is thrown to the winds and they are made into museums – in effect.

When square-rigged ships were commonplace, they did not always receive the attention they deserved, and probably few people in Gravesend Reach recognized in the Norwegian barque *Fortuna,* as she towed past with her fore t'gallant mast gone in 1906, the last of Green's Blackwall Line. A closer look at the stern windows might have provided a clue. Built in 1875, she was actually the last square-rigger built on the Thames and, since surplus man-o'-war plates were used in her construction, she may well have been the strongest ever built. Then she was the *Melbourne,* famous as a wool and passenger clipper, only to become equally famous as Devitt & Moore's sail-training ship *Macquarrie,* and Captain Corner's splendid photograph of her in this role is so well-known that there is no occasion to reproduce it here. This picture (Pl. 338) was taken shortly after she had been sold to Johan Bryde of Sandefjord, being converted to a barque beforehand. It has been recorded that her mizzen was in one piece, but the photograph disproves this.

Three years later she was sold to the Wallarah Coal Company and Pl. 339 shows her in her last, ignominious role as a coal hulk, alongside one of the Clan Line fleet in Melbourne. She should not be confused with the Norwegian full-rigger *Fortuna,* formerly James Nourse's coolie ship *Ems,* which was burnt off the Irish coast in 1927.

· Troubles could be relatively transient, as was the case with the *Minnie A. Caine* at Corporation Wharf at Port Adelaide in 1917. Of 880 tons and built by Moran Bros in 1900 and owned by Nelson's of San Francisco, her chief claim to fame lay in providing some of the inspiration for the Cappy Ricks stories. She had already been salved from a stranding on Smith Island in 1901, and was finally burnt for her metal after being blown ashore near Santa Monica in 1939.

The steel barque *Penang* was built in 1905 as the *Albert Rickmers,* and was not the same vessel as the earlier four-master of that name which became the *Herzogin Sophie Charlotte.* Rickmers, of Bremen, had a large fleet of mainly full-built vessels and this one was no exception but, at 2,046 GRT, was probably under-canvassed for her size.

After running out East like most of the fleet, she was bought by Laeisz of Hamburg for the nitrate trade in 1911 and re-named *Penang*. In the difficult times for German shipping during the First World War she was sold to J. H. Backmann of Bremen in 1917, but confiscated as war reparations, though then bought back to Bremen by Balhinaur, who soon sold her to Grimen of Hamburg who, in turn, sold her to J. Nurminen of Helsingfors in 1920. Four years later, after this chequered ownership, she came into the Mariehamn fleet of Gustaf Erikson under whose flag she remained until she was sunk in 1940.

The First World War played havoc with all tonnage, sail or steam, but there were few enough square-riggers still in trade by 1939 and, although the effects of Hitler's War were to deplete their numbers, this was rather because they were rigged down, left to rot, or lost their identities. Of the few lost by enemy action, one was the *Penang,* which loaded grain in South Australia at the rate of 130/- per ton - a rate which would have seemed incredible a year previously when most of the surviving sailers were swinging at anchor for weeks in Spencer Gulf waiting for a freight which would show any profit at all, finally loading at around 25/- per ton. It was tempting enough to load at this freight rate, but whether it was

339. *The FORTUNA eking out existence as a coal hulk.*

340. *The MINNIE A. CAINE at Corporation Wharf, Adelaide, in 1917.*

341. Loaded with grain the PENANG, painted grey, swings up into the wind to anchor after clewing up sail and heaving to for orders off Falmouth.

wise to send a barque right into the war zone – whatever the profit – might be queried. In the event, she was approaching Queenstown at the end of her passage when she was torpedoed by the U-140 and lost with all hands.

Pls. 346–7 are unique, if poor in quality, and show her sinking. In the conditions which obviously obtained, it might be supposed that lives would have been saved. It looks uncommonly as though she had also been subject to shell-fire, though this cannot be confirmed. One presumes that, as a war-time precaution, her boats were griped outboard and, in any case, sailing ships' boats were not always launched, or capable of being launched, as quickly as might be thought in normal circumstances. Equally, being a big shell with no transverse bulkheads, as previously stated, a sailing ship *does* sink very quickly indeed once she is badly holed.

This vessel had water-ballast tanks which filled very slowly. When leaving dry-dock in London in 1932 the dock was filled too quickly and before her tanks were filled, with the result that, had the master of the *Pamir* who happened to be aboard not taken very prompt action, she

342. The rape of a clipper ship – the SAMUEL PLIMSOLL as a hulk in Fremantle.

343. Sails shining in the summer sun, the PENANG tows through the Barrow Deep in 1934 bound from London towards Mariehamn.

344. After discharging a cargo of guano from the Seychelles, the PENANG leaving New Plymouth in 1940 for Port Victoria, in South Australia, to load her last cargo.

345. The PENANG (right) in her home port of Mariehamn, with the WINTERHUDE outside her. Both ships were originally units of the Rickmers fleet, the WINTERHUDE being the MABEL RICKMERS. Note the local galeass in the foreground.

346.

347. Two pictures which need no caption – of the PENANG sinking.

would have gone right over, as, indeed, she did in London during a gale in 1926. She almost went over once in 1931 in Copenhagen Sound, for she had grounded and, to get off, had pumped out her tanks. The odd thing about the ship was that water had to be pumped in to the tanks, since there were no inlet valves, and, having got off and anchored, the master decided to get under weigh to steal a march on the *Ponape* which was wind-bound nearby. However, the pump failed and, in bitter and hard weather, the barque was almost sailing on her side until, after a hair-raising interval, she succeeded in coming to anchor again, although cracking one of her hawse-pipes in the process. It was a night when the vessel might well have been lost but, once again, the circumstances can be clearly attributed to human error (or mis-judgement) and not to the ship.

Preceding the *Penang,* the first square-rigger casualty of the last war was the *Olivebank,* a fine four-masted barque which had been built for Andrew Weir's 'Bank' Line in 1892 and was sold to Norway in 1913, having four owners under this flag, the last of whom named her *Caledonia,* a name she bore until she was bought by Captain Gustaf Erikson in 1924, when she was re-named *Olivebank*.

She had discharged a cargo of wheat at Barry, and sailed on 29 August, 1939, proceeding down the Bristol Channel and up the English Channel, homeward-bound to her home port – Mariehamn in the Åland Islands. News of the outbreak of war was heard on a small personal radio and a council was held on board. Some men voted for turning back and sailing round the north of Scotland: one voice voted for sailing to the Canaries and staying there, but the wind was fair, which is always a cogent argument in a sailing vessel, and she proceeded on towards the North Sea.

Off Dover, she was hailed by a British destroyer, which told her to stop, but was answered that this was not possible in so fresh a wind in the Straits, whereupon she was told to make fast her sails and that she would be towed into Southampton. However – and unfortunately as it proved – Captain Granith obtained permission to proceed on his voyage. Nothing was said of minefields and, in the event, it was a wrong decision – viewed with hindsight. She sailed on into the North Sea, through shattered lifeboats and much other wreckage, until, on 8 September, when some 100 miles off the Danish coast, a mine was sighted right ahead.

The ship was taken down three points, but then there were many mines seen and, almost immediately, there was a violent explosion. Several yards crashed to the deck as the ship listed heavily to port and began to sink – fast. An empty ship is even more vulnerable than a loaded one being, to all intents and purposes, one vast, empty shell. Some men were injured and there was no time to launch a boat, so those hands who could jumped overboard. Some men managed to cling on to floating wreckage, and then a spar – the fore upper topsail yard – stuck up out of the water for about 3 metres. Seven men managed to reach it and lashed themselves on, one of them with a crushed foot. There they were, lashed by spray,

348. The OLIVEBANK being passed at sea by the Lamport & Holt liner VOLTAIRE.

bitterly cold, without food or water, for two days and a night before being rescued by the Esbjerg fishing boat *Talona.*

It was a sad affair. I not only knew the ship well, but all her crew since, when in the *Pommern,* we had lain long with her in South Australia that year and then made sail home together, being in close company three times and sighting her a fourth time. Indeed, some of her men were old shipmates. She was a vessel I had encountered on a number of occasions, one of them being in 1932 when she was lying in Gravesend Reach ahead of the *Archibald Russell* and *Alastor* and astern of the U.S. training steamer *Maine.* (This was on the same voyage as her encounter with the *Favell,* page 44). It is surprising how many incidents occur, even in port, which are never seen ashore. Åke Rosenius, who was in the ship that voyage, recalls how half the crew were allowed ashore, and told to be back to meet the boat at a certain time. In the event, a young Dane named Hansen missed the boat and, being a good swimmer and not appreciating the rate of the tide in the steam, hid his clothes ashore and struck out for his ship.

When the hands turned out in the morning, he was not present, and those aboard the *Olivebank* only realized his predicament when they saw a crowd of men aboard the American steamer staring with obvious interest over their foc's'le head. Using binoculars, to see what was causing their curiosity, they discovered that they were all gazing at a naked, shivering figure on the buoy — Hansen — without apparently doing anything to get him aboard. In passing, it may be remarked that there can be few more uncomfortable places to spend a night than when naked on a buoy in a strong tideway, washed by the wake of passing ships (and Gravesend Reach was a busy waterway in those days), and that it was no light matter to get onto — and stay on — it anyway!

349. the OLIVEBANK after being passed by the POMMERN on her last passage home from Australia. The fore and main braces of a four-master lead in to the bulwarks but, due to the curvature of the hull, those of the mizzen lead to a bumkin, which can be seen projecting from the POMMERN's side, level with the OLIVEBANK's foresail.

350. *In this view of Adelaide in the 1880s, there are no big ships to be seen, yet spars dominate the scene.*

Anyone who has advanced this far into this book will be well aware that those responsible for it take exception to the phrase 'Tall Ship' which is in such common currency in relation to the school-ships and small vessels which consort with them. A generation or so ago it would have ranked as a social gaffe of the same order as speaking of 'Horse Riding' – another 'Non-U' expression which is insidiously gaining its place in language.

The height of a ship is comparative, and it may be argued that a vessel is lofty in relation to her hull rather than in comparison with another. Thus a small, skysail-yard brig might be deemed to be loftier than a bald-headed four-master, although the latter would extend her trucks much higher into the air. If sailing ships had feelings, it is difficult to believe that

351. The ubiquitous LAWHILL, run by the South African government during the last World War, under her Finnish captain, Artur Söderlund, became the last square-rigger to load in Adelaide, seen here with local ketches alongside.

they enjoyed being in port, often in conditions of squalor, but it was in such surroundings that they were seen by the majority of people and, because their age was before that of the modern architects who have inflicted so many high-rise structures and skyscrapers on civilization in almost all the great ports of the world, their spars became landmarks which projected above almost all the buildings of their time. This was true almost up to the time of their demise before the 1939–45 War, and it was only in such places as Port Blakely (Pl. 352), where they lay against a backcloth of equally high forest, or where there was a range of hills behind them, that their spars did not dominate the scene.

Indeed, in most ports the masts and spars of ships were so relatively high that they could be seen from a long way off, and it was sad when, in recent years, many of the surviving school-ships were assembled in New

352. Port Blakely, in the days of sail, matched its pine forests ashore with the steel forests of the masts and spars of the square-riggers which came to load the lumber from the saw-mills ashore. In this picture, the white four-master with her stern to the camera is the German LISBETH.

353. In a picture of very poor quality, more than fifty small schooners with the odd ketch leave Falmouth together. Such sights used to be commonplace.

York to pass up the harbour, to find that they were dwarfed by the skyscrapers ashore. It conjured up little of the past (although New York was an exceptional port in the beginning of tall buildings), since all the perspective was awry. So, when the ships rallied in Oslo's Piperviken, they were similarly dwarfed by the monstrous masses of the city's Town Hall. This is a problem which presents itself (or which *should* present itself) to those who seek to preserve ships, since to provide the desired effect, they should be viewed clear of tall and massive buildings, which seldom impinged on dockland areas in the past, save only for the odd grain silo: the occasional factory chimney and other very isolated erections.

Many ports were mainly anchorages, where the ships did not go alongside to any extent – the tea clippers in the Min River: the West Coast nitrate ports (on the whole), and others. There the vessels were not usually viewed in juxtaposition with the buildings ashore and, in the more crowded anchorages, created memorable spectacles.

354. Now painted black, the LISBETH makes sail off the Columbia River bar, glad enough to be getting back to sea. Originally the PENDRAGON CASTLE, owned by the Lancaster Ship-owners of Liverpool, she was built by Williamsons of Workington in 1891 and, with her two immediate sisters, the PINDOS and EUSEMERE, made a great reputation. In 1899 she was sold to H. H. Schmidt of Hamburg who re-named her and, after being allocated to France after the war, was bought back to Hamburg by Claus Hinrichsen, and broken up in 1927.

Perhaps the most famous – and justly famous – of all ports was Sydney's Circular Quay, both because it really was circular in form in those days (and not a series of short piers, as it is today) and because it berthed some of the most thoroughbred vessels of the whole sailing ship era. Probably there was no other port where one could see so many pedigree clippers, undiluted by more mundane vessels, at any one time. Today the area is still colourful, with the ferries berthing there and, in the interim, it has had steamers and the transition vessels when sailing vessels had auxiliary engines and steamers had auxiliary sails, but Pl. 355 shows the Aberdeen White Star clipper *Star of Peace,* with her green hull and single topsails, lying in the foreground. Built in 1855 by Walter Hood, the famed clipper builder, and hulked in 1892/3, she was broken up in 1895. Behind her, with painted ports, is the *Duncan Dunbar* – a Blackwall frigate of 1,374 NRT built in 1857, which was later wrecked on the Rocas Reef, off Brazil, in 1865. The two other vessels are of the same vintage and pedigree.

Pl. 356 was taken a little later, in 1871, and shows, on the left, another Aberdeen White Star clipper – the *Maid of Judah* with the company's white lower-masts – and one must use imagination to conjure up the smart effect over the green hull with the gold stripe. Most of the Aberdeen White Star clippers took their names from ancient Greek history – *Miltiades, Aristides, Thermopylae* and the like, but some had names with Jewish connotations to attract the Jewish merchants. Over her stern, on the other side, is the famous *Sobraon:* in the foreground the *Duke of Sutherland* in which Conrad was serving when he met the original of the 'Nigger', who became James Wait in the novel: astern of the *Sobraon* is Dunbar's frigate-built Blackwaller, the *La Hogue,* which later came under Devitt and Moore: Rose's *Windsor Castle* and Devitt & Moore's *Hawkesbury.* The other ships are not positively identified but . . . what a collection! It may not be a matchless photograph, but it is pure history!

It has been pointed out elsewhere that ships became squarer in their configuration as they became bigger, and it is a fact that many of the clippers were as lofty as their larger successors – the big carriers, but the latter, in virtue of their more massive scale, gave a greater impression of a 'forest of masts and spars'. There were so many ports and so many ships that a review of only a fraction of them would fill many volumes. Perhaps

355. *The STAR OF PEACE at Sydney's Circular Quay in 1871.*

356. *Thoroughbred clippers at Circular Quay.*

357. For all its fame latterly, Port Victoria in Spencer Gulf was a bleak sort of place in reality, with the ships lying at anchor and little enough ashore. Here, in 1918, a load of wheat hauls out, with a dog atop of it, for some square-rigger. Inevitably, the horse-drawn carts were replaced by internal combustion engines.

358. The Chilean nitrate port of Antofagasta was one where many square-riggers could be seen at one time. (And see Pl. 206.)

359. The Norwegian barque CAMILLA, of 1875, was the first ship to use the Nouvelles Maritimes at Ostend on 9 September, 1904, which is why she is dressed, but the occasion does not appear to have attracted much interest!

360. Hamburg was always full of sailing ships in their era, and is readily identifiable by the big, wooden dolphins, but . . .

361. *. . . it was not necessarily confined to the bigger vessels, and . . .*

362. *With her port anchor dropped and the tug's hawser made fast to her quarter, the CRAIGISLA prepares to swing round in Cape Town Docks. She was a sister to the LIMENA and built by Doxford's in 1891 for J. Nicholls. Of 1,040 tons, she later wore Norwegian colours, under the ownership of E. Monsen & Co.*

363. ...ships of all sorts from over the world were to be found in Hamburg: the vessels owned in the port being as fine as any of them.

364. Table Mountain and its 'table-cloth' may dwarf the barque with her upper yards sent down and the full-rigger with painted ports alongside the mole, but they stand higher than the buildings ashore in Cape Town.

Calcutta is one that received less than its fair meed of attention over the years. It was a port which, on the whole, received less thoroughbred ships, but at the same time vessels which merit attention, and of it an old master of the *Glenorchy* once wrote:

> *From Garden Reach to Esplanade they lay in serried ranks,*
> *   Those old Calcutta traders, the "Falls" and "Brocklebanks".*
> *The "Bens" and "Glens", the "Fernie" ships, and others as well known,*
> *   With Jimmy Nourse's coolie ships, the SHEILA, ERNE and RHONE.'*

in a fine poem of nostalgia cataloguing so many of the vessels he knew. Indeed, Garden Reach, off the Calcutta Esplanade, could be so crowded with fine ships that one might wonder how those berthed on the inside tiers were ever shifted! Perhaps the ships there did not always look their best, since it was customary to send down the upper yards: it being mandatory in the sou'west monsoon and common practice in the Nor'east monsoon as well against the contingency of the odd cyclone which, on occasion, caused great carnage amongst the ships in port. There were other moorings in the river, one being reserved for the country craft, but all were fundamentally the same until the docks at Kidderpore came to be built, but it was never a port with much aesthetic appeal due to its overcrowding ashore: its squalor and filth; its 'bromley' kites and vultures, the myriad flies – especially in the Kidderpore area, the corpses floating in the Hooghly itself and, indeed, the sheer disenchantment of mooring there, with anchor cables crossed fore and aft, together with the whole approach to the port, with its attendant difficulties.

Ships in port at Christmas-time often displayed a miniature Christmas tree or pine sprig at each yard-arm, which was easy enough in some Puget Sound or Scandinavian ports. In Pl. 366 the *Hereford* has not only managed to scrounge leafy branches of some sort, but gone a little better with a large printed message on her fore upper topsail yard. Whereas most of Nourse's ships were named after rivers, this was not always true of those which they bought in and the *Hereford* was such a one, having been built in 1869 by Elders and bought by Nourse's about 1880. She was sold to Norway ten years later, being lost off the Horn in 1907.

Many places could show a great number of vessels in port together and,

365. *George Duncan's INDIAN EMPIRE lies inside Eyre, Evans' VELLORE in Garden Reach. Astern of the INDIAN EMPIRE is the ALBYN, a four-masted barque owned by J. Houston of Liverpool which went missing in 1921 when owned by J. Zachariassen of Uusikaupunki.*

366. *The HEREFORD at Christmas time at the Esplanade moorings off Calcutta.*

367. Square-riggers in Bristol, circa 1908.

even though many were small, they were nevertheless landmarks as a rule, but it did not take many vessels of the larger sort to attract attention – witness the three ships lying in Bristol amongst the paddle excursion steamers in Pl. 367. The date can be placed as around 1908, since the *Kilmory* (left) was sold to Norway in that year and later re-named *Cassius* and *Asgerd,* while Fernie's barque *Cleomene* alongside her was sold to the Italians at almost the same time to become the *Mincio,* while the four-masted barque *Viking,* beyond, had been built the previous year. The *Cleomene,* of 1,797 tons, had originally been a full-rigger, and the stepped topgallant-mast can be discerned on the mizzen.

In small outports a single vessel could stand out in the landscape like a Gothic cathedral in a town ashore, particularly if she was so lofty a vessel as the *Herzogin Sophie Charlotte,* and in such places she would be the focal point for the Sunday promenade – a custom now largely forgotten in an age when television tends to atrophy peoples' legs on Sundays. Could all those landsmen who so admired the sailing ships in port have

368. By no means down to her marks, the HERZOGIN SOPHIE CHARLOTTE looks to be what she was – a very lofty ship though, at 2,541 tons, she was not a really big one.

369. Maybe there was not much to do on Sunday mornings in Port Lincoln, but the sailing ships were always an excuse for a promenade to the jetty and, when so lofty a ship as the Nord Deutscher Lloyd training ship HERZOGIN SOPHIE CHARLOTTE was alongside, it became pretty crowded!

seen them swinging down the trade in all the glory of their curving canvas, shining in the sun, or glimpsed her, so relatively reduced in size in the whole elemental scheme of things as she made – or fought – her passage away down in the Southern Ocean, it would have introduced a totally different dimension into their view of them. For some men who served in the ships, ports seemed to hold superficial attractions but, for ships, they held none!

370.

371. The HERZOGIN SOPHIE CHARLOTTE was probably without peer amongst the four-masted sail-training ships, but had been built for Rickmers of Bremerhaven as the ALBERT RICKMERS. Later owned by Schlüter & Maack of Hamburg, she passed to Norway but, after a long lay-up in the slump, her good looks could not save her and she was scrapped. Erikson considered her, but . . . that was all.

372. Molicieros moored alongside.

Half a mile away from the Torreira beach whence the *Xavega* operates, on the calm and oily lagoon of Aveiro, there is another boat with a rearing bow and a high stern, although with no chance of a capsize in the boiling surf of the Atlantic. Has it illusions of grandeur above its station – that of a humble seaweed dredger; carrier of hay or reed for bedding, a muck spreader? She is a farmer's boat, if ever there was one.

Why on earth should the bows of a seaweed dredger rear up so much? and why have three times as much rudder above the water as below it? And why that curious double gunwale? Is this all tradition, merely because they have always been built that way? If so, it is crazy. But it is not so, and it never has been. Farmers they may be, but fools they are not.

The *Moliciero* dredges for *molice* – a stringy grass-like weed that grows from the bottom of the Aveiro lagoon and is harvested for fertilizer or, more accurately, to add humus to the dry, sandy soil. To raise it, the boat is driven forward by the wind with rakes reaching down to the bottom: the shafts being jammed into the gunwale so that the tines meet

373. Sailing with a fair wind and a freeboard that would have made Samuel Plimsoll blench!

the weed at an aggressive, grasping angle. Four rakes are generally used and the crew numbers two. As each rake becomes clogged and full of weed, so it is hauled to the surface and the load dragged over the low, wide gunwale into the flat bottom of the boat.

Molicieros are 55 feet long and 9 feet wide. They have no keel and their ribs are cut from grown pine. Their construction closely resembles that of their neighbours, the *Xavegas*. Carrying five tons of sopping seaweed, they are big boats with a heavy cargo and can be five miles from home when the wind drops and, like all craft that fish or dredge using the wind, the time comes when they have to work uphill again before the next series of runs. If the wind is light, even with the help of its large lee-boards, tacking will be slow and laborious, so it is much easier to point the bows into the wind, drop the sail and pole the craft.

The boat is heavy, the man is light and the water deep. Poling is all a matter of angles. How much easier it would be to punt or quant if the bottom sloped or if one had a wall against which to push the feet, or up

374. Looking down on a light moliciero as the 'poler' leaves the double gunwale to mount the high bow. There is little enough freeboard even in this condition, but the lagoon is sheltered.

which to walk backwards, for then the shove could be made with the body horizontal, or even pointing slightly downwards, and the boat would get away to a flying start and, once moving, the rest would be easy. That is the secret — or half the secret — of the *Moliciero's* bows, for the poler will walk to the top of the slope, as high as he possibly can and facing aft, and will lean at such an angle that his feet, which will move the boat, will not tend to lift in the air as he pushes on the pole, but will force the boat forward with the maximum efficiency.

If the wind is too gentle or the weed too thick, that slope to the bows will make all the difference to the power that can be applied to forward motion. Then the weight of the boat and its cargo will help as the poler moves aft along the wide gunwale, shoving as he goes. Then comes the disadvantage of quanting — the recovery — for man and pole must now move to the bows again and, lightly as he tiptoes forward, his movement is the reverse of helpful until he is once again at the top of that perilous slope, by which time, if the rakes are doing their job, the boat will be stationary again.

Thus the man and his son will carry on late into the evening until the last of the on-shore breeze has died and, perhaps, the off-shore one has failed to materialize, with the boat still five miles from home. It is only then that the other half of the secret of the bow reveals itself for, below that sloping deck and above that rearing bottom, there is a snug, dry cabin well above the oozing water slopping in the bilges.

Finally, that great blade of a rudder, which can be controlled from anywhere in the boat by a continuous rope running from yoke-arm to yoke-arm and through a block in the bows; a rudder which is a full thirteen square feet in the air and only four square feet below the water. The solution to this is easier, for we have a flat-bottomed boat, often in water too shallow for the leeboards to grip and, of necessity, with her high, wind-catching bow. Thus the high stern and rudder are part of the penalty to be paid if the bows are not to be blown away and the boat turned round by every tiresome zephyr, for they are merely to balance the lateral resistance to the wind and they do, incidentally, provide a dry place to sit when sailing.

Has some of the magic left the *Moliciero* because, after all, she is seen to be but a purely functional dredger of seaweed? Has some of the

375. Standing high in the bow, a man prepares for a quant. Note the cabin entrance in the decorated bulkhead.

376. In an age of container ships it is, perhaps, refreshing to see such methods of discharging survive. Note the exquisite carving on the yoke board between the two oxen.

377. *Decoration on ships' hulls has taken many forms down the ages. This moliciero strikes an original note.*

romance left the *Xavega* because its great sweeping stem is no more than a safety device? Has some of the majesty left those enormous oars? – and how many more riddles could have been solved for the archaeologist if only he could have seen it all happening?

378. *While one man retrieves the clogged rakes, the other quants with his body near to the horizontal. Two more rakes are working on the starboard side: others lie stowed over the port quarter.*

379. *With the lee-board — normally alongside the mast — hitched up out of the way, the moliço is discharged into an ox-cart.*

380. *The distinctive profile of a moliciero as she lies in calm.*

The Norwegian polar research vessel *Polaris* was purchased by Sir Ernest Shackleton for £14,000 in 1913 and re-named *Endurance*. She went down to the Weddell Sea, but was there beset and crushed by ice. The subsequent journey of her crew to Elephant Island, and the voyage thence by six of them in the whaleboat *James Caird* (now preserved in the National Maritime Museum at Greenwich) to South Georgia, together with the subsequent scaling of the mountains there by Shackleton, Worsley and Crean to obtain help from the Stromness whaling station on the other side of the island, are not only history, but still rank amongst the major epics of the sea.

Years later, I sailed in a schooner with both Frank Worsley, who had been master of the *Endurance*, and with Joseph Stenhouse, who took over command of the other expedition vessel, the *Aurora*, in the Ross Sea and brought her through *her* epic drift in ice; rigged her famous jury rudder after the ice had shorn off the original one, and finally arrived back in New Zealand, battered and short-handed. For my part, I have never had any illusions about that expedition or its men. It failed in its objectives, but its story, so ably recounted in print by both Shackleton and Worsley, should be compulsory reading for everyone, whether young or old.

One of my life-long regrets is that the outbreak of war in 1939 prevented me from sailing in another vessel with Worsley and Stenhouse, for never did I achieve such understanding of the sea and ships as when under their tutelage. 'Charismata' is defined as 'favours specially vouchsafed by God', and thus is a word hardly ever to be used at all, but I would not hesitate to apply it to them though, the schooner being a captious and wayward vessel, I never saw God vouchsafe to either of them the ability to make her stay!

I warrant that, had they lived a generation or so later, their ships would have had no unions (which they would not have tolerated anyway) but that they would nevertheless have been happy ones, with fine style and run to the highest standards of seamanship. Shackleton had served in the White Star full-rigger *Hoghton Tower*, Stenhouse in Andrew Weir's four-master *Springbank*, and Worsley in the New Zealand clippers *Wairoa, Rakaia, Waimate* and others. When these two latter signed on their crew for the schooner, every man had been in square-rig. One does

381. *The CHRISTIANIA frozen in, when a ship gets colder . . . and colder . . . and colder.*

not need square-rig experience to sail a schooner, but the Antarctic was the goal and there was good reason for their decision. We shall need such men when the oil runs out and wind — coupled with determination — calls the tune.

It is difficult to conjure up the so-called 'Romance of Sail' in freezing weather. Few sailing ships had a bogey stove in their foc's'les and, in general, any form of heating was totally lacking. No man, for his own safety, could wear gloves aloft and, in a ship with steel rigging and jackstays, their touch could be well-nigh intolerable. When a ship became frozen in, the cold seemed to intensify almost every day. Between snow squalls, I once saw a Banks schooner flying before the weather off Cape Hatteras like a wraith, for all her rigging was solid ice. Sailing with the speed of blown spume, she was gone almost as soon as she was sighted and, within four hours, we were in a hurricane force wind of over 100 knots. She was reefed right down, it is true, but nothing could be worked

382. The ENDURANCE on her way south on her fateful voyage. Note the patent reefing gear on the fore topsail.

383. Frozen up: only tatters of canvas left, the PRINSESSAN tows into Raumo in 1939.

in those conditions. My ship was a mass of stalactitic icicles which thickened and lengthened with every sea that broke over her. The schooner was in the same case and, even had it been possible temporarily to clear the ice from a single block, it would have been unworkable within seconds. I often wonder how she fared that wild night.

Thus, in Pl. 383, the schooner *Prinsessan* met with a severe winter gale in the Baltic in 1939 and in her case, too, all the blocks were so frozen up that her sails, seen in tatters, had to be cut away with knives. In the picture, she is being towed into the safety of Raumo harbour, the very stance of the two men forward enhancing the scene of misery. Anders Westermark, who supplied the picture, says that when his father, who was mate, went below and tried to take off his boots, the feet came away in his hands: the rest of them being frozen solid to his legs! Many such vessels as this one traded in the Baltic, the *Prinsessan* having been built in the post-war boom of 1920 at a small shipyard in Borga, on the south coast of Finland. She was a wooden vessel of 199 NRT and a deadweight of 400 tons, with a capacity for 140 standards of timber, being equipped with a small auxiliary 60 h.p. engine. Measuring 127', with a beam of

384. Sunk by a U-boat the next year, the SETH JR lies in the ice at Louisburg in 1916.

29.2′, she was later owned in Raumo and given a more powerful 120 h.p. engine which reduced her net tonnage marginally. By 1939 she was bald-headed, as shown, with small radio topmasts for receiving only.

One might say that becoming frozen in was an occupational risk of Canadian schooners. Oddly enough, the *Seth Jr* (Pl. 384) was of just the same NRT as the *Prinsessan*, but was built in the last pre-war wave of tern schooner-building at Liverpool, N.S. in 1910, and although sold to Panamanian interests was run with a Canadian crew throughout.

The 508-ton Norwegian barque *Christiania* is frozen in the River Dvina, which flows into the White Sea at Archangel, in Pl. 381. Men who sailed in the Murmansk convoys in the last war will appreciate just how much romance was to be found in sailing round North Cape and along the Murman coast in a barque like this. Originally she had been built at Medford, Mass. in 1858 and was previously named *Ottone* and *Nautilus* before she was bought into Horten in 1866, being subsequently owned in Kristiania, Tønsberg and Grimstad before being finally abandoned at sea in 1895. There was nothing very exceptional about this as a life-span for a ship of those times, as will be apparent from perusal of this book alone,

385. *The steam whaler ESQUIMAUX was built in 1865 by Alexander Stephens, creator of so many lovely clippers, and was 593 tons, measuring 157.3 × 29.5 × 18.5', being owned by D. Bruce of Dundee. She was working until well into the 1890s and here, reflected in the water, is seen 'on the job' in the far north.*

but it is nevertheless illuminating to compare the useful lives of the sailing ships of those times with the life-spans of the multi-million pound vessels of today. There was no such thing as 'built-in obsolence' in the days of sail!

'But', the reader will ask, *'are there no illustrations of the ENDURANCE in the ice?'* The answer is *'Not here'*. There are many, very fine ones, and of the vessel finally disappearing into the Antarctic depths, from the expert camera of Herbert Ponting, which must be well-known to all those who have read that saga of the sea. For those who do not know it, I have said that it is compulsory reading!

386. *With snow on her decks and snow ashore, the PLUS tows out of a Baltic port – probably Karlsborg or Båtskärnäs – just before the real onset of winter. It looks well enough in the photograph, but the man on the upper topsail yard would not have viewed it in quite the same way!*

There was something of a misnomer about the word 'split-wood', although it provided a trade for innumerable sailing craft within the Baltic and on the short-sea routes to the United Kingdom and the Continent, since the cargo concerned was generally the off-cuts from the Scandinavian saw-mills, and was brought over as firewood or for making cheap furniture, boxes and similar articles. Often enough the craft were referred to by the derogatory term 'firewood barques' but, more commonly, as 'onkers'. This really derived from the windmill pump with which so many of the wooden vessels in the trade were equipped, and which was held to make the noise: 'onkurr-onkurr' when in action, though of course there was nothing exclusive to the firewood vessels about windmills, and they were to be seen in the ice barques and many others. Indeed, vessels engaged in the trade were not necessarily wedded to it, and might well carry any other more remunerative freight which offered.

The ships in the firewood trade comprised a big variety: some were relatively modern craft built especially for the run; others were older which had made their mark in their day, but which had descended to this somewhat lowly station on account of age or because they were too small

387. The PLUS lying off Woolwich in the Thames.

to make viable deep-sea voyages in conditions changed so much since they were built.

Thus the *Plus*, already noticed in Pl. 386, had been built for the Laeisz 'Flying P' Line of Hamburg and had taken her berth regularly for the Horn passage to Chile and back until she was sold to Frederikstad in 1908, but latterly she was owned by Hugo Lundquist of Mariehamn. After some years in the split-wood trade she was wrecked in a blizzard outside Mariehamn when returning home to lie up after discharging a cargo of guano in London from the Seychelles in 1933. She was a smart-looking barque, painted light grey for many years but latterly, as she had started, was black. Pl. 390 was taken from the deck of a liner as she was starting to loose sail in Gravesend Reach and she is thus a little foreshortened, whilst her royal yards have been sent down and she is light ship. Minutes before, with yards beautifully squared, she had attracted much favourable comment as she passed Tilbury.

There were a variety of rigs to be seen in the 'onker' fleet, and one of the most modern was the *Dione* (Pl. 391) which was built in Åland in 1923 for

388. The PLUS towing up the Thames with split-wood. Thames barges beat across the river astern of her.

389. The Finnish barquentine NIMROD flying light in the Baltic. Built in 1890 at Levonme and owned by John Nurminen at Raumo, she was very typical of many vessels in the trade.

390. The PLUS towing down Gravesend Reach and starting to loose sail. Her royal yards are merely sent down: she was never stripped of them.

391. The wooden barquentine DIONE in Northfleet Hope (River Thames) with a cargo of split-wood.

392. The ESTHONIA was a barquentine of 800 tons d.w. (481 GRT) built by A. Wammus at Gutsanbach in 1921, and was bought by Gustaf Erikson at public auction at Frederikstad in 1927. Sailing in the North Sea and Baltic 'onker' trade, she was wrecked near Orskär in October 1936, when bound from Hernosand towards Portsmouth, soon after this picture was taken.

393.   The ALASTOR, painted white, still with her main royal.

local owners, passing to Gustaf Erikson in 1934 but, five years later, she was hit at sea by an unidentified steamer and, although towed into Nystad badly damaged, was soon out of the register.

In Pl. 395 the old Norwegian barque *Medusa*, built in 1862, is reducing sail as she makes port. The outer jib is coming down and the men on the downhaul wait until the sheet is slacked off a bit more. Note the portion of the foc's'le head rail which has been removed to handle the anchor. Just before she anchors, she will haul down the other two headsails and the fore upper topsail, to round to under the main upper topsail. Note, too, how beautifully the square sails which are fast have been stowed. It is a mistake to suppose that, because a ship has been cut down in her rig or relegated to a less important trade, she was any less smart in her running than others, for sailing ships were as good as the men who sailed them, even if men were not always as good as their ships! The *Medusa* had been built by W. Briggs & Sons of Sunderland, and was owned by J. F. Andorsen of Mandel, being of 860 NRT and $171.2 \times 34.5 \times 21.2'$.

The *Alastor* boasted a main skysail when she was originally fitted out in

394. Contemporary with the PLUS in the Laeisz Line, the PROMPT was built in 1887 and given double t'gallants so that, when stripped of her royal masts, she looked very stumpy. Owned by Hugo Lundquist of Mariehamn since 1908, she was broken up in 1935.

395. The Norwegian barque MEDUSA.

396. Seen from the FAVELL, the barque LOCH LINNHE makes sail in the Öresund.

Shoreham for R. & H. Penney and sent out on the Colonial run. Latterly she was owned by the Consul Schröder and registered at Hangö, although many of her shares were owned in London. Gradually she became shorn of her royals, but was a frequent visitor to the Thames. In the early 1920s, and even later, so many artists were depicting square-riggers with white yardarms that many people believed them to be the rule. Finally, Charles R. Patterson, the great American Marine artist who had served many years in sail himself, went into print to disabuse the world of this fallacy, based on his own experience.

He himself had only seen two vessels so painted, and examination of old photographs will demonstrate that he was right. However, there are exceptions to prove every rule, and sometimes a vessel such as the German *Julius*, ex *Hoek van Holland,* would be so painted due to some foible of her master. Thus the *Alastor* suddenly appeared with white yardarms for a short period in the 1930s (Pl. 397) but it was always regarded as an exceptional practice.

397. The ALASTOR with a cargo of firewood and her yard-arms painted white.

398. Barquentines like the Finnish HILDA and . . .

399. . . . such schooners as this, so common around the Baltic and Copenhagen Sound until the 1939 War, were often engaged in the 'onker' trade. One might say that a vessel like this would have been better two-masted, but she would not have been so easy to work. Note that her topmast staysail is set upside down!

400. *A good deal of the split-wood trade was directed towards the Southern Baltic and North Europe. Here the three-masted schooner MAINE of Hamina (Finland) has the Kiel pilot boat alongside as she makes port with a big deck cargo. Her fore gaff topsail is not set, but a makeshift staysail from her main. Her peak halliard arrangement is very clear. Built by A. Sunteo at Veekelaks, she was 155 tons, measuring 133.5 × 30.7 × 12.8′.*

401. The SHAKESPEARE, shown in dry-dock in London, went ashore near Norrskar in the North Quarken Channel in 1930, and broke up two days later. She was bound from Pitea towards the London river with firewood.

402. There were also many topgallant – and other – schooners from the south Swedish ports like Råå. This is the EBBA of 206 tons, built in 1891 by J. H. Halden of Butvenäs and owned by Johan Anderson of Ystad. She measured 102.6 × 25.2 × 9.1'.

403. Said to give the 'onkers' their name, the windmill pump of the barquentine FRIDEBORG, built for the China trade in 1866, is in operation as she lies with her decks piled with split-wood.

404. Sometimes a sailing ship would meet a schooner of very different pedigree in the Baltic. Here the L'AVENIR is in company with the American schooner-yacht VEMA of 234 NRT, built by Burmeister & Wain for G. A. Vetlasan of New York, who also sailed the 12-metre VEMA III.

405. Many of the Baltic trading schooners were functional rather than beautiful.

406. When, in 1933, there was a temporary embargo on Russian timber, Baltic splitwood freights suddenly soared and the grain carriers PARMA, MOZART and LAWHILL brought over a cargo each to the Thames, which was unusual for such large ships. Here the LAWHILL passes the oil installations at Thameshaven.

407. The Finnish barque AHTI of Uusikaupunki discharging firewood off Rochester in 1923, shortly before she was lost. She had been built in 1880 at Tvedestrand as the IMACOS. Her sails are unbent, stopped off and ready to be sent down.

408. The ALASTOR and LINGARD discharging split-wood in the Regents Canal Dock in the Thames. That the former has a jibboom outside her bowsprit and the LINGARD a spike bowsprit gives a clue to their years of building – 1875 and 1893 respectively.

409. *The VIMIERA has just cast off her tug and set sail. The mainsail and crossjack tacks are being bowsed down while men on the topgallant yard are overhauling buntlines.*

People frequently say that they prefer a photograph of a sailing ship to show 'what she really looked like', but this is too facile since any single picture, whether of a ship or of one of the humans who created her, can only tell part of the story. A man can be be both fat and thin in his life-span: he may be clad in cloth of gold or other finery or, if unfortunate, in sack-cloth or, in his natural state, with no clothes at all. He may be clean, or he may be dirty. He may be alternately bearded and clean-shaven. In due time, he may go bald and, as he ages, so his features may become sunken and lined but, whether in one state or another, he will look different in laughter and sadness. How, then, can one photograph portray this man for posterity?

So it is with a ship. She may be loaded or light, as a man might be fat or thin: she might be lying in some filthy dock with her yards cock-billed and braced awry, her hull rust-stained and touched with red lead, or she might be at anchor, freshly painted with yards perfectly squared and in splendid order alow and aloft. The metamorphoses in her appearance were infinite

411. The ARCHIBALD RUSSELL setting sail off the Sunk Lightship (off Harwich) seen from the yacht CARIAD.

410. Seen from fine on the port bow, the VIMIERA has a loftier look about her.

under varying combinations of sail in all the varieties of weather and points of sailing, and even the colour of her hull could affect her looks just as clothes make the man. Even the combinations of sunlight and shadow, or the sombre shades of storm, could affect the recollections of memory, because bright sunlight on sails can make the whole vessel seem more light and ethereal in an instant.

As her life advances, her rigging plan may be reduced but, in both man and ship, the ribs or frames; the backbone or keel, and all the other skeletal components, remain relatively constant, yet only the anatomist or the naval architect has the X-ray eyes to see through the decoration and veneer and, for the rest of us, in the absence of the ships themselves, photographs are the best likenesses that can be produced, always providing that they are accepted to be a good likeness at the moment they were taken, though not necessarily at any other one. Even then, whether with man or ship, there can be much distortion, according to the angle, height and distance at which the camera was held.

It may be argued that a plan is more objective and accurate than any picture and it certainly had infinite advantages to a model-maker. Yet, having used it, he all too often makes so perfect a replica of the original that he fails in his objective, because his model is *too* perfect and frequently better and smarter than the original, thereby losing the true representation for, like the plan on which he based it, it is only seldom that one senses the very personality of the original vessel. A plan of a ship does give a better idea than a scale drawing of the skeleton of a human being, but it is not an unfair analogy and few people wish to preserve the memories of their loved ones by representations of their skeletons!

The camera could sometimes catch the personality of a vessel, but it certainly recorded her mood more accurately. Let no-one sneer at the idea that a sailing ship had a personality. Some vessels exuded their very characters, for better or for worse, and even two sister ships could be utterly different in this respect. Much the same is true of many houses, although it is true that not everybody is attuned to such responses. Moods were a different matter and constantly changed in myriad variations in diverse waters and all manners of weather, as the outward appearance (if not the physical arrangements of houses and rigging) could also change, and it seems, therefore, that to understand 'what she really looked like'',

412. *As a brand new ship, the ARCHIBALD RUSSELL tows down the Clyde from her builder's yard, high in the water and with her staysails still in the stops in which they have just been delivered from the sail loft.*

413. *Deep-loaded and under sail, with her royals mast-headed, her proportions looked different. She maintained painted ports all the time she was owned by Hardies.*

one must be able to see what the ship looked like under all the conditions which she encountered, and this presents difficulties, because pictures taken from without in high gale are few and far between.

Clearly, the further forward or abaft the beam from which the ship is viewed, the loftier she will seem, and from any angle this aspect was enhanced if she was down to her marks rather than light, when the hull bulked larger to the eye in relation to her masts and spars, whilst a picture looking down from a flying machine gave yet another totally different impression, whereas those vessels which were subject to major structural changes often bore little resemblance to their former state.

One of the bigger of the last British sailing companies was that of Captain J. R. Hardie of Glasgow. His vessels were normally given painted ports over a black stripe, below which the hull was grey down to the boot-topping and, latterly, the vessels were named after battle-fields in the Napoleonic wars. Like her sister ships, the *Pyrenees* (which was beached and burnt out on Manga Reva reef and later salved and sailed as the American *Manga Reva* and Clink's *Thistle*, the *Vimiera* was given single topgallants, which looked incomparably better than the double yards which succeeded them, however much more difficult they may have been to handle. She was a successful vessel which was only broken up in 1924 due to slump conditions.

The company launched other four-masters subsequently and the last of them departed from the fairly standard nomenclature, being named *Archibald Russell*. She was, in fact, the last of the many square-riggers built by Russell & Co. of Port Glasgow and was unusual for a sailing ship in being fitted with bilge keels. With her consorts, the *Hougomont* and the three-masted barque *Killoran,* two of Hardie's other vessels, she came under the house-flag of Captain Gustaf Erikson of Mariehamn after the 1914–18 war and, although the *Hougomont* was dismasted south of the Australian coast and condemned in 1933*, the other two were still in trade at the outbreak of the 1939 war, the *Archibald Russell* being caught in Hull after discharging her annual grain cargo. She was rigged down to her lower-masts and remained at Goole during hostilities, having been requisitioned by the British government. After having been moved up to a cheaper berth on the Tyne, she was given back to Erikson, who tried to sell her without success despite one or two schemes which

*Page 305.

414.

415. Two views of the ARCHIBALD RUSSELL under short sail in a blow in the North Sea, taken from the FAVELL.

416. In 1932, Erikson had the ARCHIBALD RUSSELL painted black with light boot-topping. Here she is passing Dover with just enough ballast to get back to the Baltic and with her royals fast, a year or so later.

417. The ARCHIBALD RUSSELL being towed up Gravesend Reach by two tugs in 1932, that on the left being Watkins' famous old seeking tug HIBERNIA. It is apparent how well a white hull suits a long, open-decked square-rigger, but . . .

418. . . . here she is down to her marks and with all sail set as she leaves Spencer Gulf in a light breeze. The angle of view is relatively high, but . . .

419. . . . viewed from almost right ahead and from a low aspect, especially when loaded ship, the impression of height is enhanced.

420. *A different aspect of the ARCHIBALD RUSSELL off the Australian coast.*

were put forward, so she was scrapped in 1949, ten years after she had last been to sea.

It may be that the four-masted barque is over-emphasized in this book and in sea-literature generally, because there were probably not more than five hundred four-masted square-riggers, whether full-rigged or barques, built in the whole world together, and these varied a great deal in hull size and form. This figure was, of course, a miniscule one when set against the vast number of three-masters of various sorts and the veritable hordes of smaller craft, but in general terms they were the biggest and the rig which tended to make the last major survival. Thus there is no apology to be made for concentrating upon them in this section. They were not, for the most part, as fast or as beautiful as the clippers, which were built in a different economic climate, but, again, attention to these thoroughbreds. which were also a very small minority in the total shipping effort, has always been a disproportionate one.

The four-master survived as she did because, above all things else, she

421. The PONAPE in the Channel bound for Rotterdam, with the wind right aft.

was a large carrier and, in those last days with its attendant economic considerations, this was the most useful and viable ship. It may well prove that any large commercial sailing ship of the future may be much improved or even very different in form and rig, but it would be folly to suppose that the lessons of these last big four-masted barques should be neglected because, if the few 5-masted 'freak' ships be excepted, they did represent the ultimate development of the great age of sail.

The Italians only built 34 steel square-riggers and several of them were launched with their masts standing and yards crossed, as in the case of the *Regina Elena* in Pl. 424. The view is an unusually foreshortened – though accurate – view of a vessel, though it stands in great contrast to Pl. 421 which was taken in the Channel when the vessel was under all sail and deep-loaded in 1932. The *Regena Elena* had been bought into the Laeisz Line and named *Ponape*, but became the *Bellhouse* after the first war when under Norwegian registry (though actually owned by Sir James Bell, of Hull), and she reverted to the name *Ponape* when bought by

Gustaf Erikson of Mariehamn from Hugo Lundquist, of the same little port, in 1927.

With the wind aft, as she has in the photograph, the mizzen square sails blanket those on the main, which blanket those on the fore, and in these conditions the staysails were virtually useless and run down as a rule. In this case, there is not a lot of wind and it makes little enough odds but, in a harder wind, with a big following sea, the ship almost invariably steered badly and would yaw perhaps two and a half points each side of her course. In these circumstances the staysails became impossible. Although it was seldom done, square-riggers would probably have done better to tack to leeward: that is, to alter course a point or so to fill all the sails and derive their full driving power, since the increased speed would compensate for the extra distance sailed.

If an artist were to portray a ship running before the weather under foresail, crossjack, six topsails and a main lower topgallant-sail in a moderate gale, he would be much criticized, since the crossjack normally comes in before the mainsail. The *Moshulu* was once running in such conditions in the Southern Ocean when the mainsail was stowed and the crossjack set. While the mainsail had been set, it had blanketed the foresail to some degree, and this sail provides a great 'lift' forward but, once it was taken in and the crossjack set, the foresail took full effect and the ship sailed much more comfortably with no loss of driving power.

Reverting to the *Ponape,* Pl. 422 was taken in 1933 when she was painted black and towing through the Barrow Deep in ballast on her way from London towards Mariehamn. Under five topsails, she ran 65 miles in six hours with the towing hawser in a bight all the way. Courses were seldom set when towing in order to give the helmsman a clear view of the tug. Course has just been changed and the main staysail still needs to be taken over the main stay. 'Why', it may be asked, 'keep the tug when she was not necessary?' The answer is that, at that time, there was little bargaining between tugs and deep-water ships in London, but a contract was made by the agents before they ever arrived, and this included one tug from Gravesend to the Sunk pilot cutter.

Another Italian-built four-master which survived until she was wantonly run down at sea in 1937 was the *Emmanuele Accame* of 2093 tons, which was sold to Sweden in 1912 and successively named *Ferm,*

422.   The PONAPE towing through the Barrow Deep in 1933.

423. The HERZOGIN CECILIE following her tug off Dover with only fore-and-aft canvas set.

Suecia, Elsa Ölander and *C. B. Pedersen*, when she became a sail-training ship, as shown in the front endpaper, when she was setting the triangular courses invented by Captain Bentinck, and which were, in consequence, sometimes called bentincks. Taken from high on the bridge of a steamer, the photograph gives a very different impression of the height of a ship than if – say – it had been taken from sea-level. It will be noted that her mizzen was slightly shorter than the fore and main-masts.

In Pl. 423 the *Herzogin Cecilie,* with only her fore-and-aft canvas set (except the jib topsail) has just picked up her tug, which is out of the picture, though the tow-line is visible. The headsails were of supreme importance and acted as 'steering' sails, much as did the jigger canvas, due to their balancing effects*, but the other staysails were normally of very little use and a survival of the belief – frequently shown to be erroneous – that the more sails that were set the faster the ship would sail. In fact, when set in conjunction with square sails, they tended to

*Page 94.

424. The REGINA ELENA, later BELLHOUSE and later PONAPE, on the stocks at Riva Trigosa in 1903, being built for Pietro Milesi of Genoa. The Italians built 34 steel square-riggers and a number were launched ready rigged.

425. The Norwegian barque SØM setting sail off Cape Henry when bound for the River Plate in 1917 (see page 384).

diminish the effect of the latter, and it was usually found that a vessel made better speed when they were hauled down. In certain conditions they did have a steadying influence, and were frequently the first sails to be set when making sail under tow.

One odd illusion, both in fact and picture, was that a ship which did not have her courses set, but everything else, often looked 'taller' than would otherwise have been the case, especially when viewed from fairly fine on the bow or stern. So it is with the *Søm* in Pl. 425. She was a nicely proportioned barque built by Blohm and Voss in 1892 for Captain N. H. P. Schuldt of Hamburg as the *Antuco*, but was sold to the 'von 1896' Company in 1907, but was renamed *Maco* when bought by Marcus, Jorgensen & Co. of Grimstad in 1912. S. O. Stray of Kristianssand bought her in 1918 and had her when this picture was taken off Cape Henry. She was broken up six years later.

Because a vessel was rigged as a four-masted full-rigged ship, it might be assumed automatically that she was of considerable size. This was true of some of them, such as the *Liverpool* and *Peter Rickmers*, but it did not follow by any means, and many of them were of relatively modest tonnage and so rigged in the fallacious belief (which died hard) that the more canvas that was carried, the faster the ship would go, the argument being precisely the same as that for staysails.

As has also been mentioned, the square sails on the aftermast of a full-rigger often did more harm than good, since the additional driving power was so often counter-acted by the braking effect of the rudder, due to the tendency to carry weather helm. One might suppose, superficially, that, had the sail plan been better designed and the centre of effort further forward, this would not have occurred, but it was not so simple as this. It is broadly true to say that a sailing ship spent more time with foul winds than fair (even if this proportion of wind was not true over the distance made good, because much more time was spent making good a given distance in a foul wind than with a fair one) and it was when the yards were braced on to the backstays that the full-riggers griped the worst.

Indeed, there were never more than 100 vessels rigged in this way, since the four-masted barque was just as fast and more economical. The vessel illustrated is the *County of Peebles,* owned by R. & J. Craig of Glasgow, which did prove to be most successful, to the degree that they followed

426.

427. Two pictures showing the COUNTY OF PEEBLES. It will be seen that she has a single topsail on her jigger, clewing up to its quarters, as does the topgallant sail, while those on the fore, main and mizzen clew up to the yardarms. Her main and mizzen spencer gaffs are also visible.

her with five sisters, and later with six more four-masted full-riggers, albeit the later ones crossed double t'gallants, and this company accounted for a sizeable proportion of the building of this rig. Main and mizzen spencers were a feature of these ships and they were, rather unusually, used to a certain extent, being extremely useful when reaching in a head gale although, of course, the ship would point up no higher than her square sails allowed.

Generally the company was trading to Calcutta and the ships made some fine passages, but they made other voyages too, and the *County of Peebles,* which had been built of iron by Barclay, Curle of Glasgow in 1875, was sold to Chilean owners in 1898 and lost in a hurricane on Takaroa when bound across the Pacific from Caldera in 1905. Sometimes the Craig vessels had painted ports on a solid black hull: sometimes grey beneath the ports, as shown in these illustrations.

When a vessel carried a jibboom outside her bowsprit, it had to be rigged in when docking, for obvious reasons. Rigging it both in and out were relatively quick and simple operations, and here she is, towing to sea and even hoisting some staysails before it is rigged out again. A single-handed round-the-world yachtsman who had survived the impropriety of keeping insufficient look-out was recently induced to write a text for a picture book about commercial sail*. Amongst many other 'howlers', he averred, when confronted with a picture of a vessel with her jibboom rigged in, that it was *'broken'*. This is *not* the case where the *County of Peebles* is concerned, any more than it was in the case of the ship he cited. In fact, a clipper would reduce her length (and docking space required) by some 20% when rigging in her jibboom and, in some ports, this reduced her dock dues proportionately.

The impression given by such a vessel as this is that she must carry an enormous amount of sail, but this is an illusion. In fact, on an GRT of 1,614, her sail area was 30,610 feet, which was less than a wool clipper of lesser tonnage.

Originally from the same stable as the *County of Peebles,* the *County of Inverness* was cut down to a four-masted barque early in the century. After a period as the hulk *Dora* in Buenos Aires, she was bought by French interests in 1916 and re-rigged as the *Carmen,* in which guise she is seen drying her sails in Falmouth in Pl. 429, with a radio aerial rigged as a

*The Twilight of Sail, Robin Knox-Johnston, Sidgwick & Johnson, 1978.

428. *No point of view could disguise the loftiness of the PETER RICKMERS.*

429. *The CARMEN, ex-COUNTY OF INVERNESS.*

430. The LORD RIPON. Ships so rigged seemed to be lofty from any angle.

war-time measure. Later, she was converted to the full-powered Esthonian *Nemrac* (her French name in reverse) and, later still, she became the Italian *Amicizia,* being sunk by an allied air-raid on Hamburg in 1945. Although she was subsequently raised, she was then broken up.

No viewpoint, even when not down to her marks and with her big Liverpool section, could disguise the loftiness of the *Peter Rickmers* which, with her green hull, must have been a fine sight at sea, for she was the only four-masted full-rigger ever to cross skysails over royals and double topgallants on all four masts. Of 2,926 tons gross, she stranded on Long Island in 1908, after twenty successful years of trading to the Far East. Not many four-masted barques crossed skysails over royals and double t'gallants, but all looked lofty, even though not all were really big, as in the case of the *Lord Ripon,* later the German *Nal,* seen in Pl. 430, which was of 2,765 GRT — not small, but not to be compared with the last, bigger ships.

Aesthetically, and the more especially when under sail, the proportions aloft of a ship with skysails over royals and *single* topgallants struck

431. The WANDSBEK had a more aesthetically appealing rigging plan.

much better on the eye, as in the case of the German *Wandsbek* (Pl. 431), which had been bought by Knöhr & Burchard from England, for she was originally the *Ancyra,* built by Russell at Port Glasgow in 1892.

There is little enough to conjure up the 'Romance' of sail about the *Hippalos* as she tows in in Pl. 432, her rust-stained hull high in the water and her lower yards cock-billed, yet this was the more common sight of a square-rigger for the majority of people. How different would she seem, viewed from another vessel, running before the Westerlies! So . . . what did the ship 'really look like?' It is clear that it all depended on when she was seen! As photographic impressions, or even artists' renderings, have their limitations, so constant changes of name can be confusing to the historian. When this vessel was built for Brocklebanks in 1888, she was named *Holkar* and, with her sister, the *Sindia,* were then the two largest sailing ships afloat, being of 4,800 tons deadweight.

The *Holkar* was sold to D. H. Wätjen of Bremen in 1901, but was captured by the armed merchant cruiser *H.M.S. Caronia* in the 1914 War, being later sold to Norway and, under different owners, became the

432.   It would be sad if the HIPPALOS were remembered only by this picture.

Odessa, Souverain and *Hippalos*. **In 1924** she reached Havre from Melbourne in 116 days after a voyage in which beri-beri developed amongst her crew. Then she was laid up until she went to the knackers in Holland the following year. In the picture, she is displaying two black balls when under tow, which was unusual.

   The ugliest rig ever devised for general use was the 'bald-header', or, as it was once called, the 'Jubilee' rig, since it first appeared in the year of Queen Victoria's jubilee. With nothing above double topgallants, the whole configuration was very square and, if it had little aesthetic appeal, it was indubitably functional. The *Lawhill*, so rigged and with a midship section and under-water lines which speak for themselves in Pl. 433, was certainly no beauty, but she was never intended to be one. Her object was to earn money, and this she did very successfully since she had a long,

433. It might be said – unkindly – that the LAWHILL was almost square from her keel to her upper yards, but the fact remains that she seldom hit the headlines, for better or worse, and was economically an extremely successful vessel.

434. The ghost of the LAWHILL continually inserts herself into this book, even when breaking all the rules by towing round the Kentish coast to London in 1934 with her courses set and nothing else – the opposite of the normal practice. (Page 380.)

lucky and profitable career, with relatively little trouble, although seldom making noteworthy passages and trading right through two major wars. Finally, after the last World War, she was left to rot at Lourenço Marques.

Not only was she a profitable vessel, but a relatively comfortable one, whether in the jute or case oil trades or, latterly, under the flag of Gustaf Erikson of Mariehamn, though she was requisitioned by the South African government in the last war and never returned to Erikson's ownership. Photographs cannot tell the whole story, despite the extent to which this ship has insinuated herself into this volume!

The *Gustav* was built in 1892 for Colonel Goffey and was sister to the *Ornasia,* being built as the *Austrasia,* both being heavily-sparred vessels with 106 feet mainyards. With the crossjack sheet led round the capstan, Pl. 436 gives a good idea of a long open deck. It is sometimes said that

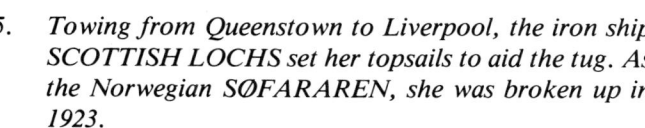

436. The long open deck of the GUSTAV, ex-AUSTRASIA.

435. Towing from Queenstown to Liverpool, the iron ship SCOTTISH LOCHS set her topsails to aid the tug. As the Norwegian SØFARAREN, she was broken up in 1923.

437. The GUSTAV sending down her sails in Gravesend Reach. She was later sunk in collision as the MELBOURNE.

438. The saloon of the GUSTAV.

439. In contrast to the four-masters, the Grimstad barque VESSORES glides past the Norwegian mountains. Note the lack of buntlines on her topsails and topgallant sails.

sailing ships would have been so much more efficient had they had the almost continuous hatches of modern vessels. This is true enough, but not with the sort of hatches then in vogue, for they were extremely vulnerable when loaded ship in bad weather. Note the protective baulks bolted down on the main hatch and see Pl. 17. She had several German owners, latterly being under the house-flag of H. H. Schmidt of Hamburg, but was sold to Gustaf Erikson in 1927, and was, somewhat unpredictably, re-named *Melbourne* but was run down and sunk by the tanker *Seminole* off Queenstown in 1932 with some loss of life. These pictures were taken in 1927, Pl. 437 showing her on arrival in the Thames with a cargo of grain from Sydney, and lying in Gravesend Reach, while sending down her sails. One of the china clay coasting schooners can be seen beyond her, between the fore and mainmasts, and one of the coal hulks is visible, while a number of Thames barges lie at anchor off Lobster Buoys.

Gustaf Erikson is associated – rightly – with the last big fleet of deep-

440. *With her main upper topsail and much of the lower topsail blown out; with rags of canvas on the foreyard, it all adds up to the wind through which the VIKING has passed, but the low viewpoint of the picture does not provide all the drama of the situation.*

water square-riggers, and it is easy to forget the smaller vessels which he owned. As television cameras can – and do – slant the presentation of documentary news, so a single photograph can colour the impression of a ship, and it might be said to be unfair to her to reproduce such a picture as Pl. 441 of the *Rigden* rotting in the Fowey River against a background of laid-up steamers but, regrettably, that is how so many people best remembered her. Built as a barquentine at Geta, in Sweden, in 1907, as the *Ingrid,* she was owned by A. F. Jansson of Mariehamn, but Erikson bought her in 1919 and used her in the 'split-wood' trade to England. After three years, he sold her to Allen, Adams & Co, whereupon she was renamed *Rigdin* (an anagram of *Ingrid),* having by then been reduced to schooner rig with an auxiliary. She passed to J. Fletcher Campbell and

442. A Danish brigantine towing out of Littlehampton.

441. The RIGDEN laid up in the Fowey River.

443. *The wooden barquentine ATHENA, of 665 tons and measuring 164.4 × 36.5 × 16.1', was built by Thos. Mosher at Newport, N.S. in 1888 and was abandoned at sea in 1915. Owned by T. C. Thomas of Windsor, N.B., she is seen here a little down by the head as she works cargo at Preston before the First World War. Pictures of ships under sail may have a greater superficial appeal, but ones like this give a far better understanding of the actual vessel, in the same way as . . .*

then, in 1927, to Stephens of Par, who re-rigged her as a barquentine, but she proved to be too big for the china clay trade for which he intended her, and was broken up in 1938 after a long lay up.

Although, as time went on, small vessels like the Danish brigantine in Pl. 442 were forced out of business due to their very small size, they were not only often happier vessels than their bigger successors, but they probably proved themselves to be the best and most concentrated school of practical seamanship of all – a point which should not be overlooked in any future resurgence of merchant sail.

444. ... this fine and detailed view of the ANNIE M. REID, which was one of the more famous four-masted barques of her day as the HOWARD D. TROOP. Built by Robert Duncan on the Clyde in 1892 for the great Troop fleet of St John, N.B., and of 2,180 tons, she was probably the finest vessel of a fine fleet – most of which had been built locally. She made the record run of 20 days from Yokohama to Astoria and a number of other good passages. On Troop's death in 1912, she was bought by James Rolph of San Francisco, and was broken up in Alameda, after some years of inactivity, in 1935.

445. *The most commonly seen craft were the various coasters. In this photograph the three-masted topsail schooner JASPER, built in 1884 and owned by A. Jenkyns, is getting along very nicely with her flying foresail set.*

446. *Ships of the age of the SOLBLOMSTEN were seldom caught by the camera. She is seen lying off Chatham in 1876, but she was built in Napoleonic times in 1807 – a real old-timer. Now she has double topsails, not introduced until the 1850s, and note the main spencer; the Bentinck boom to her foresail and stun'sail booms on the lower yard. The long jibboom is run in, with the inboard end hoisted on the forestay, which was the normal practice.*

447. Although a big, heavy ship, with her midship section, double spankers and high out of the water, a flash of sun makes all the difference to this picture of the French four-master RICHELIEU. Built for the Laeisz 'P' Line as the POLA in the First World War, she never sailed for that company, due to post-War reparations. She blew up in Baltimore in 1926, when loading pitch for L'Orient.

448. The barquentine FAIR WIND making sail, with her buntlines not yet overhauled. This fine angle of view and the fact that each yard is checked in a little more than the one below gives a false impression of a rather square configuration.

449. The HELEN DENNY about to cast off her tug in Cook Strait, and . . .

Deep water ships of all nations visited the Antipodes, but those owned locally were mainly in the Tasman Sea trade and relatively small: that is, small by the standards of the times, since some of them had seemed to be quite large when originally built. Such a one was the full-rigger *Helen Denny,* of 728 tons, which had been launched in 1866 by Robert Duncan of Glasgow and which sailed to Rangoon and other Eastern ports under Patrick Henderson's house-flag until 1874, when she was transferred to the New Zealand emigrant trade, being cut down to barque-rig the following year. Sold to Shaw, Savill & Albion in 1882, she continued on the same route, returning some smart passages, until 1896 when much larger vessels were forcing ships like the *Helen Denny* off the long hauls. 310 miles in 24 hours was her best recorded day's run, which was good for a vessel of her size and made soon after she was stripped of her mizzen canvas.

She was owned by two Christchurch firms in the next four years, during which she carried timber to Australia and coal from Newcastle or

450.   . . . having done so, to make more sail.

wheat from Sydney on the return voyage and, in 1900, was bought by Captain Frederick Holm who had always admired her, and he and his son commanded her in the Tasman trade until the competition of steamers, with their regularity of sailings, forced her out of business. Holm, who was an astute man and whose Holm Shipping Company is still in existence, finally had to sell her as a coal hulk to the Paparoa Coal Company and, in 1948, she was towed out to sea and used for target practice – more fortunate, perhaps, than some vessels which have been 'preserved' and stuffed with curios as tourist attractions.

   The *Manurewa* was another of the pretty Tasman Sea barques and, of only 335 NRT, measured 143′ 1″ × 26′ 1″ × 13′, having been built as the *Vale Royal* in 1884 at Port Glasgow and then owned by H. Sewall of London, who sold her to G. Wood of the same port, but in 1906 she took the name *Manurewa* when sold to G. T. Nicol of Auckland. Later, in 1909, she was sold to Sydney, being owned successively by J. Stewart, R. G. Holmes and, in 1920, by A. S. Patterson & Co, but she was lost in

451. *The MANUREWA in Hauraki Gulf.*

the Tasman Sea with all hands two years later when bound from Sydney towards Grafton, in the Clarence River.

Another of the many fine little barques in this trade which could be mentioned was the *Raupo,* ex-*Louisa Craig,* which had been launched in 1873 as the *Peru,* the sister ship of the *Chili.* Of 683 tons nett, she was built of iron in Aberdeen by John Key & Sons for J. W. Robertson, and her lower masts were of iron and the upper spars of wood, while she was unusual in several particulars. For one thing, her standard compass was situated half way up the mizzen lower mast, in an effort to reduce deviation errors which were still not fully understood, and her spanker was bent to hoops on a wooden spar which extended as far down as the boom on the after side of the mast. Seen in later life, the reason for this might seem to be rather obscure (Pl. 452), and it might, at first sight, be likened to the trysail arrangement of a snow. However, there can be little doubt that she was originally so rigged in order that the spanker gear would not foul the elevated standard compass and that, when this was dropped to deck level, the gunter spar remained to puzzle all those who saw her!

In 1880 both the *Peru* and *Chili* came under the house-flag of John Stewart's, of London, who, in the 1920s, were to become the last company to own square-riggers with a British port of registry, and she sailed with much success in general trade until 1906, when she was bought by J. J. Craig of Auckland, who was a merchant owning the largest fleet of sailing vessels registered in Australasian waters, most of them being smart craft and named after members of his family: *Joseph Craig, Constance Craig, Selwyn Craig, James Craig* and the like, and the *Peru* fell in with this nomenclature by becoming the *Louisa Craig.* It was soon after this sale that the standard compass was lowered to its more conventional position on deck, and she was generally employed in bringing coal back from Newcastle, N.S.W. after taking timber outwards, though she handled various other general cargoes and sometimes had keen races with other units of the company's fleet. Occasionally she went up to the Islands, but had had a successful Colonial career when she was sold to George Scales of Wellington in 1918.

Scales' name has appeared in a number of histories as the purchaser of various vessels, including the big *Rewa,* ex-*Alice A. Leigh,* but his operations have often seemed to be somewhat nebulous. In fact, he had started

452. The RAUPO, ex-LOUISA CRAIG, sending down her main lower topsail in San Francisco Bay. Note the manner in which her spanker is bent.

business in 1884 as an auctioneer and commission agent, but subsequently became manager of the New Zealand Freight Reduction Committee for the wool producers, and he had appreciated that shortage of tonnage in New Zealand waters necessitated the chartering of overseas vessels and he correctly believed that the way to lower freights was to build up a fleet of New Zealand-owned deep-water ships. Those square-riggers owned in the country *had* been deep-water vessels when built, but were no longer viable on long voyages due to their small size in relation to the ships which had come after them.

In the event, his scheme did not get off the ground until after the middle of the 1914–18 War, and the *Raupo* was his first purchase. Although he was successful with this vessel for several years, albeit not in the trade for which she was intended, there was a major shipping slump after the First World War, as is well-known, and thus he was never able to bring his scheme to fruition, being obliged to lay up the *Raupo* in 1921 and then to sell her as a coal hulk – a function she maintained until broken up in the 1930s.

Not all the Tasman and Inter-Colonial traders were barques. There were a number of barquentines and other rigs, one of the former being the *Alexa,* which was certainly neither the most attractive nor the fastest of them – and many *were* fast sailers –but she did have the distinction of being the last square-rigger to sail regularly out of Sydney. She was being built in Holland in 1904 under the name of *Voorburg,* but was bought on the stocks before launching by A. Hattrick of Wanganui and sailed out under the name *Alexa,* which she retained thereafter. Leaving London with general cargo – she was only 235 tons – she lost her rudder in the 'Roaring Forties' and a good job of seamanship was made in rigging a jury one. Then, on the last leg of the voyage, she went ashore on the Farewell Spit at the western end of Cook Strait, but managed to kedge herself off.

Unusually, at this time, she was fitted with stockless anchors, which dispensed with cat-heads and all the labour of fishing and catting the normal Admiralty pattern anchors. She was, of course, of steel construction. With a very low freeboard coal-laden, she proved to be a very wet vessel, though life aboard was easier when running out with timber, though she never had a good turn of speed and, like most bluff-bowed

454. The GLADBROOK setting sail during the brief period of her second life.

453. The bluff-bowed ALEXA with her stockless anchors.

455. No-one looking at the GLADBROOK fitting out at Port Chalmers and getting ready for sea in 1918 would have imagined her as a hulk so short a time before.

vessels, did her best off the wind. At about the beginning of the 1914 War, she was sold to a Chinese merchant in Sydney called On Chong as a replacement for his Hobart-built barque *Loongana* which had been wrecked in the Gilbert Islands, and she went into the island trade, running successfully until 1929 when, while loading copra at Butarati (also in the Gilberts) the half-loaded cargo caught fire and, with its oily nature, there was no hope of extinguishing it. She was beached — but finished.

Not all the New Zealand and Australian vessels were in the intercolonial and island trade, however, and a case in point was the *Gladbrook,* although her case was brought about by the exigencies of war. Originally built as the *County of Anglesey* for W. Thomas' Welsh County Line (which should not be confused with Craig's 'Counties', which were all Scots counties) in 1877, she was of 1,000 tons register, like

410

most of her sisters. In 1918, after acting as a hulk for a number of years in New Zealand, she was re-rigged to meet the shipping shortage and managed by the Union Steamship Company, as the *Gladbrook*. However, the boom only lasted a mere three years, during which time she had voyaged to the West Coasts of North and South America, and in 1921 she was sailed to Fiji to be hulked once again. On her first voyage in 1918 from Newcastle, N.S.W. to Callao she made the very respectable time of 45 days and went through Cook Straits — a route normally shunned by masters bound for the West Coast. She was a smart little vessel, with a monkey poop rather similar to that in the *Cutty Sark*.

There are so many craft which have claims to be mentioned, and perhaps one to be remembered is the *Quathlamba,* which was built in 1879 by Hall of Aberdeen for J. T. Rennie, who ran some beautiful little barques to South Africa, all with Zulu names. Hall, of course, built some of the most peerless of the clippers. Later, the barque passed to a Captain P. L. Francis who sailed her all over the world and remained in command when he sold her to J. J. Craig, who retained her name for quite a long time before bringing it into line with his fleet by re-naming her *Hazel Craig,* but whether under the one name or the other she was one of the fastest and finest sea-boats in Australasia, although of a mere 467 tons. Latterly, she was owned by G. T. Nicol, and finally broken up in 1922.

If there was a Romance about the age of sail, it probably existed rather in the routes and ports visited by some vessels, and it might be held that the best material lies in the brigs, brigantines, barquentines, barques and schooners trading to the Pacific Islands which, before the advent of high-rise flats and the like, were able to weave their own spells on men. There were, however, two sides to this coin, fascinating though it was, since, apart from the copra bug (invariably loaded in teeming millions with the copra), the trade showed a long trail of disaster, both from typhoon and other causes. Moreover, adequate photographs are few and far between. Nevertheless, it is a subject deserving of more research, since it not only attracted some fascinating vessels, but men of often unusual characters.

Schooners of various types were to be found throughout Australian waters, though most were of fairly small tonnage. Some, with the many ketches to be found in South Australia, became known on a more world-wide basis because they loaded the last of the deep-water square-riggers

456. Formerly the QUATHLAMBA and HAZEL CRAIG, the WHITE PINE shows what she can do.

with grain in such anchorage ports as Port Victoria although, of course, this was only a very small part of their business in a year and, for the most part, they carried varied cargoes around the coasts. Most became the recipients of auxiliaries in later years and, in consequence, this led to a 'bald-headed' appearance as they then usually dispensed with their topmasts. Thus the *Evaleeta,* of some 80 tons, which originally hailed from Hobart, seen alongside the *C. B. Pedersen* in Pl. 458. Some were owned by individuals, but more by syndicates and some by larger companies, and they varied in size over the years from about twenty to, perhaps, eighty tons. Some had black hulls, more white and some were green, which made them very smart in appearance.

As usual, some were conversions. Watching the three-masted schooner *Waimana* threshing through a fleet of anchored square-riggers in half a gale in fitful moonlight, as she passed our double-reefed lifeboat as if we were going the other way, she looked enormous — size being so relative — but in fact she was but 93 NRT and had, in fact, been built in 1899 in Whangaroa as a twin-screwed scow. (The New Zealand scows were remarkably handy chine-built craft with flat bottoms and centre-boards.)

457. *A typical South Australian ketch under sail and power. She is taking a party out to Port Victoria anchorage to 'see the wind-jammers'.*

458. *The EVALEETA loading the C. B. PEDERSEN off Port Victoria. When there was much wind, the square-riggers would haul out their spankers and haul up the sheets to make a lee for the ketches.*

459.   The ROOGANAH off the Adelaide Semaphore.

Another schooner of about the same size was the *Rooganah,* built in Tasmania in 1909, which caught fire the year after the photograph in Pls. 459–60 were taken when her engine back-fired on starting and when she was carrying 198 cases of benzine to Whyalla, near the head of the west coast of Spencer Gulf, and her four men had to abandon her.

Some of these craft became altered, like the *Coringle,* which had been built in North Sydney in 1909. In Pl. 461 which gives the impression of some strange arboretum amidships, she is actually being lengthened. The purist may say that, latterly at all events, so many of these craft had auxiliaries that they were no longer real sailing craft. Nevertheless, the sailing vessels on the Australian coast were a very mixed bunch: some had been bought in; some had been built locally, and some were conversions, ranging from barques downwards through all sorts of schooners, but perhaps the most pleasing to the eye were the jack-yard ketches of Tasmania which, in their annual regatta, presented a sight to vie with the

460. The ROOGANAH *sailing through the sun as she passes a P. & O. liner*.

461. Lengthening the CORINGLE, which had been built in 1909 in Berry's Bay, North Sydney. Of 128 NRT, she had various Adelaide owners and was returned to that port after being requisitioned in the Second World War, but latterly operated out of Darwin with twin-screw auxiliaries.

yachts of any age. The photographs do not make it obvious that they had flat bottoms, rather like the New Zealand scows, and one or two were fitted with lee-boards. Their sail areas were prodigious for their size, and a vessel of $69' \times 1' 2'' \times 5' 2''$ would have a main gaff of 25 feet – only 2 feet shorter than the boom – while the mainmast was 75 feet and the mizzen 65 feet. Often termed 'barges', purely on account of their hull form and in no sense of derision, a number of them *did* capsize when caught in a sudden squall or funnel of wind through the hills.

One schooner from New Zealand seems to have achieved almost immortal fame – perhaps because she was the subject of a book. This was the *Huia,* mainly employed in the Tasman and South Australian trade. Rigged as a topsail schooner, she had been built of kauri wood in 1894 and was a nice-looking little vessel in fine weather, when she steered like a witch, but in heavy weather she was treacherous and needed a good deal of handling. Latterly, her crew were a tough, hard-drinking crowd and

462. The Tasmanian jackyard ketch FOAM and . . .

463. . . . the FLEET off Hobart.

464. Jackyard ketches off Hobart – the SPEEDWELL in the foreground.

465. The ALMA DOEPEL, of 150 tons and built on the Bellinger River, N.S.W., was the last merchant craft in South Australia to set a square sail until 1939, when she was reduced to a pure bald-headed fore-and-after.

466. *The WAIMANA's engines were removed at Fremantle in 1907 and she was owned in Hobart when this picture was taken. During the 1939–45 War she was taken over by the Navy.*

almost violently efficient, knowing the vessel and determined to master her. Similar to her, but more heavily built and with a raised foc's'le forward which housed her seven crew and provided shelter when the wind was forward of the beam, was the *Piri*. When the two ships were lying together, she appeared to be larger than the *Huia,* yet the latter was in fact 166 NRT and the *Piri* 114, demonstrating the illusions of appearance. Men who sailed in both vessels aver that the *Piri* was much the better behaved of the two in bad weather. Her main boom was 45 feet long and of about the same diameter as the cargo derricks of the big steamers of her era. She too had been built in 1894 – as the *Tangaroa.* Her main topmast was lost in 1927. The pictures give some idea of such a craft at sea and the weather so often encountered in the Tasman Sea.

467. The pretty brigantine WOOLAMAI of 151 tons, measuring 181.4 × 36.9 × 20.7 feet.

468. The PIRI, ex-TANGAROA.

469.
The PIRI slipped at Auckland. Note the stockless anchor to starboard and the Admiralty pattern to port.

470.

471. The PIRI at anchor.

In those days, one section of the Auckland waterfront was reserved for steamers, and the rest was used for the coasting trade — the word 'coasting' having a fairly wide application in view of the distances involved. Latterly, most of these 'coasters' were built of wood, being ketch or schooner rigged, and generally ranging from 50 to 75 tons NRT. According to the custom of the times, the crew worked all cargo, mostly with cargo booms rigged on the masts and a bull-rope on the hook controlled by one man who would take a turn round a cleat secured to a hatch coaming. Sometimes a lizard was used on the fall. Most of these craft were heavily rigged, as weather was often bad on the New Zealand coast, so short, stocky masts with sails of heavy canvas tended to be pretty standard.

Some vessels were smaller, like the *Miro* (Pl. 485) which was only 29½ registered tons, and owned by the Nobels Explosives Co. This was a sturdy, nice-looking vessel with gaff topsails, a coppered bottom and a centre-board which was armoured against striking any under-water

473. ... looking down and aft from the fore rigging.

472. Wind in the PIRI's topsails ...

474. Blowing up in the Tasman Sea, the PIRI still has her square foresail set.

475. Soon she is shipping water — a view looking forward.

476. *Looking forward.*  477. *Looking aft.*

As the weather worsens, the little schooner is hove to under a close reefed foresail.

478. Without her main topmast. The square-sail is set on the weather side.

obstruction and cut away so that it would automatically raise itself when it touched bottom.

Frank Walker, who took the pictures in the *Piri,* joined the *Miro* as junior hand in 1926. Leaving Maratai for Gisborne, the explosives depot, he was at the wheel while all sail was set with the engine running, the centre-board down and with a good breeze on the beam. Suddenly he found himself alone, the master, Captain M. Himaire, an Esthonian, calling out as he went below: *'Keep a good look out. Call me at your peril. If the wind freshens too much for the gaff topsails, steady her on course, lash the wheel and clew up the topsails: then go aloft and make them fast. Don't worry, she knows the way to the Cape anyway.'* She did, too! But to a young man coming straight out of deep-sea square-riggers, this was a contrast in approach. Soon after leaving Gisborne, she was nosing her way into all sorts of small creeks to isolated gold mines which could only

479. With the wind aft, flying foresails on both sides of the fore-yard give the schooner a good push.

480. Fine sailing with the wind on the starboard quarter.

Two views from the PIRI's bowsprit.

481. *Boarding seas were a common enough condition in the Tasman.*

482. *The PIRI's decks could not hold the water of a big square-rigger, but were just as uncomfortable in bad weather.*

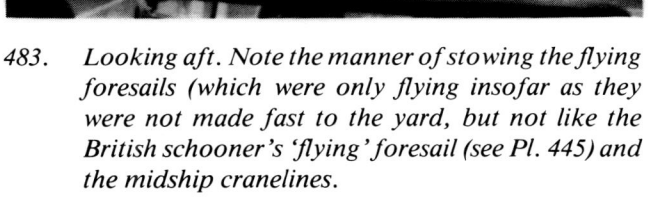

483. Looking aft. Note the manner of stowing the flying foresails (which were only flying insofar as they were not made fast to the yard, but not like the British schooner's 'flying' foresail (see Pl. 445) and the midship cranelines.

484. Surprisingly, perhaps, the mainsail is reefed in this photograph.

Two weather side views aboard the PIRI.

485. *The MIRO alongside at Maratai. A bogie of explosives is alongside.*

486. *The PIRI in dry-dock at Auckland in 1926.*

be reached by craft like her, for she only drew six feet when loaded, and delivered, amongst other things, detonators which were specially stowed in the lazarette aft. In contrast with the British coasters of that period, it may be noted that the crew all berthed aft and that they had a recreation room (also used as a mess-room) with an ironing board: electric iron, refrigerator, shower and good feeding! These things may be taken for granted today by seamen who have little idea of the work of a sailor but, in those days, the local seamen's unions *had* obtained conditions ahead of any other nation (except, perhaps, in Norway) yet, in return, they did ensure that their members not only knew their jobs but accomplished them properly. It was not the 'take everything and give nothing' attitude which has become so common amongst unions since the last war.

487. The topgallant-yard schooner ALPHA was built at Nambucco in New South Wales in 1903 and measured 92.4 × 25.1 × 7 feet.

488. Another view of the brigantine WOOLAMAI, which was built by R. Kennedy of Jarrah Bank, South Australia, and owned by R. Tulloch of Adelaide.

489. *A stern view of the YSABEL when slipped. Originally built in 1875 with an auxiliary and Cunningham's patent topsail on the fore as the mission schooner SOUTHERN CROSS, she passed to Captain W. Ross of Auckland who named her YSABEL and gave her double topsails, whilst removing the auxiliary. Later she came under French ownership.*

If this second volume were extended to fifty volumes it could never cover the multiplicity of merchant sailing craft that plied the seas in the last era of sail – perhaps from the 1850s – since, although some types remained in much the same form that they had maintained for centuries, the deep-watermen embarked on a series of changes and modifications at about that time. Moreover, it was the beginning – just – of the photographic era and, for better or worse, these books are described as 'A Camera Record'.

Perhaps – who knows? – there *will* be fifty volumes in due time, but many readers will not live to see them, and it may therefore be of interest to take a kaleidoscope view of a few of the medley of craft which passed through the registers during the epoch of the camera, taking them at random and without favour to one or another, for each had her function and, if the little Genoese wine trader, sailing no further than nearby Elba, may seem inferior to a threshing Cape Horner, it is undeniable that the Cape Horner could never have done the job of the little Mediterranean craft.

Thus, whilst the bigger or famous ships often have stories or epic tales accruing to them, the outrigger canoe, the individual dhow of whatever form, or numerous local craft of various sorts, usually lived out their lives usefully and well, but only passed into history as a type rather than as an individual vessel in its own right, since their more humdrum careers tended to maintain their anonymity. They were none the worse for that.

Nine square-riggers in company today would bring all hands tumbling out on deck, however cold the weather! Pl. 490, taken in the early years of this century, shows units of the Alaska Packers Fleet beating through the Unimak Pass, past the Aleutian Islands, bound for the Alaskan salmon canneries. Famous though this fleet became, since it was one of the last big ones comprising square-rigged ships to survive, and included many famous wooden Down-Easters; iron and steel medium clippers, former big oil sailers and others, the fact is that the vessels were laid up in San Francisco for the winter, and then made the passage to Alaska, where they lay with their two bower anchors down and the cables on a swivel, whereupon the upper yards were sent down until the homeward trip began. Thus their actual sailing time was little enough, but it was a bad area with plenty of fog, currents and hazards, with the result that losses in

490. Nine of the Packers' ships beating through Unimak Pass after the turn of the century.

491. Shortly before 1939, one of the last wine traders of Sestri Levante, near Genoa, lies on the beach. She and her consorts brought wine in barrels back from Elba.

492. *When the old Down-Eastern ABNER COBURN was forced ashore by ice (which may be seen) on Menshikott Point in 1918, some of her crew – and only a portion of them are in view – gathered ashore. Like many another of the Packer's ships, she survived her experience and was not broken up until 1929. One of the most splendid of the Down-East sailing ships, she was built by W. Rogers of Bath, Me. for Pendleton, Carver and Nicholls in 1882.*

relation to sailing time tended to be rather high. One may be sure that this scene did not attract much attention at the time, although the ships' complements were extremely large, including great numbers of Chinese cannery hands who never stopped gambling en voyage, and also many fishermen, who were mainly Scandinavian.

The square-riggers carried the tins and shucks for the cases up to the canneries and, while they remained at anchor, the fishermen went out in the small, sprit-rigged gill-netters, two men to a boat. Gill nets were a form of drift net with the mesh big enough to allow the passage of the fishes' heads, but not their bodies, so that they were caught by their gills. In Pl. 494 the boats are ready to leave – witness the crude star on the shed which is the signal for the tow-boats. These pictures were actually taken in 1929, after the days of the square-riggers were over, but things had not altered and there was probably as much sailing, in aggregate, in these gill-netters as there had been in the mother ships!

The Portuguese have a great seafaring tradition and were one of the few nations to send schooners and barquentines to the Grand Banks of

493. *The gill-netters fan out from Nannek.*

494. *Gill-netters ready for a tow out.*

495. *Returning to the Tagus after a six months voyage and with 600 tons of fish in her holds, the ARGUS has sixty dories on deck stowed in nests of six. Normally white, she and the CREOULA arrived in Sydney, Cape Breton, in 1941 with red hulls, which did not suit them.*

496.   Another view of the ARGUS.

Newfoundland in quest of cod, one man going out in each dory (against two in French and North American vessels) to catch them with hand lines. A multiplicity of craft were engaged in the trade, some being real 'old characters', but the last to be built before steam took over altogether were the sisters *Argus, Creoula* and *Santa Maria Manuela,* built by De Haan and Oerleman at Beuden, in Holland, shortly before the 1939 War. With a length of some 200 feet, masts 130 feet above their double bottoms and with spoon bows, they were equipped with Sulzer diesels of 400 BHP and represented, in a sense, the transition from sail to screw, with modern refrigeration plants and many advances on the pure sailers. Note their big, square-nocked fishermen's topsails.

   The world of the whaler was a lonely one, and no other vessels kept the sea for so long at a time. Speed was no great object and the ships were generally bluff in the bow and of extremely robust construction. Unlike

497. The laid-up whalers ROUSSEAU and DESDEMONA represented a class of ships with their own fascination.

the Dundee and Hull whaling ships in the United Kingdom, which were latterly given fairly powerful steam auxiliaries*, the Americans clung to sail. They were only to be seen in port in such places as Nantucket which participated in the trade, and no-one seeing a whaler would be in any doubt about what she was, if only by the number of davits along her side to take her whale-boats — boats which were permanently outboard. In Pl. 497 the *Rousseau* and *Desdemona* are laid up, with their jibbooms rigged in, all their spars and gear sent down save only the futtock shrouds which hang forlornly from the lower tops, which are themselves raised above the trestle trees to allow a free passage of air and thus prevent any rot, and boats, upper masts and spars are all ashore. In this condition they lie very high in the water, and the copper strips below the waterline are plainly visible. Astern, another whaler prepares to join them: her boats are gone and she is drying sail — and note the old, deep single topsails — before they, too, are sent down.

Of all square-riggers, some of the full-rigged clippers were undoubtedly the most pleasing to the eye, and those with masts of unequal height, crossing a main skysail over royals and single t'gallants, looked the best of all. As all ships got larger, they tended to lose some of their looks. Skysails became abandoned: masts of equal height became the rule and Liverpool sections appeared amidships and, finally, they became lower and squarer. Spike bowsprits had long supplanted jibbooms and it is undeniable that the last, very powerful and large vessels were heavy to work, although utterly inspiring when they really got going in the hard winds of the westerlies, which were their true *mètier*. Ships were not built for the purpose of gladdening the eye of bystanders though, by a happy coincidence, many of them did no less, even though not every beholder saw beauty in the same vessel. For my part, had I been walking round the dockside in Melbourne at the time that Pl. 498 was taken, I should have gone straight aboard to apply for a berth. Yet other men I know are not drawn by the picture at all. It is true she is in dock: that her mizzen yards have not been braced round since she hove to — perhaps off Port Phillip Heads: that her hull is scarred, that sails are being sent down and that there is little trim about her and, indeed, I may be in a minority of one, but of all the thousands — nay, tens of thousands — of photographs of square-rigged ships which I have seen, no other (and I have seen plenty of

*Pl. 385 — The *Esquimaux*.

498. *The QUEEN MARGARET.*

others of the same ship) has exercised so strong a hold over me, and it has not diminished my desire to sail in the ship over half a century.

Unfortunately, she was wrecked before I was born. She is no less than

499. *The wheel of the QUEEN MARGARET. The helmsman is very short in this photograph and would normally be standing on the grating. The relieving tackles can be seen, but are too slack.*

the *Queen Margaret,* of 2,144 tons, which was built in 1893 by McMillan for John Black & Co. of Glasgow and, indeed, she was a vessel which earned a reputation for speed and smartness and whose name became well-known on the lips of all seamen who saw her or who had served in her. In 1913, when this fine skysail-yarder stood into the Lizard to read the flags on the signal station under all sail, she came in *too* close, became caught by the tide, and went ashore only a quarter of a mile off the point, to be lost. Few wrecks came about so unnecessarily.

It is interesting to notice in the picture of her changing sail* that the upper topsail yard has been left at the masthead for there is little wind, but the point is that her upper topsail sheets are long enough to permit this to

*Pl. 500.

442

500. Changing the main topsails for the tropic passage in the QUEEN MARGARET.

501. *Seen towing into Cape Town, the Norgweian barque IRENE was built in Lubeck in 1891 and, of 1111 GRT, was owned by H. Jeremiassen of Porsgrund. She was sold in 1923.*

be done, which was unusual at any time, and the more unusual in ships of her date*. The port clew is still shackled on. The port clew of the lower topsail has been hauled back over the yard, between the two men.

All too often views of sailing ships were as they were arriving or leaving port, as in the case of the French barque *Bérengère,* seen making Hobart on her maiden voyage in 1902. There is little enough wind and all her buntlines have been broken prior to clewing up sail, with the result that the canvas is badly pinched. She was built by the Chantiers de St Nazaire at Rouen for the Soc. des Voiliers du Sud-Ouest of Bordeaux, but was sold to the Soc. des Voilers Dunkerquois in 1904. The following year she distinguished herself signally when homeward bound from New Caledonia towards Glasgow, under Captain Beaudouart, for, when making the Horn passage, she came on MacVicar, Marshall's full-rigger

*Page 240.

502. Bending the crossjack.

503. Looking forward, as a sea is scooped over the maindeck.

The QUEEN MARGARET.

504. The COLONEL DE VILLEBOIS MAREUIL.

Garsdale, built in 1885 as the *Fort James,* totally dismasted and on her beam ends – a condition in which she had been for the past five days. This vessel was outward bound from the Tyne towards Portland, Ore. and in sorry case. It took some twelve hours of hazardous boat-work to rescue the British crew, and there might be doubt whether they would have succeeded had it not been for the experience of many of her Breton hands who had learned their trade in the Terre-Neuvas on the Grand Banks of Newfoundland. Sailing ships taught men a much better idea of the very run of the sea than any steamer, and it was sad to see the very bungling which characterized the abandoning of so many vessels sunk in convoy in the last war and, indeed, in certain instances during the intervening years. The ubiquitous helicopter may not always be available to winch off personnel in sailing ships of the future, and boat-work is one of the arts that will need to be re-learnt. The *Bérengère,* whose crew exhibited such consummate seamanship on that September day in 1905, was sunk by a U-boat south and west of the Fastnet in 1917.

    Pl. 504 of the *Colonel de Villebois Mareuil* is reproduced because,

505. The BÉRENGÈRE.

506. The LILLY G, built in 1891 by Antonio Valle at Camogli for F. & A. Bartelotto, of 510 tons, became a total loss off Cape Kelibia in 1936. Oddly, surviving square-riggers in the Mediterranean created little interest when those elsewhere were becoming 'news'.

507. *The smart Boston pilot schooner VARUNA tows past Goat Island, S. Boston, at the end of the nineteenth century astern of one of the Boston Towboat Company's tugs, while a coasting smack makes her way in. Note her large mainsail and low freeboard.*

although it exhibits a great deal of detail, it does not otherwise show the ship at her best, but it does give the lie to (probably) every sailing ship history which has mentioned the vessel, since it has always been stated that, of thirty virtually identical barques of some 2,300 GRT launched by the Chantiers Nantais between 1900 and 1902, she alone was bald-headed. Indeed, there is quite a well-known photograph purporting to be her, which shows her so rigged. On the other hand, there is a series of her towing across the Columbia River bar, of which one is world-famous, for the hull is behind the sea and the effect is most dramatic, but . . . she is crossing royals.

Often though this picture was published, it seems that it was never queried – possibly because it was a 'dramatic' picture rather than of a ship – until an American reader of one of our books*, Mr Norbert Tocszko, queried her royals. He would have been flattered to discover the number of individuals and institutions which became involved in the controversy which raged for a very long time, since the French historians had all made a point of the fact that the vessel was 'jubilee-rigged', and the inference was, therefore, that the Columbia River bar pictures must be of some other ship. Indeed, experts at the San Francisco Maritime Museum, which owned the plate, found themselves in something of a dichotomy,

*Square-Riggers – The Final Epoch, 1921–1958.

448

508. Some of the British naval training brigs (illustrated in Vol. 1). Here four of them lie off Dartmouth, opposite Kingswear – a splendid sight in a lovely river. A coasting schooner lies astern, while a brig-rigged steamer is beyond. Beautifully kept, these Symondite brigs answered their purposes perfectly.

509.   Local sprit- and lateen-rigged craft in the Bosphorus in 1933.

because they were certain, on the one hand, that the negative was properly labelled yet, at the same time, believed the ship to have had no royals. It was thus a relief to all concerned to discover this picture, in which the fore royal yard is admittedly sent down, though it obviously exists. Later, two old men who had served in the ship were discovered, and they confirmed that she always crossed royals and that all the French historians were wrong! It may seem a small point, but it does demonstrate how an error, once made, becomes perpetuated, and a recent checking of very many ships' logs by Mr Richard Cookson has exposed innumerable errors in the works of Lubbock, Lacroix and others. This is not to denigrate their tremendous efforts, but it is true that very few works – if any – are *wholly* accurate, even though the author has worked from what he believed to be unimpeachable sources. As to the *Colonel de Villebois Mareuil,* she had several Nantais owners and traded up until 1922, when she was laid up until she went to the knackers in 1929.

The *Sound of Jura* was a sister to the barquentines *Westfield, Oberon* and *Titania,* all illustrated in Volume 1, and owned originally by Charles Walker. She was 1,009 tons and built by Russell & Co. in 1896. Twenty

510.

511. *The SOUND OF JURA was sister to the barquentines WESTFIELD, OBERON and TITANIA, illustrated in Vol. 1. In 1916 she was equipped with a steam engine and funnel which gave her 2–3 knots in calm. Latterly she was owned by the Kerguelen Whaling & Sealing Co, taking coal south from Cape Town and then acting as a store ship for seal oil for the rest of the season. She was broken up in 1928.*

512. The SOMALI.

years later, in 1916, she was equipped with a steam engine and funnel which gave her 3–4 knots in calms. Latterly, she was owned by the Kerguelen Whaling & Sealing Co. taking coal south from Cape Town, and then acting as a store ship for the seal oil during the rest of the season. She was broken up in 1928.

The *Somali,* of no less than 3,537 NRT, was built in 1892 for Gilbert R. Steeves, who also owned the four-masted barques *Simla, Saratoga* and *Stanley,* besides the barque *Senegal.* The *Somali* was the longest lived, passing to the Aktien-Gesellschaft 'Alster' in 1900 to become the *Alsterdamn,* being then the largest German sailing ship afloat after the *Potosi.* In 1912 she became the *Adolf Vinnen* of Bremen, but was at sea when the 1914 War broke out and received word of it when speaking the *Potosi* at sea. She made her destination, Santa Rosalia, without incident and became interned, becoming the *Mae Dollar* when subsequently allocated

513. *Wearing the Austro-Hungarian ensign, the barque AMOR makes sail out of New York. There are many interesting features about this vessel which reward close study. She is flush-decked: there is the position of the martingale, the lack of buntlines to her upper topsails and, indeed, her whole layout. It will be noted that the lee gaskets have been made up on the main lower topsail and that a man is aloft making up those to windward.*

514. The late Captain Archie Horka, who contributed to this book, served in the SKAREGROM.

to the United States. However, she never went to sea again and eked out 40-odd years of existence as a barge – the *Crown Zellerbach No 1*. Originally she had crossed three skysails above her royals, which are sent down in Pl. 512, which is a good example of how the angle of a photograph can belie the size of a ship.

Built by A. Rodger of Port Glasgow for T. Beynon of Cardiff, the bald-headed full-rigger *Castleton* was one of the last square-riggers built in the United Kingdom and was a far cry from the clippers in her sail plan. Of 1,971 GRT, she was nevertheless quite a good carrier which passed to S. O. Stray of Kristianssand in 1915 to become the *Svalen*, but later passed to Grimstad owners and was re-named *Skaregrom*, as she was when this picture (Pl. 514) was taken. In 1926 she was dismasted off Madeira when outward bound with a timber cargo from Halden towards Melbourne and, after reaching the Azores under jury rig, was condemned.

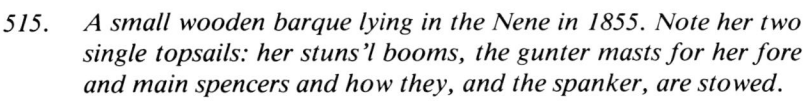

515. A small wooden barque lying in the Nene in 1855. Note her two single topsails: her stuns'l booms, the gunter masts for her fore and main spencers and how they, and the spanker, are stowed.

516. With her fore royal and t'gallant yards sent down, the Norwegian barque SMART, built in 1898 by A. Aaronsen of Arendal and owned by J. Petersen of Holmestrand, was 154.5 × 31.2 × 12.3' and another of the legion of unsung sailing ships.

517. Milne's little 'Inver' barques were generally painted light grey, but here the INVERNEILL has painted ports as she lies at Port Victor (not to be confused with Port Victoria, also in South Australia). Later she passed to Sir William Garthwaite...

518. ... to become the GARTHNEILL, being hulked in Adelaide in 1926. (See Pls. 321/2). Above, with the wind right at as she passes Lowestoft, and with the sea almost cut out of the picture, she has the appearance of a model.

519. *The topgallant-yard schooner ELLEN of Marstal (See Pl. 521).*

520. *The detail of rigging in this picture of the full-rigger SCHLIEBRACHT towing out to sea leaves nothing to the imagination and gives an excellent idea of a ship of her period. Probably taken about 1860, she was one of the earlier vessels with double topsails.*

521. *Although owned in Marstal until lost in 1928, the ELLEN was not typical of the schooners of that port, being steel with stockless anchors and, in fact, built by H. G. Bodewes at Mertenshoek in 1914 of 305 tons. In a sense, she represented the final development of the merchant schooner – if not in terms of size.*

522. *With her upper yards on deck, a barque makes sail as she tows down to Sandy Hook: the lightship being visible ahead. A ship of the past, unfortunately unidentified, she is typical of that great armada of forgotten square-riggers which have sailed into the limbo of time. Clearly an American-built vessel, it will be seen that her side-light brackets are right aft, which was common practice then (late 1850s and afterwards) although the lights could have been of little enough use to any ship fairly fine on her lee bow. In those days, lights were not carried much in deep water, but usually only in busy lanes or around coasts.*

523. *Some eagle eye can fault almost any picture. In this one the criticism can be made that the lower t'gallant gaskets are not made up to equal lengths. So it is equally possible to fault a book like this in which the twin forces of quality of illustration and of interest pull in opposite directions. Is it better to have a professional photograph of a ship casting off her tug with her gear not made up and her buntlines not overhauled, or some apprentice's effort with a 'box' Brownie when all was 'ship-shape and Bristol fashion'? Does the interest of the sinking of the PENANG outweigh the lack of clarity of the pictures?*

At all events, the Publishers hope that this Medley has struck the right balance and been enjoyed, and that all readers will be wafted by as fair a wind as the LADYE DORIS has in this picture to come and join the ships once more in Volume 3 of this work, when we shall all examine yet more masts and sails of the past in another excursion through the seas and ports of the world.

―――――oOo―――――

INDEX

Aaronssen, A. 455
Aberdeen White Star Line 29–312–328
Abner Coburn 435
Abraham Rydberg 95–244/5–294
Actie 298
Ada 312
Adelaide, Port 325
Admiral Karpfanger, see
   L'Avenir
Adolf Vinnen, see *Somali*
af Chapman 1
Ahti 369
Aid 220
Alaska Packers Assn. 433
Alastor 323–360–369
Albatross 173
Albert Rickmers (bq.), see
   Penang
Albert Rickmers (4-m. bq.), see
   Herzogin Sophie Charlotte
Albyn 337
Alcaeus Hooper 255
Alexa 408/10
Alexandra 232
Alfen 142
Alice A. Leigh, see *Rewa*
Allen, Adams & Co. 396
Alma Doepel 418
Amasis, see *Schulschiffe*
   Pommern
Amelia 232

Ames, Oliver 257
Amicale Internationale des Cap
   Horniers 4
Amicizia, see *Carmen*
Amor 455
Ancel, Mr. 208
Ancyra, see *Wandsbek*
Andersen, Johan 366
Andorsen, J. F. 360
Anemone, see *MacCallum More*
Anirac 296–298
Anne Comyn 266
Annie M. Reid 399
Antofagasta 189–332
Antuco, see *Søm*
Arcadia, tug 103–292
Archibald Russell 302–304–323–374
Ardencraig 300
Ardente 68
Arethusa, see *Hippalos* (bq.)
Argus 437/8
Aristides 330
Ark, Noah's 212
Arthur Seitz 255
Asgerd, see *Kilmory*
Asia Island .. .. 36–40 *et seq.*
Assn. Maritime Belge .. 69–71
Asteria, s.s. 32
Astrea 39
Astur, see *Anirac*
Athena 398

Atlas, see *Bertha L. Downes*	
Aurora	349
Austrasia, see *Gustav*	
Backmann, J. H.	316
Baghla	122
Bago, see *Pajala*	
Balhinaur	316
Baltimore clippers	248
Bandi, see *Elizabeth Bandi*	
Barclay, Curle	212–386
Barco de Mer, see *Xavega*	
Barcore, see *Songvaar*	
Barron, Joseph	209
Barteletto, F. & A.	447
Bear	287
Beaufouart, Capt.	444
Beethoven	216
Bell, Sir James	216–379
Bellhouse, see *Regina Elena/ Ponape*	
Bentinck, Capt.	225–382
Bentincks	225–382
Bentinck booms	225–229
Bérengère	444
Berge Istra m.v.	14 f.n.
Bergen Schoolship Assn. ..	142
Bergesen, Sigval	202/3
Berge Vanga m.v.	14 f.n.
Bertha	40
Bertha L. Downes	281
Bertoletto, Capt. Vittorio ..	210
Besian	83
Bessfield	40–43
Beynon, T.	454
Bhyalkshmy	136
Bianca	270
Bianca Shipping Corporation ..	270
Binne (of Paimpol)	54
Birmah .. ..,	203
Bisean	81/2

Black, John	442
Blacksmith	234/8
Blohm & Voss	140–384
Bodewes, H. G.	458
Bolt, Aileen	xix
Bolt, Daniel	xx
Bordes, A. D. et fils	29–69–186–301
Borge, H.	146
Boston Tow Boat Co.	448
Bowen, Frank	xvii/xx
Boy Clifford	114
Boyd Bros.	22
Box-hauling	102
Bradford C. Jones	275
Brech, Carl	95
Bridgetammal ..	126/7–129/32
Brigs, collier	228 et seq.
Hermaphrodite	221
H.M. Training	449
Indian	126 et seq.
Brigantine(s)	128–130–132/4–398
Briggs, W., & Sons	360
British Governor, s.s. ..	292
British Shipping Controller ..	22
Brocklebank, T. & J. ..	389
Brodin, O. A.	220
Browne & Watson	182
Bryde, Johan	315
Bruce, D.	354
Brunel, Isambard	212
Burmeister & Wain	367
Caboteurs	49–57/8
Cadiz, s.s.	301
Caisley, Wm.	297
Calcutta	336
Caledonia, see *Olivebank*	
California, State of	285
Camilla	333
Campbell, J. C.	95

Campbell, J. Fletcher	396
Carmen (bq.)	304
Carmen (4-m. bq.)	386
Carpenter	171
Caronia, H.M.S.	389
Carrier Dove, see *Ungdoms Venner*	
Cassius, see *Kilmory*	
Castleton, see *Skaregrom*	
Cavour, see *Sofia*	
C. B. Pedersen, see *Emmanuele Accame &*	382–412
Cecil P. Stewart	266
Champigny, see *Fennia (2)*	
Chandler, Ralph J., Shipbuilding Co.	266
Chantiers de St. Nazaire ..	444
Chantiers Nantais	448
Charles A. Briggs	252
Charles Racine	203/7
Charlotte, see *Diego*	
Chasseurs	48–56–58
Chili	406
Chiltonford	165
Choli	126
Christiania	353
Cidad de Porto, see *Tango/Hans &*	283/7
City of Orange	266
Cleomene	338
Cleta, see *Frideborg*	
Clink, J. D.	374
Club-hauling	104/6–276
Colbert, see *Prinzess Eitel Friedrich*	
Coles, Adlard	11
Colling & Pinkney's reefing gear	46–226
Collins, Miss Clema	273
Colonel de Villebois Mareuil	.. 446/50
Commerce	229/30
Commonwealth, see *Sofia*	
Comte de Smet de Naeyer	69–77/8
Concorde	55
Connells (of Glasgow) ..	109
Conqueror, tug	292
Conrad, Joseph ..	18–208–210–312
Constance Craig	406
Cookson, Richard M.	450
Cooper & Co.	231
Cora F. Cressey	260
Coringle	414
Corner, Capt. F. W.	315
County of Anglesey, see *Gladbrook*	
County of Inverness, see *Carmen* (4-m. bq.) &	386
County of Peebles	384/6
Coupland, J.	199
Courses, triangular ..	225–382
Court, W. H.	225
Craigisla	334
Craig, J. J.	406–411
Craig, R. & J. ..	384/6–410
Crane	242–244
Crawford & Rowat	300
Crean, Thomas	349
Creoula	438
Crocodile, tug	xx
Cromdale	212–310
Crowell & Thurlow ..	255–274
Crowinshield, Benjamin	272–274
Crowley, Capt. John ..	258–274
Crown Zellerbach No. 1, see *Somali*	
Cuatros Hermanos, see *Sofia*	
Cumberland Queen	270
Cunningham's patent reefing gear	46–226–432
Cutter	122
Cutting away steel rigging	.. 106/8
Cutty Sark	411

Daniels, Capt. H.	xx
Daphne, s.s.	292
Dar Pomorza, see *Prinzess Eitel Friedrich*	
David Dows	257
de Cloux, Capt. Reuben	303/4
de Freitas, A. C.	218
de Haan & Oerlemann	438
Deryksen (of Dunkerque)	61
Desdemona	440
Deutscher Schulschiff Verein	138/51
Devitt & Moore, Messrs.	22–69–315–330
Dharma, see *Ladye Doris*	
Dhows	14–122/6
Diego	216
Dione	356/60
Dogger Bank, Battle of	206
Dollar, Wm. & Co.	285
Domino	51–62
Dora, see *Carmen*	
Dovrefjeld	262
Dow, Capt.	278/80
Doxford, Wm.	334
Drago, E.	216
Dreadnought, see *Moshulu*	
Drogden, see *Nina Podesta*	
Duen	298/300
Duke of Sutherland	209
Dunbar, Duncan	330
Dunboyne, see *af Chapman*	
Duncan, Geo.	337
Duncan, R.	210–399–403
Duncan Dunbar	330
Dundees	49–56
Dunkerque	69
Dunn & Elliott	270
East African, see *Ada*	
East India Co. Hon.	314
Eckford Webb	250
Edmiston & Mitchell	300
Edna Hoyt	258–270
Edwin Fox	314
Elder & Co.	210
Elder, J.	336
Eleanor A. Percy	258–262–264
Elfrieda, see *Schulschiffe Pommern &*	144/5
Elizabeth Bandi	196/7
Ellen	457/8
Elliott Shipbuilding Co.	270
Elsa Ölander, see *C. B. Pedersen*	
Emerett, see *Cumberland Queen*	
Ems, see *Fortuna* (sh.)	
Emmanuele Accame, see *C. B. Pedersen &*	380
Endurance	349/51–354
Erikson, Capt. Gustaf	28–71–74/5–216–283–303–316–322–340–359/61–374–380–392–395/6
Erikson, Capt. Sven	303/6–308
Esmeralda	300/1
Esquimaux (aux.)	354
Essburger, J. T.	197
Esthonia	359
Ethel	309/11
Eufrozine	257
Eusemere	329
Evaleeta	412
Eva Montgomery	163
Eyre, Evans	308–337
Evertsen, see *Tellus*	
Fastnet Race	12
Favell	20–22–27/37–40–43/4–102–323–375
Fennia (1)	22
Fennia (2)	25/7
Ferm, see *C. B. Pedersen*	
Fernie Bros.	338
Finnish Schoolship Assn.	22

Finska Ångfartygs AB	22–34
Finska Rederi Aktiebolaget	22
Fiona Shell, see *Fennia (1)*	
Fire welding	236
Fitzjames	163
Flora, see *Potosi*	
Flugge, Carl	95
Fore River Ship & Engine Co.	274
Forest Dream	266
Forest Friend	266
Forest King, s.s.	266
Forest Pride	266
Förlig Vind	219
Fort James, see *Garsdale*	
Fort Laramie	268
Fortuna (ex *Ems*)	316
Fortuna (ex *Macquarrie*)	315
France (2)	7–283
France, Fenwick Ltd.	309
Francis, Capt. P. L.	411
Frank A. Palmer	254
Frederikshavn's Shipyard	198
Frexas, see *Anirac*	
Frideborg	367
Fritz, see *Ellen*	
Fuller Palmer	258
Full-riggers	10
Garth, Lancelot Silver	206
Garthneill, see *Inverneill* &	164 f.n.–457
Garthsnaid	302
Garthwaite, Sir William, Bt.	457
Garsdale	444/6
G. D. Kennedy, see *af Chapman*	
Genoese wine trader	433
Gerd, s.s.	216
Gerda	219/23
George W. Wells	258–274
German Schoolship Assn., see Deutscher Schulschiff Verein	
Getelli, Luigi	281
Getting under weigh	95 *et seq.*
Gill-netters, Alaskan	435
Giuseppina Accame	204
Gladbrook	410/11
Glenard	22/6–28/9–40–106
Glen Line	22/6
Glenorchy	336
Glycine	62
Goëland	64/5
Goelettes	54/6–62
Goffey, Col.	392
Golden Fleece	212
Goodrich, see *Fennia (1)*	
Goss, Sawyer & Packard	252
Govansan, B.	298
Governor Ames	257
Grace Harwar	164
Grangemouth & Greenock Dockyard Co.	69–218
Granith, Capt. Karl	322
Grays Harbor Motorship Corporation	266
Great Eastern, s.s.	212
Green, R. & H.	315
Grefstade, B. J.	105
Grimen (of Hamburg)	316
Grossherzogin Elisabeth	139–142–150
Grossherzog Friedrich August, see *Statsraad Lemkuhl* &	141/2–146
Guano	36 *et seq.*
Gustav	392
Halden, J.	366
Hall, Alexander	411
Hamburg	333/5
Hamburg–Amerika Line	76
Hampshire, Charles	xx
Hans, see *Tango/Cidad de Porto* &	283/4
Harbinger	xx
Hardie, Capt. J.	302–374

Haroldine 254	Howes patent topsails 47
Hattrick, A. 408	*Huia* 416/9
Hawaiian Isles, see *Abraham Rydberg*	Hull painting 28–57–69
	Human factor (fallible) 18
Hawkesbury 330	Hunier à rouleau .. 45 *et seq.*
Hay, Capt. John 164/5	
Hazel Craig, see *Quathlamba*	*Ideal* 67
Heaving to 108/114	*Ikala*, s.s. 206
Helen Denny 403/4	*Imacos*, see *Ahti*
Henderson, Patrick 403	Indian country craft 121 *et seq.*–219
Henriette, see *Anirac*	*Indian Empire* 337
Hereford 336	*Ingrid*, see *Rigdin*
Hermann 56	*Inverkip* 294/6
Hero, see *MacCallum More*	*Inverneill*, see *Garthneill* & .. 457
Heros, tug 148	*Inversnaid*, see *Garthsnaid*
Herzogin Cecilie 76–303/8–382	*Inverness* xx
Herzogin Sophie Charlotte 303–316–338/40	Iquique 183/8–190/2
	Irene 444
Highland Chieftain 229	*Iris* 54
Hill, C. & Co. 29	Irvin, Dixon & Co. 298
Hill, Miss Favell 20	*Isabel Llusa* *312*
Hill, W. H. 225	*Isobel Browne* *182*
Himaire, Capt. M. 426	*Isis*, see *Narcissus*
Hine Bros. 29	*Islandais* 48–56
Hinrichsen, Claus 329	Ismay, T. H. 301
Hippalos (sh.) 109	
Hippalos (4-m. bq.) 389	*Jacob M. Haskell* 253
Hoek van Holland, see *Julius*	*James Caird* 349
Hoghton Tower 349	*James Craig* 406
Holkar, see *Hippalos* (4-m. bq.)	*Jane Palmer* 258–261
Holley & Bean 274	*Janes*, see *Diego*
Holm, Capt. Frederick 404	Jansson, A. F. 394
Holm Shipping Co. 404	Jarvis, Capt. F. C. B. .. 234–244
Holmes, R. G. 404	*Jasper* 400
Hood, Walter 330	*Java* 314
Hooghly pilots 208	*Jeanie Landles*, see *Linlithgowshire*
Hoppet, see *Novo*	
Hougomont 302/6–374	Jenkyns, A. 400
Houston, J. 337	Jeremiassen, H. 444
Howard D. Troop, see *Annie M. Reid*	Jibbooms 386
	Johanna, tug 74

466

Johannesen, J. W.	204
Joseph Craig	406
Joyce & Co.	199
Julius	362
Junks, Chinese	116/20
Junks, Japanese	115
Kagosima	226–228
Karima	128
Kate Brigham	250
Katherine Mackall	266
Kelly, W.	226
Kenilworth, see *Star of Scotland*	
Kennedy, R.	431
Kerguelen Whaling & Sealing Co.	452
Kerroch	57
Ketches, Tasmanian jackyard	414/6
Key, John & Sons	406
Killoran	374
Kilmory	338
Kineo	262
Kirkby & Co.	231
Knight of the Thistle, see *Novo*	
Knöhr & Burchard	389
Knox Johnston, Robert	386 f.n.
København	15
Kommodore Johnsen	8/9
Koranton, s.s.	294
Kortum, Karl	xx
Kotia	118–120–122/6
Krogius, Lars	22–30–33/4
Krusenstern, see *Padua &*	29
Kurt, see *Moshulu &*	301–305
La Belle Poule	62
La Croix, Capt. Louis	450
Ladye Doris	163/95
Laeisz, Rhed. F.	29–193–288–292– 301–316–356–379–401
La Hogue	330
Lambo	90

Lancaster Ship-owners	329
L'Avenir	69 *et seq.* –367
Law, Thomas	69
Lawhill	95–234–240/4–305–328– 370–392/4
Lawson, Thomas W.	274
Leicester Castle, see *Vik &*	197/200
L'Étoile	62
Letterewe, see *Anirac*	
Lever Bros.	216
Lille, Capt. Sten	28/39–102
Lilly G	447
Limena	334
Lindfors, Capt. Harald	303/4
Lingard	216–369
Lisbeth	329
Linlithgowshire	69
Liverpool	384
Llusa & Co.	312
Loch Broom	296
Loch Carron	294/6
Loero & Bucelli	41
Loongana	410
Lopi	82
Lord Ripon	388
Louisa Craig, see *Raupo*	
Lubbock, Basil	450
Luckner, Count Felix von	198
Lundquist, Hugo	218–356–360–380
Lundquist, M.	208
Lwow	141
Lyra	231
McAteer Shipbuilding Co.	268
McCallum More	95
McColm, Capt.	214
McCulloch, Capt.	208
MacGillivray, D.	146
MacMillans	207–442
Maco, see *Søm*	
Macquarrie, see *Fortuna*	

MacVicar, Marshall Bros.	444
Madby Ann	297
Mae Dollar, see *Somali*	
Mahamadeli, Capt.	131
Maid of Judah	330
Maine	365
Maine, s.s.	323
Magdalene Vinnen, see *Kommodore Johnsen*	
Malaboo, see *Tellus*	
Manga Reva, see *Pyrenees*	
Manning (U.S.C.G.)	270
Manurewa	404/6
Maple Leaf	252
Marblehead schooners	248
Marcus, Jorgensen & Co.	384
Marine Coal Co.	196
Marjorie Brown	256
Mary Dollar, see *Hans/Tango*	
Mary H. Diebold	258
Masefield, John	301–313
Mattson, Capt. J. M.	308
Medusa	360/1
Meia Luas	158
Melbourne (sh.), see *Fortuna*	
Melbourne (4-m. bq.), see *Gustav*	
Mercator	71
Mermaid	225/6
Mertie B. Crowley	274
Middleton	225
Milesi, Pietro	383
Milne, George	302
Miltiades	330
Mimi, see *Bertha*	
Mincio, see *Cleomene*	
Minnie A. Caine	316
Miro	422/30
Mneme, see *Pommern*	
Modoe (U.S.C.G.)	270
Molfetta	266
Moliciero	152–341/348
Montgomery, A.	164
Montgomery, W.	163/4–169
Monroe, President	248
Monson, E. & Co.	334
Moran Bros.	316
Morten Jensen, see *Niobe*	
Morutiers	48–57/8
Mosher, Thos.	398
Moshulu, see *Kurt &*	283–286/91–380
Mount Hamilton	268
Mount Stewart	74–212/6–310
Mount Whitney	268
Mozart	216/8–368
Nal, see *Lord Ripon*	
Nancy	273
Narcissus	207
Nathaniel T. Palmer	258
National Maritime Museum	xix/xx–349
Nautilus, see *Christiania*	
Nettinhas	158
Nelly and Mathilde, see *Frideborg*	
Nelson, Chas.	316
Nemrac, s.s., see *Carmen*	
New Zealand Freight Reduction Committee	408
New Zealand Shipping Co.	349
Nichol, J.	208
Nicholl, G. T.	404–411
Nicholls, W.	334
Nina Podesta	281
Niobe	198
Nithyakalyani	135
Nobels Explosive Co.	422
Nord Deutscher Lloyd	22–75 303–339
Nordeas, L.	298
Norma	300
Norman, tug	61–66
Norske Seilskute Klubb	216

Northland 254	*Patrie* 300
Nourse, James 316–336	Payne, Arthur xx
Nurminen, John .. 316–357	*Pear Branch*, s.s. 195
	Pearson (of Whitby) 225
Oberon 450	*Pehr Ugland* 216
Ocean 231	*Peking* 288–291
Oceana, s.s. 292	*Penang* 316/322
Oceanide 56	Pendleton, Carver & Nicholls .. 435
Odessa, see *Hippalos* (4-m. bq.)	*Pendragon Castle*, see *Lisbeth*
Ohlsson, Martin 222	Penney, R. & H. 362
Ohlsson, Capt. Per .. 220–222	Percy & Small 260–274
Oldenburg, Grand Duke of .. 139	Perforated sails 10
Oliva, see *Ladye Doris*	*Peru*, see *Raupo*
Olivari, Paolo 301	*Peter Rickmers* 384–388
Olivebank .. 44–306/10–322/4	Petersen, J. 455
On Chong 410	Pettersen, H. H. 300
O'Neill, Eugene 205/7	Phillips, Joseph B. 252
Oriente, see *Isabel Llusa*	*Pindos* 329
Ornasia 392	*Pinisi* 82/3
Ottone, see *Christiania*	*Pinnas*, see *Fitzjames &* .. 193
Outrigger canoes (Ceylon) .. 122	Piaggio, Henry 266
	Pintado 178
Pacific Freighters Co. 266	*Piri* 419/29
Padewakang 80–82–86	*Pisagua* 292
Padua, see *Krusenstern &* .. 29	*Plus* 356/58
Pajala 90	*Polaris*, see *Endurance*
Palari 90	*Pola*, see *Richelieu*
Palgrave 212	*Pommern* 109–323
Palmer, Nathaniel 254–258–272–286	*Ponape* 321–380
Palmer, William 273/4	Pontes, E. 210
Pamir 10–17/19–106–240/1–318	Ponting, Herbert 354
Paparoa Coal Co. 404	*Port Logan*, see *Bertha*
Parma 303/4–368	Portuguese Grand Bankers .. 435/38
Parvathavarthaniamma .. 135	*Potosi* 6–452
Passat 292/3	Potter, W. H. 298
Pass of Balmaha, see *See-Adler*	Poyser, Capt. Fred. .. xix/xx
Passos, R. 210	Prahu craft .. .. 80 *et seq.*
Paterson, Robert R. 210	*Preussen* 4/5–32–240
Patorani 82	*Prinsessan* 352
Patterson, A. S. 404	*Prinz Eitel Friedrich* (cruiser) .. 182
Patterson, Charles R. 362	*Prinzess Eitel Friedrich* 140

Priwall	308
Proas, flying	80
Prompt	360
Protector	227–230
Pugsley, J. N.	270
Pungue, s.s.	286
Pyrenees..	374
Quathlamba, see *White Pine* & ..	411
Queen Margaret..	440/3
Race Relations	206–214
Rahouix, A.	257
Rakaia	349
Raupo	406/8
R. C. Rickmers	69
Regena Elena, see *Ponape* &	379–383
Reid, E.	196
Rendova..	216
Rennie, J. T.	411
Revenge	289
Rewa	406
Rex, see *Star of Scotland*	
Ribiero, Julio	285
Richelieu	401
Rickmers, R. C. Rhed.	29–69–76–316–340
Rigdin	396
Risør, see *Ada*	
River Indus	166
Roberts, E. F. & W.	208
Robertson, J. W.	406
Rochambeau	11
Rodger, A.	454
Rogers, W.	495
Roller topsails (Breton) ..	45 *et seq.*
Rolph, James	399
Romance	1
Rooganah	414
Rose, W.	330
Rose Mahoney	272

Rosenius, Åke	323
Ross, Capt. W.	432
Rousseau	440
Ruth E. Merrill	264
Russell & Co.	146–300–374–389–450
Rydman, Capt. Gunnar ..	22
Sailing ships of future ..	8–16
Sail training ships	21
St. Patrice, s.s.	23
Samuel L. Groucher	261
Samuel Plimsoll	312–319
San Francisco Maritime Museum	448
Sanita, see *Anirac*	
Santa Maria Manuela	438
Saratoga	452
Sauvage (of Dunkerque) ..	51
Saxon, see *Schulschiffe Pommern*	
Scales, George	406/8
Schiaffino, C.	296
Schliebracht	457
Schlüter & Maack ..	218–340
Schmidt, H. H. ..	40–329–395
School-ships ..	21–138–326
Schooners:	
Baltimore	248
Banks	251–254–350–435
Breton	45 *et seq.*
Giant ..	18–248 *et seq.*–283
Marblehead	248
Tern ..	250–254–353
Topsail	45
Schröder, Consul	362
Schuldt, Capt. N. H. P. ..	384
Schulschiff Deutschland	142–146–150
Schulschiffe Pommern ..	146/8
Scinde, tug	208
Scows, New Zealand ..	412
Sedov, see *Kommodore Johnsen*	
See-Adler	198

470

Seeute Deern, see *Elizabeth Bandi*	
Seileren, see *Loch Carron*	
Selwyn Craig	406
Seminole, m.v.	395
Senegal	452
Seth Jr.	353
Sewall, Arthur	262
Sewall, H.	404
Shackleton, Sir Ernest	349
Shakespeare	397
Shanghai-ing	200/202
Shaw, Savill & Albion Co.	403
Shelter decks	10–256
Ship preservation	287/88–328
Side lights	459
Siemers, G. J. H.	283
Simla	452
Sindia	389
Single-handed sailing	12
Sivasurmaniapuravny	137
Sixth sense	16/18
Skaregrom	454
Skomedal, see *Ada*	
Slater, D.	232
Slieve Gallion, s.s.	270
Smart	455
Smith, R. A. & Co.	199
Snow/brigs	220 *et seq.*
Sobraon	330
Soc. des Voiliers Dunkerquois	444
Soc. des Voiliers du Sud-Ouest	444
Söderlund, Capt. Artur	326
Söderlund, J. W.	22
Sofia	41
Solblomsten	400
Søm	384
Somali	452
Songdal, see *Loch Broom*	
Songvaar	307/8
Sorensen	146

Sound of Jura	450/2
Souter & Co.	230
Southern Cross, see *Ysabel*	
Souverain, see *Hippalos* (4-m. bq.)	
Springbank	349
Statsraad Lemkuhl, see *Grossherzog Friedrich August &*	142
Standard Oil Co.	278
Stanley	452
Star of Greenland, see *Abraham Rydberg*	
Star of Peace	330
Star of Scotland	285
Star of the Ocean	328
Staysails	10–380/4
Steeves, Gilbert R.	452
Stenhouse, Capt. J. R.	349
Stephens, Alex.	354
Stephens (of Par)	398
Stevens, W.	229
Stewart, J.	404
Stewart, John & Co.	41–406
Stobart, Fenwick & Co.	309
Stray, S. O.	296–308–312–384–454
Suecia, see *C. B. Pedersen*	
Sullivan	209
Sunlight	216
Sun Oil Co.	278
Sunteo, A.	365
Susanna	291
Svalen, see *Skaregrom*	
Tacking ship	98/102
Talona, m.v.	323
Tangaroa, see *Piri*	
Tango, see *Hans/Cidad de Porto*	
Tarapaca	301
Tecklenborgs	139–141/2
Tellus	40
Terrier	226/7

Thermopylae 330	Vigilant (ketch) 61
Thistle 374	*Vik*, see *Leicester Castle*
Thomas, T. C. 398	*Viking* 13–113–338
Thomas, W. 410	*Vimiera* 374
Thomasina, see *Thomasina McClellan*	Vincent, Mildred xix
Thomasina McClellan 207/8	Vinnen Gebr. 144–146
Thomas W. Lawson . . 272–274/82	*Vittoria*, see *Anirac*
Thomson & Gray 207	*Voorburg*, see *Alexa*
Thorsten 298	von 1896, Rhed. Act. Ges. 109–163–384
Thørvesen, Captain 206	
Timandra 206	
Titania 450	Waage, Capt. Gustav . . 29–203/6
Tocszko, Norbert 448	Waage, Capt. Severin xv
Tomaso Drago, see *Diego*	*Waimana* 412
Topsail (roller), see Hunier à rouleau	*Waimate* 349
	Wairoa 349
Torrens 210	Wait, James 209
Troberg, August. . . 182–208	Walker, Charles 450
Troberg, Capt. K. 310	Walker, Frank . . xvii–426
Troop & Son 399	Walkers (of Greenock) 294
Tulloch, R. 431	Wallarah Coaling Co. 316
Tyholm, see *Niobe*	Wammus, A. 359
	Wanderer xx
U-140 318	*Wandsbek* 389
Ugland, J. L. 216	Water, fresh 13
Under weigh, getting . . 95 *et seq.*	*Wathara*, see *Lingard*
Ungdoms Venner 298	Wätjen, D. H. 389
Union S. S. Co. 411	Watkins, William & Sons . . 292
	Wave Length principle 123
	Wearing Ship 102/4–124
Vale Royal, see *Manurewa*	Weir, Andrew & Co. 349
Valle, Antonio 447	Wencke, B., Sohne . . 109
Vane, A. P. 272	Wencke, Friedrich . . 109
Varuna 448	Wentmore & Meritt . . 298
Vellore 337	Westermark, Anders . . 352
Vema (sch. yt.) 367	*Westfield* 450
Vema III (yt.) 367	Whalers 354–438
Vernon, T. H. 301	*White Pine* 456
Vesores 395	White Star Line 349
Vetlasan, G. A. 367	*William C. Carnegie* 282
Viceroy of India, s.s. . . 75	*William L. Douglas* . . 260–274

William L. White 252	Worsley, Capt. Frank 349
Williamsons 329	*Wyoming* 281
Windmill pump 257–355–367	
Windsor Castle 356	*Ysabel* 489
Winslow, J. S. 255–258–264–272/4	*Yvonne*.. 41–47
Winterhude 151–345	
Wood, Captain G. G. 164	
Wood, the Misses 172	*Xavega* 154/62
Woods, Capt. E. A. xx	
Wild, G. 404	
Woolamai 467–488	*Zealandic*, s.s. 321

MOSHULU *in wild weather in the Skaggerak.*